THEOLOGY ON FIRE

THEOLOGY ON FIRE

Sermons from the Heart of J.A. Alexander

Joseph Addison Alexander

Solid Ground Christian Books
Birmingham, Alabama

SOLID GROUND CHRISTIAN BOOKS
PO Box 660132, Vestavia Hills, AL 35266
205-443-0311
sgcb@charter.net
http://www.solid-ground-books.com

Theology on Fire:
Sermons from the Heart of J.A. Alexander

by Joseph Addison Alexander

From the 1860 edition by Charles Scribner, New York

Published by Solid Ground Christian Books

Classic Reprints Series

First printing of paperback edition September 2004

ISBN: 1-932474-50-1

Special thanks to Dr. David B. Calhoun of Covenant Theological Seminary in St. Louis, MO for his excellent biographical sketch of Dr. J.A. Alexander.

Manufactured in the United States of America

Biographical Sketch
of
Joseph Addison Alexander

Joseph Addison Alexander was born in Philadelphia, Pennsylvania, on April 24, 1809. His father, Archibald Alexander, was pastor of the Third Presbyterian Church of Philadelphia, to which he had been called in 1806 from the presidency of Hampden-Sydney College in his native Virginia. The new baby's mother, Janetta Waddel Alexander, was the daughter of the famous blind preacher of Virginia, James Waddel. Joseph Addison Alexander was the third son of Janetta and Archibald. He was named for the noted English statesman and writer, Joseph Addison, the cofounder of the *Spectator*. Addison, as he was called, had seven siblings, a sister and six brothers.

The Alexander children probably learned more at home than they did at school. Their father taught them spelling, arithmetic, geography, algebra, geometry, the classical languages, and especially the Bible. When Addison showed unusual interest and ability in languages, his father wrote out the Hebrew alphabet for the six-year-old boy, and a little later prepared a manuscript grammar adapted to his age. By the age of ten Addison had mastered the rudiments of Latin, Greek, and Hebrew. He found an old copy of an Arabic grammar on the top shelf in his father's library and was soon reading the Koran.

Recognizing Addison's ability and initiative, his parents postponed his formal education, allowing him freedom to study with family members and private tutors or on his own. When he was fifteen years old he entered the junior class at the College of New Jersey (also called Princeton College; now Princeton University). There he amazed both his teachers and fellow students with his knowledge.

Declining a position as tutor in the college, Addison Alexander spent the next three years in private study. He took special delight in oriental languages and literature and read French, Italian, Spanish, and German. He began the study of Chinese. When he was not studying languages he was writing stories, political editorials, and poems.

Alexander taught at the Edgehill School in Princeton for a year while he completed a master's degree at the College of New Jersey. It was during this year that Addison put his trust in Christ. Earlier his father had written to a family friend, "His views and feelings on the subject of religion are known only to himself. He is so reserved that nobody attempts to draw him out; but his whole deportment is as correct as it easily could be." Dr. Alexander gave the good news of Addison's conversion to Robert Baird, seminary graduate and one of Addison's early tutors, and then "covered his face with his handkerchief, and gave way to his deep emotions of joy and hope" (Baird wrote). Addison's journal, with its scholarly notes and records of his study and writing, now showed a new interest. Addison wrote: "In addition to literary pursuits, I have been deeply engaged in a study new to me, and far more important than all others—the study of the Bible and my own heart. I humbly trust that I am not what I was. Intellectual enjoyment has been my idol heretofore; now my heart's desire is that I may live no longer to myself, but in Him in whom I have everlasting life." Addison wondered whether his early interest in languages was, in God's providence, a preparation for foreign missionary service. His reading now included Augustine, Jonathan Edwards, John Owen, Henry Martyn, and John Newton, among other great Christian writers. He found these books valuable but imperfect; sometimes there was "an overstraining of some one point of view in preference to others," he wrote. "It is only in the Book—the Book of Books, that all is symmetrical and consistent; Oh may I love it more and more!"

In 1830 the twenty-one-year-old Alexander became adjunct professor of Ancient Languages and Literature at Princeton College. For the next two and a half years he taught his courses, continued his study of languages (adding Portuguese, Danish, and Turkish), and began theological studies with his father. He set a new goal for his life: "to become thoroughly acquainted with the

Scriptures; philologically, theologically, practically; and so to qualify myself for interpreting them properly to others." Every day he memorized portions of the Bible, in English, Greek, and Hebrew.

During the years 1833 and 1834, Addison studied in Europe at the University of Halle and the University of Berlin. He impressed his European teachers, especially Friedrich Tholuck, professor of theology at Halle. Tholuck said that young Alexander was the only man he knew who could always give him the right English word for one in German "apparently untranslatable."

In May 1834, J.A. Alexander was appointed assistant to Charles Hodge, professor of Oriental and Biblical Literature at Princeton Seminary. The next year he was elected by the General Assembly as associate professor. Alexander declined the chair of Oriental and Biblical Literature in Union Theological Seminary, just established in New York City, and was inaugurated professor at Princeton on September 24, 1838.

The seminary students were in awe of the new professor, knowing he was "a great scholar." They were also a little afraid of him. He is "as unsociable as a comet," one wrote. The campus children, however, loved him, and he delighted in playing with them, telling stories and singing songs for them in many languages.

J.A. Alexander impressed everyone as a superb exegete. He was an able speaker. His prayers reminded his students of Calvin's prayers. He was often impatient and sharp with slow students, however, and scorching and sarcastic in his review articles for the Princeton journal. But he deplored this tendency in himself and prayed that God would make him "humble, simple-hearted, tender, guileless, and confiding."

Addison became a candidate for the gospel ministry in 1838 and was ordained by New Brunswick Presbytery on April 24, 1839—his thirtieth birthday. In 1845 he was awarded an honorary doctor of divinity degree by Franklin and Marshall College.

J.A. Alexander quickly emerged as a leading evangelical scholar who could ably discriminate between the helpful linguistic research and learning of European biblical scholars and their harmful presuppositions and conclusions. Alexander began to produce his impressive commentaries, beginning with two volumes on Isaiah (published in 1846 and 1847).

For six months during 1847, Addison Alexander was the regular preacher at Tenth Presbyterian Church in Philadelphia. The following November he began another six-month preaching engagement, this time at Second Presbyterian Church in Philadelphia. Charles Hodge said that Addison's sermons "were always instructive and often magnificent. He would draw from a passage of Scripture more than you ever imagined it contained."

In 1851 J.A. Alexander was transferred to the Chair of Ecclesiastical History, succeeding his brother J.W. Alexander, who had accepted a call to the Fifth Avenue Presbyterian Church in New York City. Addison Alexander, as always, impressed his students with his knowledge but frustrated them, as well as himself, with frequent changes in his approach to the study of church history. He continued to teach both Old and New Testament courses. Charles Hodge explained to a friend that "our rule here is to urge Addison to do whatever we can find he is willing to do." He continued to produce commentaries: *Acts* was published in 1857 and *Mark* the next year.

Alexander suffered from diabetes, and in 1859 his health worsened. He had to give up teaching, but continued to work on a commentary on Matthew. The commentary ends with chapter sixteen, but, anticipating his death, he completed an analysis of the remaining chapters. He read with great joy the passage on the resurrection in Charles Hodge's commentary on Romans. During his last days he went about his room repeating softly the words of Isaac Watts's hymn—"Show pity, Lord, O Lord forgive; Let a repenting rebel live." He died on January 28, 1860. Charles Hodge wrote, "We have lost the greatest and one of the best men I ever knew." Hodge believed that there was not a man in the Presbyterian church "who had a more simple childlike faith in the entire Scriptures from Genesis to Revelation" than J.A. Alexander, Princeton's great linguist and scholar.

David B. Calhoun

CONTENTS OF VOLUME I.

PAGE

I.

MARK 1, 1.—The beginning of the Gospel of Jesus Christ the Son of God, ... 7

II.

MATTHEW 2, 2.—Where is he that is born king of the Jews? . 27

III.

JOHN 13, 7.—What I do thou knowest not now; but thou shalt know hereafter, ... 46

IV.

JOHN 1, 29.—Behold the Lamb of God, ... 66

V.

ROMANS 1, 25.—They worshipped and served the creature more than the Creator, ... 85

VI.

JOHN 3, 36.—He that believeth on the Son hath everlasting life: and he that believeth not the Son shall not see life, but the wrath of God abideth on him, ... 106

VII.

LUKE 17, 32.—Remember Lot's wife, ... 124

CONTENTS OF VOLUME I.

PAGE

VIII.
1 JOHN 3, 2.—It doth not yet appear what we shall be, . . 144

IX.
LUKE 11, 26.—The last state of that man is worse than the first, 167

X.
ROMANS 16, 27.—To God only wise, be glory through Jesus Christ forever. Amen, ... 188

XI.
LUKE 14, 17.—Come, for all things are now ready, . . . 209

XII.
PROVERBS 22, 2.—The rich and poor meet together; the Lord is the maker of them all, ... 227

XIII.
ROMANS 11, 22.—Behold therefore the goodness and severity of God; on them which fell, severity; but toward thee, goodness, if thou continue in his goodness; otherwise, thou also shalt be cut off, ... 249

XIV.
1 CORINTHIANS 15, 33.—Be not deceived! 264

XV.
ACTS 28, 28.—Be it known therefore unto you, that the salvation of God is sent unto the Gentiles, and that they will hear it, 280

XVI.
1 PETER 1, 5.—Kept by the power of God through faith unto salvation, ... 302

CONTENTS OF VOLUME I.

PAGE

XVII.

TITUS 2, 11–15.—For the grace of God that bringeth salvation hath appeared to all men, teaching us that, denying ungodliness and worldly lusts, we should live soberly, righteously, and godly, in this present world; looking for that blessed hope, and the glorious appearing of the great God and our Saviour Jesus Christ; who gave himself for us, that he might redeem us from all iniquity, and purify unto himself a peculiar people, zealous of good works. These things speak, and exhort, and rebuke with all authority. Let no man despise thee, ... 317

XVIII.

LUKE 22, 32.—When thou art converted, strengthen thy brethren, 335

XIX.

LUKE 9, 60.—Let the dead bury their dead; but go thou and preach the kingdom of God, ... 354

XX.

MARK 13, 37.—What I say unto you, I say unto all: Watch! . 377

XXI.

MATTHEW 24, 6.—The end is not yet, ... 395

SERMONS.

I.

MARK 1. 1.—The beginning of the Gospel of Jesus Christ the Son of God.

AMONG the incidental disadvantages attending the inestimable privilege of early and life-long familiarity with the Word of God, is the habit of confounding things really distinct, and especially of overlooking the characteristic peculiarities of the sacred writers, which were not at all destroyed by inspiration, and a due regard to which is often necessary to their just interpretation. In no part of the Bible is this error more common or injurious than in the Gospels, which the great majority even of devout and believing readers are too much in the habit of regarding as precisely alike in plan and purpose, whereas no other books on the same subject could be more distinctly marked by individual peculiarities, some of which are of the most minute and unimportant nature in themselves, but for that very reason less likely to have been invented or contrived for any purposes of deception.

Many who have read the Gospels all their lives,

would be surprised to hear that Matthew uses the word "then" more frequently than all the others put together—that Mark is almost equally exclusive in his use of "immediately"—that John alone has the double Amen Amen—and a multitude of other minute differences equally unimportant in themselves, but equally demonstrative of individuality and independence in the several writers. The same thing is true as to other differences more important in themselves, and relating not to mere forms of expression, but to plan and method. Thus Matthew cites the prophecies, and points out their fulfilment so much more frequently than Mark and Luke, that his gospel is by some regarded, not so much as a history, as a historical argument, intended to show that Jesus was the Messiah of the prophets. Mark is distinguished by his use of Latin words and explanation of Jewish customs, showing that he wrote immediately for Gentile readers; on the other hand, he frequently records the Aramaic or vernacular expressions used by Christ, with a Greek translation; such as Talcumi, Ephphatha, Corban, Abba father. Another peculiarity of this evangelist is, that to him we are indebted for almost all our knowledge of our Saviour's looks and gestures; as we are to Luke for many interesting glimpses of his devotional habits; such as his spending whole nights in prayer, his praying at his baptism, and before the choice of his apostles, and in other cases. John, besides the general differences, arising from the commonly admitted fact that he wrote to complete or supplement the others, dwells chiefly on our Lord's discourses, and relates his actions chiefly as connected with them. On the other hand, it is to him we owe our knowledge of the chronology or dates of our Lord's ministry—it is he that enumerates the passovers and several other feasts included in that period, and thus shows us that his ministry or public life on earth continued for above three years.

These points of difference between the gospels are selected out of many that might just as easily be given, in illustration of the general statement, that while all were equally inspired and all are perfectly harmonious, each writer has his own peculiarities, not only of expression, but of plan and method. This is a matter not of learned criticism, but within the reach of every careful and attentive reader, and if properly noticed, would greatly tend not only to elucidate the gospels, but to make them interesting—in other words, to aid both the understanding and the memory. A due regard to these peculiarities would lead to the correction of another error, far too prevalent in reference to this delightful part of the Scriptures—that of regarding the four gospels not as complete histories, but as mere collections of materials, out of which we are to frame the history for ourselves; a mistake which has occasioned not only a vast waste of time and labour in attempts to reduce the four accounts to one continued narrative; but has also contributed directly to the disregard of those peculiarities which have been already mentioned as belonging to the several books, but which of course are overlooked and confounded in the process of condensing four books into one.

The simple truth appears to be, that God, for wise

and holy purposes, which are only in part visible to us, or discovered by us, was pleased to put the life of Christ on record for the edification of his people, and the glory of his own name; not in one, but in four distinct accounts, each complete in itself, with reference to its own specific purpose, and the definite impression it was meant to make upon the readers' mind, yet all completing one another in relation to the general aggregate or sum total of the impression meant to be conveyed. In this respect they have been likened to four portraits, or four landscapes, exhibiting one and the same object, but in different lights and from different points of view, yet all of course harmonious and consistent. As it would be absurd to cut up and amalgamate the paintings, so is it no less absurd to destroy the individuality of the gospels by reducing them to one. They are, indeed, to be harmonized in order to elucidate their meaning, and exhibit their consistency, but not in such a way as to destroy their separate existence, or confound their individual peculiarities. No harmony can, or ought to take the place of the original gospels, which were meant to be read separately to the end of time, and with a careful observation of their several characteristics, even of such as in themselves may seem to be wholly unimportant.

Among these is the way in which they open, and the point from which they set out, in recording the biography of Jesus Christ. Matthew begins with his genealogy, and shows by a formal and authentic pedigree, perhaps extracted from official records, his descent from Abraham and David. This is not so much a part of his narrative as a documentary introduction to it, after which he sets out from the conception and nativity of the Saviour. Luke goes back to the previous conception and nativity of John the Baptist, his forerunner. John goes still further back, to teach the doctrine of his pre-existence; while Mark omits all this, plunging at once into the midst of his subject, and beginning with the official life or public ministry of Jesus; "the beginning of the Gospel of Jesus Christ."

These words admit of several constructions, each of which has something to recommend it, and none of which are utterly exclusive of each other; so that all of them may be allowed to suggest something to the mind of the reader.

The simplest construction, and the one most probably intended by the writer, is that which makes this a description of the whole book, or a statement of its subject. This is the beginning of the life of Christ, or here beginneth his recorded history. It is equally grammatical, however, to connect the words with what follows, as a part of the same context; "the beginning of the Gospel of Jesus Christ was as it is written in the prophets;" or, "the beginning of the Gospel of Jesus Christ was John the Baptist preaching in the wilderness." These are not only positive constructions, but suggest important facts in the life of Christ, as will be afterwards particularly mentioned.

In the mean time I invite your attention to two topics, suggested by the words themselves, however they may be connected with what follows; one of which is really included in the other, or is a mere specification of it. The first and most general of these topics is *the gospel;* and the second and more specific, is *the beginning of the gospel.* Either of these would be sufficient by itself to furnish ample food for meditation and instruction, even if we merged the mere beginning in the whole, of which it is the part, or considered the whole only with respect to its beginning. I prefer, however, to present the two precisely as they lie together in the text, only giving the precedence to the general subject, and the second place to its specification. Or, in other words, first considering the gospel as a whole, and then the beginning of it in particular.

In carrying out this suggestion, it may be convenient to resolve each of these topics into two inquiries, under the general subject of the gospel: Considering first, What it is?—then, Whose it is?— Under the more specific head, Of the beginning of the Gospel, asking first, Where it began of old? And secondly, Where it begins now? By this division and arrangement, I may hope to assist both your understandings and your memories in the brief examination which I now propose to make of this interesting passage, not as a matter of mere curious speculation, but as a source of instruction and improvement.

I. Our first theme, then, is the Gospel; and our first inquiry, What it is!

This may seem, to some, too elementary a question, and to others, too extensive; but I merely ask you to consider for a moment, and in quick succession, the elements really included in this most familiar term, which, like others of the same sort, often conveys very vague ideas even to the minds of those who most familiarly employ it.

There are few kinds of knowledge, and religious knowledge is certainly not one of them, in which it is not often both agreeable and useful to go back to elementary ideas and first principles, and even to the simple definition of the most familiar terms. I do not scruple, then, to put the question both to you and to myself; *What is the Gospel?*—and to answer, in the first place : (1.) That the word, both in Greek and English, originally means, good news, glad tidings—a delightful phrase, expressing a delightful thing; awakening a thousand sweet and tender recollections. Who has never heard good news? Who cannot call to mind the thrill of joy which such intelligence once darted through him? To some the experience may be fresh, to others, faded; perhaps dimmed and neutralized by many an intervening alternation or vicissitude of bad news and of mournful tidings. Yet even in this case it is often possible to look back through these intervening changes, and to reproduce in some degree the exquisite delight occasioned at some distant period, by the reception of good news from some beloved object, perhaps far removed. This is an experience which never can grow obsolete. Increasing facilities of communication only multiply its causes and occasions. Even now, how many are rejoicing in glad tidings by the last arrival from some distant shore; how many anxiously, yet hopefully, expecting to receive them by the next! I appeal to these associations, not for any rhetorical or sentimental purpose, but simply to awaken the appropriate feeling which belongs to the very definition of the gospel—good news—good news—not in some abstruse or transcendental sense, but in the plain, homely, every-day sense of the same words, as employed in the dialect of common life. Why is it that the very terms and phrases which inflame or agitate us in our ordinary parlance, fall so lifeless on the ear and heart, when uttered in connection with religion? Partly because our whole state of feeling on religious subjects is too cold and dead; partly because we wilfully divorce religious terms from their natural association, and treat them as belonging to another.

Gospel, I tell you, is good news, in exactly the same sense that it was good news when you heard of the recovery or escape of a parent or a child, a husband or a wife, a brother or a sister, from some fearful peril. Recall that feeling, and then use it to explain the phrase good news as a definition of the gospel. If you leave this out, your whole conception is a false one. Whatever else may yet be added, and it is much, this is the original, essential, fundamental notion. There can be no gospel without good news, though there may in a restricted sense be good news where there is, alas! no gospel.

(2.) Having settled this as the primary, elementary idea of the gospel, as glad tidings—just as the same words are used to signify good news from man to man—from house to house—from one place to another, such as burdens our mails, and thrills along our telegraphic wires. Let us now take another step, and add to this simple definition of the gospel, as a term of Scripture and religion, that it is good news from God to man—from heaven to earth—from the infinitely blessed and the infinitely holy, to the lowest depths of human wretchedness and sin. It is no good news from America to Europe, or from the old world to the new; it is a voice from heaven, breaking through the silence or the discord of our natural condition. Oh, if we were half as sensible of this condition as we are of temporal anxieties, and fears, and wants—instead of listening coldly to this news from heaven, we should wait and watch for it, as eagerly as any mother now lies sleepless listening for the signal of a new arrival to relieve her fears and fill her cup to overflowing by glad tidings from her distant child. Oh, could the tumult of this life cease to fill our ears even for a moment, we might hear another sound, to which we are now deaf—good news, good news from heaven—from heaven to earth—from God to man—to·us—to you—to me—glad tidings. This is gospel, but is it the meaning of that word to you, my hearer?

(3.) Now let us make our definition more precise, by adding still another term. Good news, glad tidings, from the upper world, would be delightful if they related only to our natural necessities. If the voice of God were heard proclaiming peace instead of war, abundance in the place of want, and health for sickness—how might we rejoice, nay, how do we really rejoice in the sure though silent pledge of fruitful seasons and abundant harvests. But these, however free and entitled to our warmest thanks, can never meet our chief necessities—can never satisfy the soul. Its cravings are for spiritual good; its worst pains are the consciousness of guilt, remorse of conscience, and a fearful looking for of judgment. These may be smothered for a time, but not forever. Worldly prosperity may hide them from the view, and drive them from the thoughts, just as the excitement of business or of pleasure may distract the mind of the diseased and dying; but only to rush back again with tenfold anguish, when the momentary interruption shall have ceased. My hearers, no good news is good news in the highest sense, unless it reaches these necessities—supplies these wants, and remedies these evils. Without this, good news, even though sent from heaven, even though uttered by the voice of God, would be but like the good news of some half-forgotten, social or political success, at which your heart has long since ceased to beat, your eye to sparkle, and your blood to boil.

With such experiences, and who is utterly without them, no good news is good news to your sober judgment and your immortal soul—but good news in relation to your sins and your salvation, your future, your eternity. Oh, if the mask could now be taken from every heart, it would be seen that many who appear engrossed with temporal and secular intelligence, are really longing for good news of a very different kind—for the glad tidings of forgiveness, reconciliation, safety—for the joyful news that God is not their enemy, that hell is not their portion, that they may be, that they are entitled to a share in that perpetual inheritance—that indefeasible possession which lies far beyond the changes, and panics, and convulsions of this present life. You must hear such news sooner or later, or be wretched; and such, such news you may hear now, in "the gospel of Jesus Christ the Son of God."

2. This leads me to the second question under the general topic of the gospel: We have seen what it is—good news, good news from God to man—good news of spiritual good, forgiveness and salvation; but even this view cannot be complete without considering whose, as well as what it is. It is not an impersonal or abstract gospel; it is not the gospel of man, nor yet of an absolute and distant God; it is the gospel both of God and man; it is described expressly in the text as the gospel of Jesus Christ, the Son of God. I know of nothing in the Scriptures more habitually slighted and imperfectly apprehended than the names or titles of the Saviour. I could scarcely have repeated half a dozen words conveying less to multitudes of minds than those just uttered; which some of you perhaps regard precisely as you would the names and surnames of a friend or enemy; or even if you do admit the dignity of him who is thus described, it is only in the general, and without any definite perception of the importance of the terms employed. So inveterate and hurtful is this habit, that it may be well, occasionally, to remember what we all know, if we would consider and apply it; that all names are originally significant—that divine names are especially and always so; that the names of the Redeemer were designed to be descriptive and expres-

sive, not conventional and formal; and that when they are accumulated and combined, it is not without meaning, but every name is really suggestive of some great truth or important feature in the person or offices of Christ, and in the method of redemption. This, which is true in general, is emphatically true of the solemn nomenclature with which Mark begins his Gospel.

(1.) It is "the Gospel of Jesus," i. e., the good news of a Saviour: "Thou shalt call his name Jesus," said the angel who announced his birth to Joseph, "for he shall save his people from their sins." Even Joshua, whose name is identical in Hebrew, was so called prophetically, as the saviour or deliverer of Israel from enemies and dangers; and in this he was a type of him who was to come, not as a military conqueror and earthly prince, though men so expected him; not as the deliverer of the Jews from Roman vassalage, and the restorer of their ancient independence; but as a Saviour from a far worse bondage, and a more terrific ruin,—from perdition, from damnation, not of angels, not of devils, not of men without exception or discrimination; but of those predestinated to belief in him; his people, the Saviour of his people; not from temporal or physical distresses, but from sin; not from the sins of others, but their own; not from its effects, but from itself; not merely in the life, but in the heart; not merely in the stream, but in the spring, the source, the principle, the essence. Yes, the gospel is not only good news of a Saviour, but of him who came, of him who was called Jesus, because he was to save his people from their sins.

(2.) But the gospel is also the gospel of Christ; to many ears a mere tautology, an irksome repetition, an unmeaning pleonasm or superfluity, or at the most, a simple combination of inseparable names, like Julius Cæsar or George Washington. But I rejoice to know my hearers, that "ye have not so learned Christ," not even the name of Christ. The very children in the Sunday School know better, for they know that Christ in Greek, and Messias in Hebrew mean anointed, and that anointing was the Scripture symbol under the Old Testament for spiritual effusions, especially for those which qualified men for the great representative office of Prophet, Priest, and King, and that these offices themselves represent corresponding parts of the Redeemer's work; in other words, that he was in the highest sense to be the Prophet, Priest, and King, of his people. Their Prophet to reveal the will of God respecting them; their Priest to expiate their guilt and intercede for them; their King to govern and protect them; that in Him these offices before divided among many individuals and generations, were to meet and for the first time to be fully realized; all which is really expressed by calling him the Christ or the Messias.

These are not scholastic subtleties or technical distinctions, as some would fain persuade you; they are real, real—essential to a clear and full view of the office and person of the great deliverer; the source and subject of the gospel, who was called Jesus as the Saviour of his people; and Christ as the Prophet, Priest, and King forever.

(3.) But who is sufficient for these things, or who

is equal to the great work shadowed forth by these signs, and more than royal titles. If the highest earthly wisdom is evinced in separating legal and judicial functions; in dividing among many what would too severely task the powers and try the integrity of one, what human subject can combine in his own person, all that is expressed by these names. It is clearly impossible. Their very application excludes the thought of mere humanity. The necessity of a divine person to assume this trust would be apparent, from the nature of the trust itself, even if it were not expressly added, that this gospel is the gospel of the Son of God, not in the attenuated sense which heresy would put upon it, but in that which the unbelieving Jews themselves attached to the expressions when they charged our Lord with blasphemy, for calling God his father, and thus making himself equal with God. The Son of God, not merely as a creation, or an object of affection, or a subject of adoption; but as a partaker of his nature, one with him in essence, the same in substance, equal in power and glory. This is the last particular included in the description of the gospel. It is good news, from God to man, of deliverance from suffering and sin; the good news of a Saviour, of a prophet, of a priest, and of a king, not human but divine, *the Gospel of Jesus Christ the Son of God.*

II. Having thus seen what the gospel is, and whose it is, it remains to consider still more briefly its beginning, under the two distinct questions:
1. Where did it begin of old?

2. Where does it begin now?

In answer to the first of these inquiries, I remark:

(1.) That the gospel as a message of salvation, may be said to have begun in the eternal counsel of the divine will; in the eternal purpose of the God who sent it. There is no more injurious mistake than that of looking on the gospel as a sort of afterthought, or series of experiments intended to make good the failure of another method of salvation, and continually modified to meet emergencies as they arose. Known unto God are all his works from the beginning of the world, and though it may not be expedient to expatiate too freely in the bewildering mazes of this great truth, and especially to speculate upon it as a mere abstraction, apart from its connection with human duty, character, and destiny, we neither may nor can displace it as the deep and adamantine basis, upon which alone our hopes are founded. The Gospel of Christ could never terminate in our salvation, if it had not first begun in God's decree; let this then lie at the foundation, and from this let us ascend to explore the superstructure, and inquire what was the beginning of the gospel as a part of human history, and a phase of man's experience.

(2.) I remark, then, in the next place, that the beginning of the Gospel of Jesus Christ, was not in the New Testament, but in the Old; it began in the simple first promise to our fallen parents; in their sacrificial offerings; in the bleeding lambs of Abel's altar; in the simple faith and worship of the Patriarchs. It began afresh in the Mosaic legislation, in the ceremonial law, with its passover and pentecost, and great day of atonement; with its sabbaths and its jubilees, its priests and levites, its animal and vegetable offerings, its smoking altar and its shed blood. All these were worse than useless, worthless to man and insulting to God, except so far as they were typifying and symbolizing the "beginning of the Gospel of Jesus Christ the Son of God."

Once more it may be said to have begun in the predictions of the prophets, who declared in words, as the legal service did in acts, the coming Saviour, and not only foretold, but exhibited to all believers, "the beginning of the Gospel of Jesus Christ the Son of God."

(3.) Passing over the long interval between the Old and New Testaments, and coming nearer to the actual appearance of the promised Saviour, his gospel may be said to have had a new beginning in the preparatory ministry of John the Baptist. If not expressed, it is at least implied and necessarily indicated in Mark's introductory expression, that John the Baptist's preaching in the wilderness the baptism of repentance, with a view to the remission of sins, was the beginning of the gospel; its immediate precursor, the appointed preparation for its full disclosure, so that John's instructions and his baptisms derived all their worth and meaning from the fact that in the verse explained, they were the actual beginning of the Gospel of Jesus Christ the Son of God. We find accordingly, that when John's ministry was closed, and that of Christ himself succeeded, it was at first a mere continuation of John's preaching, that the burden of both cries was, Repent, for the kingdom of heaven is at hand! From this beginning, and from those already mentioned lying further back in all the prophecies, the ceremonies of the law, the religion of the patriarchs, and the decrees of God, from these beginnings, the gospel in the hands and in the mouth of Him who was at once its author, and its subject, and its finisher, was developed by degrees—in his divine instructions, in his miracles of mercy, in his perfect example, but above all in his faultless obedience and atoning passion, in his crucifixion, resurrection, and ascension, in his session at the right hand of God, in the effusion of his Spirit, the erection of his church, the diffusion of his doctrines, and the conquest of the world; that system whose beginnings we have traced, became the glorious gospel of the grace of God, even the gospel of your salvation.

2. This reference to the bearing of the gospel upon human destiny, brings us to the last remaining question suggested by the text, to which the answer must be still more brief than to the one before it; serving rather as a practical improvement than a further explanation of the subject.

Where does this gospel begin now? There is a sense in which this question would be senseless and irrelevant. The foundation is already laid, and neither need nor can be laid again. The sacrifice for sin has been already offered for all, and if that be rejected, there remaineth no more sacrifice for sin, but a fearful looking for of judgment and fiery indignation, which shall destroy the adversary. It were worse than vain, my hearers, to seek any other gospel than that which has begun already in the divine decrees, in the law, in the prophets, in the preaching of John, and in the saving work of Christ himself. There are other gospels, but of such, and of such as preach them, though it were an angel from heaven, Paul has said, let him be anathema.

But although the gospel can, in this view, have no more beginnings, yet in the subjective sense of something which may be embraced in the personal experience, and must be so embraced to secure salvation, we may ask in conclusion, as we asked before, *Where does the gospel begin now?* Without repeating what has been already said as to its ultimate source and indispensable foundation, I may say,

(1). That it begins for the most part in religious education; in that simple teaching at paternal knees and on maternal bosoms, which in our happy, highly favored times, supplies the place of those remote and long protracted means by which the world was prepared of old for the appearance of a Saviour. How many children of the church forget, how many pious parents insufficiently consider, that these lispings of religious truth to infant ears, which may even seem to be to themselves superfluous, may be intended by divine grace and realized by those, who scarcely can be said to hear them, as the beginning of the Gospel of Jesus Christ the Son of God.

(2). I say intended by divine grace, for I need not add that even these distilling dew-drops of infantile training can avail nothing without superhuman influence, without the moving of the spirit and the waters; sometimes in immediate succession to the early training without any interval of vice or unbelief; sometimes after peaceful interruptions, during which the seed sown seems to have long perished; but no, sometimes when least expected, a new life is infused into the dead mass of apparently unprofitable knowledge, the seed long buried shows itself, the tears of the departed glisten still about the leaves of the plant, and under heavenly culture and divine direction it springs up, first the blade, then the ear, and then the full corn in the ear. To that man the gospel has a new beginning, as in one sense the original instructions of his childhood, so in another the first movement of divine power on his heart and conscience, is to him the beginning of the Gospel of Jesus Christ the Son of God.

(3.) Lastly, in addition to these doctrines and gracious beginnings, there are what may be called providential recommencements of the gospel, both to communities and to individuals. I need not specify under the latter head, seasons of affliction, or under the former, seasons of revival. These I must leave with a bare suggestion to your private meditations. I will only hint in closing the subject, that to a whole church, even trivial incidents or epochs in their history, may mark such a revival of the gospel in its power as I have suggested. A change of local situation, or of pastors, the return of one after a temporary absence, nay, the very reassembling of the people after periodical dispersion, though entirely insufficient of themselves, may, under the divine direction, be the signal for new zeal upon the part of true believers, and for new attention in the unconverted, and to both, in an important sense of the expression, a beginning of the Gospel of Jesus Christ the Son of God. That I may not close without a word of application to the individual as well as the collective audience, let me say to you, my friend, who may be here to day apparently by accident, or if a stated worshipper in this place, yet a stranger to the covenants of promise, that you have only to accept of that which is so freely offered; you have only to repent and to believe and to throw yourself into the outstretched arms of mercy; you have only to consent to be made holy and happy in the way of your own choosing, and this favored hour, this otherwise imperfect service, shall be remembered by you to eternal ages, as having been to your soul, through divine grace, the beginning of the Gospel of Jesus Christ the Son of God.

II.

MATTHEW 2, 2.—Where is he that is born king of the Jews?

WHEN these words were originally uttered, the Jews, though still a nation in the popular sense—*i. e.*, not only a people but a state, not only a distinct race but a body politic—had for centuries had no king of their own royal lineage. The throne of David was still empty and awaiting his successor. He who did reign over them was regarded by them as an alien in blood and an apostate in religion. And even he was the tributary vassal of a foreign state, the last of the great powers to which the Jews had been successively subjected. The first days of their monarchy were in all respects its best days. It had scarcely surmounted the horizon when it reached its zenith. The best and greatest of the theocratic kings was David. Even under Solomon the symptoms of decline began to show themselves. He was scarcely dead before the great schism took away a large part of his kingdom. The apostate monarchy of Israel waxed worse and worse, and fell at last before the power of Assyria. Its people were carried into exile, and their place supplied by heathen settlers. The captives themselves vanish all at once from history,

and are still sought after by the name of the Lost
Tribes. The kingdom of Judah lasted longer, but
the progress of decay was constant. Now and then a
king arose, who seemed to raise them for a time, but
it was only to sink deeper by reaction and collapse.
The Babylonian empire had supplanted the Assyrian
and become the mistress of western Asia. Before the
host of Nebuchadnezzar, Judah fell as Ephraim had
fallen long before. The holy city was dismantled,
and the temple burnt with fire. The king
and the best part of the people went into captivity.
From this they were delivered by the fall of Babylon
and the rise of the Persian power on its ruins. Cyrus
the Great favoured and restored the Jewish exiles.
The temple was rebuilt in troublous times. But the
renovated commonwealth was weak and insignificant,
compared with the old kingdom, even in its latter
days; much more when compared with its pristine
glory under Solomon and David. The colony could
only exist by the protection of foreign powers. It
passed under the successive domination of the empires
which so rapidly supplanted one another in the interval
between the Old and New Testaments. First
the Persians, then the Macedonians, then the Greek
kings of Egypt and Syria. The oppressions of the latter
roused the old Jewish spirit and led to the erection
of a native monarchy. The Maccabees, or Hasmonean
Princes, united in themselves the kingly and the
priestly office. For several generations they maintained
the independence of the Jewish state, even
against formidable foes. But they were not the
legitimate successors of David; they were not even

children of Judah, but of Levi. At length a family dispute was referred to foreign arbitration.

The Roman Empire in the meantime had become the ruling power of the world. Syria and Eygpt were already under its dominion. Its agents eagerly embraced the opportunity of gaining foothold in the land of Israel. Under the pretext of pacification, Pompey the Great took possession of Jerusalem and about half a century before the language of the text was uttered, the Roman eagles were conspicuously planted upon Zion and Moriah. With their usual wise policy, the conquerors left with the conquered the appearance of self-government. Their religious institutions remained undisturbed. An Idumean family, personally favoured by Augustus, was exalted by the Senate to the royal dignity. The first that took the title was "Herod the king, in whose days wise men from the east came to Jerusalem, saying, Where is he that is born king of the Jews?" At this question, we are told the king was troubled, and all Jerusalem agitated with him. But it was not the agitation of mere wonder. The very effect produced shows that a corresponding expectation was already in existence. The Jews still held fast to their ancient Scriptures, though with many traditions. These taught them to expect the restoration of the throne of David. From them, or from an old collateral tradition, other nations were now looking to Judea as the scene of great events. The world was agitated by a vague foreboding. War for a time had ceased throughout the Roman Empire. Men had leisure to attend to predictions and prognostics. The Jews believed that the Star foretold by Balaam was about to come out of Jacob. Their heathen neighbors shared in the belief of and expectation of strange heavenly phenomena announcing the approach of great catastrophes and the rise of some extraordinary personage. At this critical juncture in the history of the world, when Roman power and Greek civilization had attained their height in the Augustine age, when heathen religion and philosophy had both reached the period of decrepitude and men began to feel the need of better consolation, when the schools and the oracles alike were dumb; when the heathen were looking for they knew not what, and the Jews expecting a son of David to restore their ancient monarchy; at this very crisis wise men from the east: the cradle of science and the home of occult superstition, came to Jerusalem, saying, " Where is he that is born king of the Jews?

They did not ask for the actual sovereign of the Jews. It was to him that they addressed the question. But they ask for the hereditary rightful king, not one to be born, but as born already. No wonder that the Edomite who held possession of the throne by the grace of a heathen sovereign, was alarmed. No wonder that his people were excited, when they heard these strangers asking : " Where is he that is born king of the Jews? for we have seen his star in the east, and have come to worship him." The question was not one of local or temporary interest. It was to give complexion to the history of all after ages. It has received or been susceptible of various answers, as the state of things has gradually changed. To some of these I now ask your attention, as a proof that the demand is still a stirring one, "Where is he that is born king of the Jews?"

When the question was originally asked, the answer might have been, In Bethlehem of Judah, in a stable, in a manger. Yes, the hereditary king of Israel, he who was to sit upon the throne both by divine and human right, was born in poverty, and to the eyes of men in shame. This was surprising in itself, but it was more—it was the first in a long series of surprises, of enigmas, of apparent contradictions. He that was born king of the Jews not only passed through all the pains of infancy and childhood, in an humble station, but in mature age had not where to lay his head. Dependent on the charity of friends, despised and rejected by his enemies. These privations and these sufferings become darker and more complex as we trace his history, until at last, betrayed by one disciple, denied by another, and forsaken by the rest, we seem to lose sight of him amidst a cloud through which the spears of Roman soldiers and the Urim and Thummim on the High Priest's breast are seen flashing in unwonted combination. From this scene of condemnation and disgrace we turn away, saying, "Where, then, is he that is born king of the Jews?"

When the cloud has once more been dispelled, this question may receive another answer. For on yonder hill, without the walls of Jerusalem, three crosses are erected. On these crosses three living sufferers are even now suspended. Two of them are ordinary convicts, malefactors.—But over the head of him suspended in the midst there is a superscription. The characters are legible enough, and that all who pass by may comprehend them, they are written in the three sacred languages of earth—in Greek, in Hebrew, and in Latin. Draw near and decipher them. Is it a record of some common-place iniquity, on which society has wreaked its vengeance? No, the words are strange and seemingly misplaced—as if some wanton hand had torn them from the walls of a palace, or the canopy of a throne, and in mockery, transferred them to this scene of execution, this Calvary, this Golgotha, this place of a skull—" Jesus of Nazareth, king of the Jews!" Yes, the very words!—In vain did the Jews plead for a change of form—Rome, the mistress of the world, through the hand of her procurator, has become witness to the truth, and the testimony cannot be recalled. "What I have written I have written!" Read, then, above the head of that expiring sufferer, the answer to the question—"Where is he that is born king of the Jews?"—There, there, upon that cross.

In this case too, the answer does but touch one link in a long chain of paradoxical events, disappointing, blasting, the long-cherished hopes of Israel. Instead of a conqueror presenting them a sufferer, accused, condemned, and put to death in due course of law. Even his followers and friends could say, in deep despondency: "We trusted that it had been he which should have redeemed Israel." Even they are slow of heart to learn, believe, and understand that this redemption must be purchased by the sacrifice of life—that Messiah must suffer these things before he could enter into his glory. Yes, the whole doctrine of atonement and salvation by the death of the incarnate Son of God is summed up and concentrated in the answer given at this awful moment on the top of Calvary, to the question—"Where is he that is born king of the Jews?"

But Calvary is not the only height about Jerusalem. There is another on the east called Olivet—the Mount of Olives. On the acclivity of that hill what do you discern?—Eleven men gazing at the sky—A moment ago and there was another with them, and they might have been heard anxiously inquiring of him—"Wilt thou at this time restore again the kingdom to Israel?" He has scarcely spoken in reply, when he is taken up; a cloud receives him out of their sight. At first perhaps they doubt the testimony of their senses; then indulge the hope that he has only vanished for a moment—but they are soon undeceived—and if the question were now put to them; "Where is he that is born king of the Jews?" they would with one accord point upwards, and reply, "He is in heaven!" Yes, he who once lay in the manger at Bethlehem, and lately hung upon the cross on Calvary, is now in heaven, beyond the reach of persecution and privation; and the same is still true. Even the youngest children who are taught the name of Christ, know well that he is not here now, as he was here of old—they know too, that he is in heaven. They know not, and the wisest of us know not, where, or what heaven is; but we know that wherever it is, he is there, and that where he is, there is heaven. And thither our thoughts naturally turn at the question—"Where is he that is born king of the Jews?"

This might seem to shut the door upon all further inquiry, but it does not. Men may think, as the eleven thought at first, that he is now beyond our reach, and we beyond his; but, like them, we may be mistaken. No, before he left them he commanded them to wait for the promise of the Father, and the baptism of the Spirit, and when that had been received, to go as witnesses of him not only through Judea and Samaria, but to the uttermost part of the earth; and they were not to go alone—for he was to go with them, and remain with them—"Lo I am with you alway, even unto the end of the world." In some sense, then, he is on earth—he is here—if we are indeed gathered in his name. "For where two or three are gathered in my name, there am I present in the midst of them." Here then is still another answer to the question: "Where is he that is born king of the Jews?" He is in heaven, but he is also upon earth; not visibly, yet really—and one day he will reappear, and then another answer still—or the same, but in a new sense, or at least with a new emphasis, must be returned.

For look again upon the Mount of Olives, and behold the eleven gazing steadfastly toward heaven. Who are those that stand beside them, clothed in white apparel? and in what terms do they accost them? "Men of Galilee, why stand ye gazing up to heaven? This same Jesus which is taken from you, shall so come in like manner as ye have seen him go into heaven." And is this not still true?

Did his coming at the downfall of Jerusalem exhaust this precious promise? Is it not one of the great doctrines that the Church through all vicissitudes, has held fast as a part of her unalienable heritage that Christ shall come again not in spirit, but in person, to the eye of sense as well as that of faith. However we may differ as to the time of this epiphany, we all believe that it will certainly take place, and that when we are asked, "Where is he that is born king of the Jews?" we shall no longer be obliged to point to a far distant heaven, or to look fearfully around us as if seeing one who is invisible—but with open face beholding the bright cloud as it descends, and him who sits enthroned upon it, we shall see amidst the halo that surrounds his head, in living characters of light, the same inscription that the hand of Pilate once appended to the cross, "Jesus of Nazareth, king of the Jews."—For when he comes he shall come in glory—the cloudy throne will be only a figure of that throne which he already occupies. His seat at the right hand of his father. All power in heaven and earth is already committed to him. We are assured not only that he is in safety, but that he is in possession, and in the active exercise of power, of all power, of infinite, almighty power. He who was humbled, is now exalted. He who lay in the manger, and hung upon the cross, and ascended from Olivet, and is to come to judge the world at the last day, is even now at the helm, guiding the complicated movements of God's providential government. Yes, he is even now upon the throne of the universe, and to that throne we may look up and to it direct the eye of others when they ask, whether as friends or foes, "Where is he that is born king of the Jews?"

This question therefore, is of interest, not merely in relation to the place of Christ's abode at any period of his history, but also in relation to his dignity and office. The question, Where is he? really means, What is he? Where is he that is born king of the Jews? What part does he now fill? In what character, under what aspect, is he now revealed to us? In this, as well as in the local sense, we may ask, Where is he? We have seen already, in reply to this interrogation, that he is upon the throne of universal ecumenical dominion. But this throne, though real and exalted, is invisible. Hereafter, we shall see it, but as yet we see it not. Yet even now, and even upon earth, his throne is standing. By a strange transmutation, he who was born king of the Jews is now king of the Christians. He came to his own, and his own received him not. The Jews as a race, rejected him. They still reject him. After eighteen hundred years, the language of their hearts, and lips, and lives, is still the same that Christ, in one of his parables, puts into the mouths of their fathers: "We will not have this man to reign over us." Even at the time, and to his face, they rejected his pretensions, crying, "We have no king but Cæsar." Even that they soon lost. The Cæsar whom they chose to be their king was their destroyer. The successor of Cæsar levelled Jerusalem with the earth, threw down its walls, and tried to obliterate its very name, while no Jew was permitted even to tread the soil. In course of time, the throne of the Cæsars crumbled. The Eternal City lost its secular supremacy. But the Jews continued, and do still continue aliens to the land of promise. They have sought the favor of Mohammedans, of Christians, and of heathen, and, in turn have enjoyed each. But all have turned to be their enemies. Even now, when a better spirit has arisen with respect to them, they are without a country, without a government, without political or national existence. In them the prophecy has indeed been verified. They have continued "many days without a king, and without a home, and without a sacrifice." Where then is he that was born king of the Jews? Has he been thrust out of his inheritance? Has the promise to David of perpetual succession been completely nullified? By no means! He who was to come has come and been enthroned, and is at this moment reigning. He reigns not only in heaven, but on earth. He reigns over an organized and constituted kingdom. He reigns over the Israel of God. The Christian Church is heir to the prerogatives of ancient Israel. The two bodies are morally identical. It was the remnant according to the election of grace, that formed the germ of the new organization. The new edifice was reared upon the old foundation. It was only the carnal Israel, the nation as a nation, that rejected Christ. Over them as Jews he is not reigning. But he is not a Jew that is one outwardly. All are not Israel that are of Israel. They may still claim to be the chosen people. But this is "the blasphemy of them which say that they are Jews and are not, but the synagogue of Satan." "We are the circumcision, which worship God in the Spirit, and rejoice in Christ Jesus, and have no confidence in the flesh. Over such Christ does reign, and in reigning over such he is really and truly, in the highest sense, and in the true sense of the prophecies and promises respecting him, "King of the Jews." He reigns in the heart of every individual believer. He reigns in the church as a collective body. He is theoretically acknowledged as the head, even by many who in words deny him. By every pure church, and by every sincere Christian, he is really enthroned and crowned, acknowledged and obeyed. He who was born king of the Jews, has become the king of the Christians, without any change of character or office, without any failure in the plan or the prediction. We have only to point to the throne of the Church and to the crown of Christendom, when any ask, in doubt or scorn, "Where is he that is born king of the Jews?"

This kingdom, it is true, is not yet coextensive with the earth, but it shall be. It is growing, and is yet to grow. The kingdoms of the earth are to become the kingdoms of our Lord, and of his Christ. The mountain of the Lord's house is to be established above every other, and all nations are to flow unto it. The stone cut without hands from the mountain is to fill the earth. The watchword of its progress is Overturn, overturn, overturn, until he shall come, whose right it is to reign. However the great men and the wise men of the world may be affected by this revolution, it shall come to pass. They may despise the day of small beginnings—but the time is coming and perhaps at hand, when the providence, if not the voice of God shall say to them, Behold, ye despisers, and wonder, and perish—they may imagine that by constitutions, and by legislative acts, or by the reorganization of society, they have secured themselves from all intrusion upon Christ's part.—But before they are aware, his hand may be upon them, and his arrows sharp in the hearts of the king's enemies. Resistance and revolt will be forever unavailing. The heathen may still rage and the nations imagine a vain thing— the kings of the earth may set themselves, and rulers take counsel together against the Lord and his anointed. They may still say as in ages past they have said, Let us break their bands asunder, and cast their cords from us. He that sitteth in the heavens shall laugh. The Lord shall have them in derision. Then shall he speak to them in his anger, and confound them in his hot displeasure. He has already set his king upon his holy hill of Zion. He will give him the heathen for his heritage, and the uttermost parts of the earth for his possession. If rebellious he will rule them with a rod of iron, he will break them in pieces as a potter's vessel. Let kings then learn wisdom, let the judges of the earth be instructed. Let them pay allegiance and do homage to this sovereign, lest they perish in his anger, which will soon be kindled. And as his grace is equal to his power and his justice, blessed are all they that put their trust in him. Christ's kingdom is not of this world, in its origin or character. He came not to be a judge or a divider, a secular ruler or a military chieftain. But he must, even here, reign. His reign must and shall be universal. And the prospect of this issue is the hope of the world.

There is no more cheering anticipation than that Christ is one day to be king of nations; that his realm is not to reach, like that of David, from the Red Sea to the Mediterranean, and from the Euphrates to the desert, but from sea to sea, and from the river to the ends of the earth. To this vast empire, and to Him who rules it, we, or they who shall come after us, may one day point in triumphant answer to the question, "Where is he that is born king of the Jews?" He that was born king of the Jews, and who never literally carried even that crown, shall be seen seated as it were upon the throne of all the ancient emperors and imperial sovereignties—Sesostris and Cyrus, Alexander and Cæsar; the lost empires shall revive in him, and all the crowns of earth shall meet upon the brow of him who was "born king of the Jews."

To this general confluence of nations there shall not be even one exception. Even one, however slight, would seem to mar the triumph. There is one especially which could not but have this effect. The people that rejected him—the seed of Abraham—to whom were committed the oracles of God—to whom once pertained the adoption, and the glory, and the covenants, and the giving of the law, and the service of God, and the promises—whose were the fathers, and of whom, as concerning the flesh, Christ came, who is over all, God blessed for ever. If these should still remain aloof, the glory of Immanuel's coronation might seem to be obscured or tarnished.

Not that the promises of God would even then fail of their accomplishment. Not that the Israel of God would even then cease to exist, or the perpetual succession of its members be at all interrupted. But the hearts that pant for the Redeemer's exaltation might feel something to be wanting. As they stood around his throne, and looked beyond the brilliant circle that encompassed it, if they still beheld the lost sheep of the house of Israel refusing to return to the Shepherd and Bishop of their souls, they might recall the promise, " All kings shall fall down before him, all nations shall serve him ;" and then say, " all nations? Ah, yes, all but one, and that, alas, the very one that he was born to rule. The kings of Tarshish and the isles do bring presents; the kings of Sheba and of Seba do offer gifts; they that dwell in the wilderness have bowed before him; and all his other enemies have licked the dust;—but where is little Benjamin, and Ephraim, and Manasseh? where is Judah, with his lion? where is Levi with his Thummim and his Urim? where, oh, where are the tribes of his inheritance? The Gentiles are here, but Israel still dwells alone. Our King is, indeed, the King of nations; the King of kings;—but " where is he that is born king of the Jews?"

Even in this respect, the answer will eventually be auspicious. He that was born king of the Jews shall yet reign over them. He shall be not only their rightful but their actual sovereign. As such he shall be acknowledged by them. As he reigns already king of the Jews, over the Israel of God which is perpetuated in his Church, so shall he one day reign king of the Jews, over those who are such outwardly, over Israel according to the flesh. This the promise of his Word entitles and requires us to expect. It is the cherished and exciting faith of some, that the seed of Abraham are to be literally gathered from the four winds, and from all parts of the earth, once more to take possession of the land bestowed by covenant on their fathers. Whether this be expressly promised in the Word of God or not—a question which will probably continue to be agitated till it is resolved by some event—there are providential signs which seem to point to such an issue. The land of promise almost empty of inhabitants; the Jews dispersed without a country of their own; their slight connexion with the countries where they dwell; the nature of their occupations tending to facilitate a general removal; and in many instances their social position making it desirable;—all this, together with a re-awakening of their interest in the land of their fathers, and the birth of a new interest in them upon the part of Christians, may be plausibly interpreted as providential indications of precisely such a change as some interpreters of prophecy suppose to be predicted. If these anticipations should be realized, and Israel should again take root downward in his own land, and bear fruit upward, how conspicuously would the regal rights of the Redeemer be asserted and established by the visible subjection of the Jewish nation to his peaceful sway? In every new accession to the swelling population of the Goodly Land from other nations, we should see repeated the acknowledgment of Jesus as the Son of David by his hereditary subjects, and his kinsmen according to the flesh—from every caravan and every fleet that bore them homeward—we might hear the voice of Israel coming back to his allegiance, asking, Where is he that is born King of the Jews?

But however joyful such a consummation might be, and on some accounts devoutly to be wished, the final exaltation of our Lord is not suspended on it, even with respect to his acknowledgment by Israel. Though Israel be not gathered, and externally re-organized upon the soil once gladdened by the presence, and still hallowed by the tombs of patriarchs, and prophets, and apostles; though perpetual exclusion from that precious spot of earth be part of God's irrevocable judgment on the race as such considered, still, we know that they shall be restored to a participation in the honours and advantages which were once exclusively their own, and from which they have fallen by rejecting the Messiah, we know and are assured that the exsiccated branches of that ancient olive shall again be grafted in—and that in some emphatic sense all Israel shall be saved; and in the glorious fulfilment of this promise, whether accompanied or not by territorial restoration, Christ's crown and sceptre shall be honoured. Every Jew who names the name of Christ as a believer, whether at the holy city or among the Gentiles, and in the very end of the earth, will individually do him homage as the Son of David. As soon as the spirit of inquiry shall begin to be diffused among that people, and the veil to be taken from their hearts in the reading of the Old Testament; as soon as the eyes of those now blind shall see clearly, and the tongue of the stammerer speak plainly; even though they should continue still dispersed among the nations; there will be something like a repetition of the scene presented eighteen centuries ago, but on a vastly wider scale, for the children of Israel will then be seen uniting with the fulness of the Gentiles in the question: "Where is he that is born king of the Jews?"

Such, my hearers, are the answers which, at different stages in the progress of Christ's kingdom, have been, or might have been, or shall be yet returned to the question originally asked by the wise men, who came from the east to Jerusalem in the days of Herod, Where is He, that is born king of the Jews? Where is he? in the manger as a helpless infant. On the cross, as a sacrifice for sinners. On the cloud, ascending into heaven. On earth invisibly partaking in the prayers of even two or three devoutly gathered for his worship. At the right hand of the Father. On the throne of universal providental sovereignty. On the throne of Christendom. On the throne of the Gentiles. On the throne of Israel. From every such view of his exaltation let us gather fresh assurance that the purpose and promises of God can never fail, that whatever clouds may hide the sky, shall, sooner or later, be dispelled; that, however long the rights of the Redeemer may appear to be relinquished or denied or in abeyance, they shall yet be openly asserted and universally acknowledged, that he who was born to reign, shall reign, that his dominion shall be endless, that the very things which seem to threaten its extinction shall eventfully further it. If even the apostacy and casting off of Israel, the chosen race with whom the church of old appeared to be identified, did not prevent its continued existence and progressive growth until the present hour, what disaffection or resistance, personal, or national, can now arrest its onward march to universal empire. No, let Bethlehem, and Calvary, and Olivet, and Paradise, and Christendom, and Jewry all bear witness, that what he was born to bring about must come to pass; the day, though distant, shall arrive when the kingdoms of the world are to become the kingdoms of our Lord, and of his Christ; and when the joint Hallelujah of angels and men, of the church on earth, and of the church in heaven, of Jews and Gentiles, shall proclaim the final and eternal answer to the question, Where is he that is born king of the Jews?"

III.

JOHN 13, 7.—*What I do thou knowest not now; but thou shalt know hereafter.*

THESE words relate to an astonishing act of condescension in our Saviour just before he suffered. Not contented with the proofs he had already given of his lowliness and willingness to be abased that we might be exalted, at his last meeting with the twelve, he crowned all by performing the most humble act of service to his own disciples. He took water, as the slaves in those days were accustomed to do for their masters and their guests, and washed the disciples' feet. It is impossible for us even now, to read of this without a keen feeling of disapprobation. For a moment at least, it seems as if the Saviour did too much, as if he went too far; no wonder then that it took the apostles by surprise, and that the boldest and most freespoken of them dared to say as much; nay, even ventured to refuse compliance, saying, Lord, dost thou wash my feet? And even after Christ had answered this inquiry in the language of the text, he persevered in his refusal, saying with some violence of feeling, Thou shalt never wash my feet. Nor was it till our Lord had solemnly declared that, unless washed he could have no part with him, that the bold and ardent Peter overcame his repugnance to this humiliating honour, and said, Lord, not my feet only, but also my hands and my head.

What I wish you to attend to now is not the particular design and meaning of his strange proceeding, but the way in which our Saviour dealt with Peter's difficulties and reluctance. He knew that Peter did not understand what he was doing, and because he could not understand it, he was not willing to explain it to him. It might have seemed that the simplest way to overcome his scruples was by telling him exactly what he wished to know, by saying, "What I mean by this preaching is to teach you such and such a doctrine, or to produce such and such an impression on you." But he gives him no such satisfaction. He only intimates that it will be given at some future time; "What I do thou knowest not now, but thou shalt know hereafter." This is in perfect agreement with our Saviour's customary method of proceeding. He requires implicit confidence in him and unconditional submission. What he did on this occasion is precisely what he is continually doing in his church. He requires his people to walk by faith and not by sight; to believe what they cannot fully comprehend; to do what they cannot altogether approve except on his authority. This is true of some of his most sacred institutions. What he did to his disciples upon this occasion was not meant to be repeated as a public ceremony of the church, although many have imagined that it was, and have continued to this day as a superstitious form.

But there are *other* things which *were* designed to be perpetual, and which men are sometimes disposed to slight or quarrel with, because they do not fully understand their meaning or their use. This is the spirit which has led some who call themselves Christians to tamper with the sacraments which Christ himself has instituted and required to be observed until his second coming. Some do not see the use of washing with water in the name of the Father, Son, and Holy Ghost, and therefore discontinue it, professing to rely upon inward spiritual baptism, although many soon dispense with this, because having once determined to do nothing and submit to nothing which they cannot fully comprehend and explain, they are forced to give up every thing in turn, because in fact there is nothing at all which they can fully understand and account for. In like manner, some begin in changing the form of the Lord's Supper, and end with setting it aside altogether as a useless and unmeaning form. And some who do not meddle with the administration of the ordinance, refuse to partake of it, and thereby publicly profess their faith, although they claim to be believers and true Christians. They cannot see why such a form is necessary, or what useful purpose it can answer, either to themselves or others, if they have the right religious views and feelings, not observing that obedience to Christ's positive commands is one of the most certain tests of true or false religious views and feelings, and that if this obedience is withheld there is no conclusive proof that inward piety exists at all. The spirit of all such disaffection to the ordinances of

God's house is that which actuated Peter when he said "Thou shalt never wash my feet," and to all who cherish it or act upon it, Christ himself may be heard saying, "If I wash thee not, thou hast no part with me," but yet adding, with a gracious condescension to the weakness of the true believer, "what I do thou knowest not now, but thou shalt know hereafter."

Such is God's method of proceeding not only in this case but in every other. We cannot live without taking many things on trust, without believing and obeying where we do not fully understand. What is there that we do thus understand? The world is full of mysteries and wonders. The very things that seem most simple and with which we think ourselves most perfectly acquainted are really beyond our comprehension. The heavens and the earth, the water and the air, are full of strange and surprising objects. We cannot explain fully how the slightest change takes place among the thousands that are going on around us. How does the grass grow? or the fruit ripen? or the seasons change? Because we know that these things do take place we think we comprehend them; but we only know that they are, not how they are. And those who have gone furtherest in discovering and explaining what are called the laws of nature, only differ in degree from the most ignorant, and are often the readiest to acknowledge that they have not reached the bottom of those mysteries, that after all their explanations and discoveries, there is something yet to be discovered and explained. This is the general rule and law throughout the universe, that what God is and what God does, is and must be beyond the comprehension of his creatures. We cannot find out the Almighty to perfection—such knowledge is too wonderful for us—we cannot attain to it—his counsels are unsearchable and his ways are past finding out. He lets us know and understand enough, not only to provide for our own safety and enjoyment, but to make us anxious to know more, and sensible how little we know now—and at the same time to fill us with an awful reverence for Him who is producing all these changes and carrying on these mighty operations in our own world and in all worlds, without even making a mistake or failing to effect his purpose.

True, to us a large part of these wonderful works are neither seen nor heard, and if we saw and heard them, we should not comprehend them. It is not certain how far we shall ever fully comprehend them. Even after ages have elapsed, when we have grown in knowledge and capacity beyond our highest thoughts and expectations, there will still be much, not only in God himself, but in his works which we do not understand. We shall know more and more to all eternity, but never can know all. And this is one of the most gracious hopes set before us, that if saved we shall never cease to rise and make advances in the knowledge and admiration of God's works and of himself. If this was to cease, even millions of years hence, the promise might seem to be imperfect and unsatisfying. But it is not to cease—at any point which we can fix upon—however much we may have learned there will be something to learn still. And yet it is encouraging to know that much that now seems strange and unaccountable in the world by which we are surrounded and of which we form a part will one day be made clear to us. If the universe, instead of being silent, had a voice, or rather if we had ears to hear the voice of God himself speaking to us in the winds, the waves, in the earth and in the skies, in beasts and birds, and in the growth of plants, we might distinctly hear him saying to all these things which now surprise us most, "What I do thou knowest not now, but thou shalt know hereafter."

This may be said to be a law of nature, but it is also a law of providence. However often we may witness or experience God's dispensations, they still take us by surprise. Even those which are most frequently repeated, and which seem most alike, still have something to excite our wonder. A destructive fire still affects us as if no such had occurred before. A prevailing sickness may appear, and disappear, and reappear, and after all seem something new. The wicked world in Noah's time was just as much surprised when the flood came as if they had received no warning. All this is really produced by a secret unbelief. But besides this, there is always something in these great calamities and general visitations which is contrary to what we look for. When we hear of the pestilence as raging elsewhere and approaching, we may expect it to arrive, but when it does arrive, it takes a course or takes a shape which we were not prepared for. We wonder why this place is visited and that passed by. We try to ascertain the cause of what we see, but all our speculations are in vain.

Those who seemed likely to be swept away survive, and those who seemed safest fall the first. And so it is in some degree with other great catastrophes. A riot suddenly breaks out in a great city, and the troops are called out, and the first shot fired strikes the heart of one who merely happened to be passing. An explosion takes place and destroys the lives of some who did not know of the existence of the danger, while those who knew it and perhaps produced it, are miraculously saved. Disease invades a household and destroys its members one by one, whilst all around escape. The young, the healthy, those upon whom most are dependent, fall by accident or sickness, while the old and helpless, who have long been waiting their discharge, still linger even when deprived of those by whom they were sustained and comforted. Examples of this kind are continually occurring, and exciting, even in the minds of Christians, a secret discontent and inclination to find fault, which often lurks at the bottom of their hearts even when they seem to acquiesce in the divine dispensations, and indeed until their minds are so far cleared, and their excited feelings so far calmed that they can hear God saying even in the fire, and the earthquake, and the tempest, and the pestilence, "What I do thou knowest not now, but thou shalt know hereafter."

And if this is the case of those who merely look at the calamities of others as spectators, how much more natural is such a feeling on the part of those who are themselves the objects of these providential visitations. Oh how hard, how hopeless, does the task seem, to suppress all risings of rebellious discontent, when we are touched ourselves by what appears to us to be a cruel and untimely stroke. How natural and reasonable does it often seem to say, as some do say to themselves or others, "I could have borne this without a murmur, a little sooner or a little later, but at this moment it is hard indeed." Or the language of the heart may be, I should not have resisted or repined under a severer stroke but of a different kind. If it had been my business, not my health; or my health, but not my reputation; or myself, but not my family; or this friend, but not that, and so on through a thousand suppositions of what might have been but is not true, I could have bowed without a murmur. In all this there is certainly a great delusion. Had the stroke been different, the effect would still have been the same. And even where there would have been a difference, that difference may itself have been the reason of the choice, because a stroke which is not felt, or which is felt too lightly, would not answer the severe but gracious purpose of the Lord in smiting us at all. But even when this is acknowledged and believed, it may be hard to see wherein the gracious purpose lies, and therefore hard to acquiesce in the benevolence and wisdom of that Providence which causes us or suffers us to suffer. Such submission may be wrought and is continually wrought by sovereign grace without imparting any clearer knowledge of God's immediate purpose by inspiring strong faith in his benevolence and truth, so that the soul is satisfied with knowing that it is the will of God, and therefore must be right, best for his honor and his creatures' welfare.

Even such, however, may derive a pleasing solace from the hope that what seems now so unaccountable, will one day be intelligible even to themselves. And when they look at the most doubtful and perplexing circumstances of their case, at which perhaps their faith was staggered, and their hope sickened, but in which God has now enabled them to acquiesce, they may find it easier to do so when they call to mind that, although they are bound to yield whether they ever knew the meaning of these strange dispensations or not, they are permitted to believe that they shall yet know at least something more, perhaps much more, perhaps as much as they could wish to know, or need to know in order to be perfectly contented with their lot, and as this quieting persuasion takes possession of their souls, their ears are suddenly unstopped, and made to tingle with these sweet but solemn words, "What I do thou knowest not now, but thou shalt know hereafter."

The application which I have been making of these words to God's providential dispensations when they take the shape of personal or national calamities, may all seem natural enough and be received without a doubt of their correctness, not because the text itself includes all this directly, but because the principle, the rule which it lays down is not confined to the original occasion, nor to religious rites and institutions, but extends to every case in which men can be called to acquiesce and to obey from general trust in God, or deference to his will, without fully knowing for what reason or what purpose in particular. Now of this there are no examples more familiar or affecting than those furnished by severe afflictions, whether such as affect only individuals and families, or such as more or less affect a whole community, and therefore there will probably be little disposition to dispute the application of the text to all such cases.

But there is another application not so obvious, to which I am anxious, for that very reason, to direct your thoughts, lest the instructions and the warnings here afforded should lose a part of their effect from being too much confined in their application, so that those perhaps in most need of the lesson which the Spirit of God teaches, may depart without it. You admit perhaps that with respect to God's works, and the changes continually going on in nature, you must wait for clearer light, and you are willing so to do, perhaps are well content to wait forever. You also admit that in reference to the meaning and design of God's afflictive dispensations, with respect both to the many and the few, both to others and yourselves, it is right and necessary to be satisfied with knowing in the general that God is just and merciful, that what he does not only is, but must be right, not only right but best, best for him and best for you, and that therefore you may rationally wait for any further explanation or discovery. But has the thought occurred to you that this is no more true of affliction than of any other state or situation? that the only difference arises from the fact that suffering makes men think of this and feel it, but does not make it any truer or more certain than it was before; and that this very circumstance makes it peculiarly important to remind men of the truth in question, when they are not so reminded by their outward circumstances. There is no time when men need less to be warned against intemperance and imprudence than a time of general sickness and mortality, for this very state of things is a sufficient warning. But when health prevails, we are peculiarly in danger of forgetting our mortality and neglecting the precautions which are necessary to preserve us from disease and death. So too in the case before us, when men actually suffer, either one by one or in large bodies, they have but occasion to be told that God may have some purpose to accomplish which they cannot understand at present, but which may perhaps be understood hereafter.

Now let us ask ourselves the question; May not God have purposes to answer, of which we have no suspicion, when he grants us undisturbed prosperity? Does he cease to reign as soon as men cease to suffer? Is his only instrument the rod? Is it only the afflicted that are subject to his government? And are the rich, the healthy, and the honoured, the cheerful, the thoughtless, and the gay, exempt from his control? Perhaps this is the secret of the coldness with which most of us contemplate God's strokes till they touch ourselves, despising the riches of his goodness, and forbearance, and longsuffering, not knowing that the goodness of God leadeth to repentance. And how few really regard this as the great end of prosperity; to lead men to repentance! How many do indeed believe that health and wealth and comfort are all means employed to bring men to repentance? And if this is so, how seldom does prosperity accomplish its design: I mean its purposes of mercy; for alas! it has a twofold tendency. It is like some desperate and potent remedies for bodily disease. It either kills or cures. Are we sufficiently convinced of this? Do we feel it as we should if God were pleased to lift the veil that overhangs the hearts and inner lives of men, and show us what is passing at this moment, and to what results hereafter it is tending? If you, my hearers, could be made to see that your prosperity is just as much a state of discipline as the affliction of your neighbour; that your heart, if not subdued and softened by God's goodness is continually growing harder; that the frivolous and exciting pleasures which engross you, or the violent passions which inflame and agitate you, or the sordid appetites which enslave and master you, are all combining to prepare you for changes which you do not now anticipate: if I could shew you God looking down upon this fearful process, and permitting it to go on, as a righteous recompence of those who do not like to retain him in their knowledge, but revolt from his authority and trample on his mercy, and treat the very blood of Christ himself as an unclean thing: if I could show you that sleepless and untiring eye forever fixed upon your individual heart, which neither wrath nor mercy, hope nor fear have yet sufficed to break, when breaking might have saved it, and which, if it ever breaks at all, is likely to break only with incurable anguish and despair: if I could show you how completely you are at God's mercy in the height of your prosperity, and how severely he is trying you by means of it, you might perhaps be brought to hear him say, as he does say with solemn emphasis "What I do thou knowest not now, but thou shalt know hereafter."

The dangers thus attending a state of high prosperity have led many, who were destitute of true faith, to repeat the prayer, Give me neither poverty nor riches. And some who hear me now may be ready to congratulate themselves that the extremes of joy and grief are equally unknown to their experience. They are glad perhaps that though they do not suffer, they are not the slaves of passion. They do not seek their happiness in violent excitement. They enjoy tranquillity, and thank God for it. They are comfortable and content with their situation. Perhaps too contented. Yes, unless possessed of a good hope through grace, they are certainly too well contented. They have no more reason to be satisfied than the sufferer with his sufferings, or the man of pleasure with his sinful joys. Especially is this the case if they imagine that, while God directs the lot of others, he is letting them alone, *i. e.* allowing them to be at ease without those dangers to which others are exposed.

There is a sense in which he may indeed be letting them alone, giving them up to themselves, allowing them to stagnate and to putrify, if not in vice, in selfish indolence, spiritual sloth, and carnal security. Because they are exempt from sore distress on one hand, and from gross sins on the other, they imagine themselves safe and even happy. They forget that although they may be idle, Satan is at work, employing every art to shield them from the light and make them sleep more soundly; that the world around them is at work to render them more drowsy by the hum and murmur of its business and its pleasures, so that when they open their eyes for a moment, they immediately fall back again and dream on as they have dreamed before.

Nor is this all. While evil spirits and a wicked world are thus at work upon the stupid soul, it may be said without irreverence that God himself is not inactive. He is not an indifferent spectator, but a sovereign and a judge. "Let no man say when he is tempted I am tempted of God; for God cannot be tempted with evil, neither tempteth he any man. But every man is tempted when he is drawn away of his own lusts and enticed. Then when lust hath conceived it bringeth forth sin, and sin, when it is finished, bringeth forth death." "The sting of death is sin and the strength of sin is the law." And the law is the law of God, and neither men nor devils can offend against it unless he suffer them. And when he suffers them he may comply with their governing desire. But at the same time will he take vengeance on them. To a sinner no divine stroke can in this life be so fearful as the stroke of letting him alone. As God is not and cannot be the author of sin, the worst he can in this life do is to let men do as they please. Beyond this nothing is required to ruin them. Their native tendency is downwards. There is no need of creating it. It is sufficient not to stop or change it. Nothing can possibly do either but divine grace. And in multitudes of cases it does both. And in the case of all who hear the gospel it is offered. And in the case of some that offer is long continued and frequently repeated. But its being offered even to a single soul, or for a single moment, is a miracle of mercy. If no one has a right to it at first, much less has any one a right to it forever. For then the longer men refused God's mercy, the more would he be bound to offer it, which is too absurd to be believed. And if this offer, even for a moment, is an act of God's free grace, and might have been withheld without the slightest imputation on his justice or his mercy, who will charge him with violating either if, when a man has long despised the Son and quenched the Spirit, he should be permitted by the Father to go on as he desires and is resolved, to do precisely what he wishes, to be just what he intends to be. Is this unmerciful, unjust, or cruel? What, unjust to let him have what he claims as his right? Cruel to leave him undisturbed? When he has over and over refused to accept God's invitation and importunately prayed to be let alone. Can he complain that God should take him at his word, and now withhold what he might have withheld from the beginning? Such an abandonment is doubly just. It gives the man precisely what he claims, and at the same time asserts God's sovereignty and vindicates his justice by allowing it to take its course.

It seems then that of all conditions in the present life, there is none more terrible than that of being let alone. And when this is the secret of men's calmness or contentment, they have just as little reason to congratulate themselves that they are thus left undisturbed, as the drowning man has to congratulate himself that he is left to sink without the trouble and vexation of seizing on the saving hand held out for his deliverance, or the poisoned man that he is not required to take an unpalatable antidote, or the convict on his way to execution that he is not interrupted by a pardon or reprieve, but suffered to continue his journey in tranquil indifference. My hearers, if I could convince you that the ease which you enjoy is such as I have described, I am sure that you would instantly hear him who would have saved you, but who now perhaps consents to leave you to yourself as you desire, saying, "What I do thou knowest not now, but thou shalt know hereafter."

In all these views we have been looking forward, trying to anticipate that which is still future. But the time is coming when we shall look back at the same objects from a very different point of observation—and look at them no longer as mere possibilities, but actual realities. It is a fearful supposition, but it cannot make your danger any greater than it is, to suppose, my hearer, that your soul is to be lost, and that when it is lost you will still be able to retrace the steps by which you travelled to perdition. When you thus look back—among the various feelings which will struggle with each other for predominance in your soul, one of the strongest must be wonder at your own infatuation in not seeing to what end your purpose and conduct here were tending—in not knowing that the world and the devil and your own corruption were at work to make affliction and prosperity and even tranquillity all contribute to your ruin—and that God himself, by every gift and every judgment, and even by his silence and forbearance, was still warning you that, though the end of your course was not yet visible, it certainly would have one, and that every thing you did, enjoyed, or suffered, was contributing to give that end a character, to make it forever either good or evil. This, I say, will be an astonishment to any lost soul—that he did not see all this beforehand—if not as certain yet as possible—and did not act accordingly. And in addition to this wonder at the general course pursued in this life, there will no doubt be particular conjunctures, with respect to which it will appear incredible and almost inconceivable that any rational and moral being should have still continued so insensible and blinded when the gifts of God were so peculiarly abundant, or His judgments so peculiarly severe—or the comfort and tranquillity enjoyed so perfect, that to one reviewing it from that distant point of observation it might seem that even sin itself could not have plunged the soul in such insensibility, or roused it to such madness, as to hide from it the fatal course which it was taking, or to stop its ears against the warning voice which was continually sounding from the death-bed and the grave, and the devouring jaws of hell, as well as from the cross and the throne, the mercy seat and judgment seat of Christ. Ah, my hearers, may it not be that among these recollections will be that of the very opportunity which you are now enjoying, and that, although now in looking forward you may see no sufficient reason for alarm or even for solicitude as to the end, a sovereign God is now afflicting you or sparing you—yet when you come to look back at the same things from the world of woe, you will regard it as a prodigy of spiritual blindness that you did not see what you will then see so distinctly, and of spiritual deafness that you did not hear what will then sound in your ears, in every echo from the vaults of your eternal prison, "What I do thou knowest not now, but thou shalt know hereafter."

Having gone so far as to transport you into the eternal world and to anticipate its solemn recollections, let me not conclude without presenting the reverse of that distressing supposition upon which I have been speaking. Thanks be to God the power of recollection is not to be monopolized hereafter by the lost. While it will, no doubt, add to the intensity of future torment, it will magnify and multiply the joys of heaven. Yes in both worlds memory will survive. There will be memory in hell. There will be memory in heaven. And on what will the blissful recollections of that holy, happy place be more intently fastened, than those mysterious but effectual means, by which a miserable sinful soul was stopped short and turned round in its career of ruin, and while others still refused to be arrested, or were arrested only long enough to give them a new impulse in their downward course, you, yes, my friend, it may be you, were taken off from all corrupt attachments and from all false grounds of hope that you might be saved through Him who loved you.

If permitted thus to look back at the way by which you have been lead, what occasion for rejoicing and thanksgiving will be furnished by the thought that your Saviour did not suffer you to wait till you could fully understand his requisitions, before trusting and obeying him. The difference between you and the lost will not be that the lost could not see the end from the beginning, and that you could; but that the lost insisted upon seeing, and that you through grace were satisfied with believing; that the lost would only walk by sight, and that you were enabled and disposed to walk by faith; that the lost could trust the care of their salvation only to themselves, and sunk beneath the load, while you had wisdom and humility and grace enough imparted to you to think God stronger than yourself, and a Saviour's merit greater than your own, the Holy Ghost a better comforter than the world, the flesh, or the devil. When Jesus with divine condescension proposed to wash their feet, they replied, with Peter, in his want of faith and of understanding, "thou shalt never wash my feet;" but you replied with Peter, in the strength of his renewed love, "not my feet only, but my hands and my head." This is all the difference, but it is enough, for it determines your eternal destiny. Happy the soul that is now upon the right side of a question which to men may seem so unimportant. Happy, forever happy, he who shall look back and see with wonder how his own plans were defeated, his most cherished wishes crossed, his favorite opinions contradicted, his highest hopes completely disappointed, and himself entirely set at nought, if thereby he has saved his soul; for what is a man profited if he gain the whole world and lose his own soul, or what shall a man give in exchange for his soul? The loss of all these things is to gain a new heart, to gain a heaven, to gain a God. It is the loss of God, as a consuming fire, to gain him as he is in Christ, a fountain of life. When possession is secured, my hearer, it will be a sweet or bitter recollection to our soul, that in this place and at this hour, although some around you still refuse to look beyond the immediate fruits of their misconduct, or to be persuaded that its effects would extend into eternity, the scales, through mercy, fell from your eyes, and the veil was gathered up from off your heart, and the noise of this world of a sudden ceased to fill your ears, and in the place of it a still small voice, a voice both of kindness and of authority, stole in upon your spirited senses, saying, "What I do thou knowest not now, but thou shalt know hereafter."

IV.

JOHN 1, 29.—Behold the Lamb of God which taketh away the sin of the world.

How long our first parents remained innocent is not revealed, and cannot be conjectured. The space allotted to that portion of their history in God's Word is extremely small. But this is no proof that the time itself was short. It is Bacon's maxim that the best times to live in are the worst to read about, *i. e.*, the worst for entertainment as affording least variety of incident. Certain it is, however, that we scarcely enter on the history of man before his ruin is recorded. But then, upon the other hand, we scarcely read of his fall, before we read also of his restoration. The gates of Paradise are scarcely closed, before the altar of atonement is erected at the entrance. The flame of the cherubic sword is blended with the flame of the consuming sacrifice. Cain was a tiller of the ground. His gentler brother was a slaughterer of animals. The promise of salvation to lost man was sealed and symbolized by blood—not the blood of bears and lions, but the blood of sheep and oxen—not of vultures, but of turtle doves. Was this accidental or a mere caprice? Is there any thing even in man's fallen nature which disposes him to seek the death of brutes for its own sake, without any view to food or even to amusement? And is this propensity so doubly perverse as to choose the harmless and the unresisting as its victims, rather than the fierce and ravenous? If not, the ancient sacrifices must have had a meaning; and they had, for they were meant to teach by signs and emblems the essential doctrine that without shedding of blood there is no remission—Blood being put for life, and its effusion for the loss of life by metaphors so natural as scarcely to be metaphors. The lesson taught by this perpetual spectacle of death, was that nothing short of death could save the life which man had forfeited by sin. And this implied that sin incurred a penalty, because it was the breaking of a law, and that the penalty of this law could not be evaded by the breaker, or by him who gave it. It implied that the distinction between moral good and evil was a distinction running back beyond all arbitrary positive enactments; that the righteousness of God made it impossible that sin should go unpunished; and that as the sinner's life was forfeit on account of sin, that forfeit must be paid by the sacrifice of life.

But all this might have been revealed and understood if no remedial system had been introduced at all, if no Saviour had been promised.—There was more than this implied in the ancient rites of sacrifice. They taught not only that man was a sinner, and that sin must be punished, but (that man) what seemed to be at variance with these truths, that sin might be forgiven and the sinner saved. The very forms of oblation taught this. Of these forms we have no exact account in the beginning or throughout the patriarchal age. But they were no doubt in essential points the same with those which were prescribed and practised in the law of Moses. And among these there was one too clear to be mistaken if regarded as significant at all, and if it was not, the whole system became merely a confused array of vain formalities.

Imagine that you see the host of Israel gathered in that vast enclosure, with the altar smoking in the midst, and by it the anointed priests in their official vestments.—To some, perhaps to most, in the surrounding multitude, the sight is a mere spectacle, a raree-show; but there were never wanting some who walked by faith and not by sight; and even now, though man may know it not, there beats among that breathless crowd some heart which feels the burden of its sin too sensibly to be content with outward show, however splendid. It sees, it wonders, it admires, but is not satisfied. Its language is, Oh what is this to me—how much of that oppressive weight which crushes me can this imposing spectacle remove or lighten? But the crowd divides. The offerer approaches with his victim. Mild and dumb it stands, speechless it awaits its doom. But see! before the stroke can be inflicted, there is yet a solemn rite to be performed. The offerer must first lay his hands upon the head of the poor victim and confess his sins—a simple rite, but full of solemn import to the mind of the spectator burdened with a sense of guilt and taught by God to understand the sight which he beholds. For he sees that in that simple act of imposition the believing offerer transfers his guilt, and in that transfer he beholds the only possible alleviation of his own distress. If the whole system be not merely a theatrical display, its rites must be significant; and if that solemn imposition has a meaning, it must signify a transfer of the curse and penalty from one head to another; and if such a transfer be conceivable in one case, why not possible in all? and if in all, then in mine, and if in mine, then I am free. For, all I ask is the removal of this burden from my conscience—I care not whither it is carried, only let it pass from me.

But here the question would suggest itself, how can the guilt of my sin be transferred to a dumb animal? Can sheep or oxen bear the weight of my iniquities, or their blood cleanse the stains which sin has left upon my soul? It cannot be. The voice of nature and of reason cries aloud—It is not possible. "It is not possible, that the blood of bulls or of goats should take away sins," Heb. x. 4. And yet the voice of the whole system cries in tones of equal strength, that "without the shedding of blood there is no remission." How shall these discordant sounds be tempered into unison? How shall these testimonies, seemingly so opposite, be made to stand together? How shall the burdened soul which has discovered that its only hope is in the transfer of its guilt, be enabled to go further and to see how that transfer may be really effected? Only by looking far beyond the innocent but worthy sacrifice before him to another which it represents. Only by seeing in its blood the symbol of a blood more precious than silver and gold, a blood speaking better things than the blood of Abel; not invoking vengeance but proclaiming pardon, as it streams from every altar. It is indeed impossible that the blood of bulls and of goats should take away sin: wherefore when HE cometh into the world he saith, "Sacrifice and offering thou wouldest not, but a body hast thou prepared me. In burnt offerings and sacrifices for sin thou hast had no pleasure. Then said I, Lo I come, in the volume of the book it is written of me, to do thy will, oh God." Here is the doctrine of sacrifice expounded by the Sacrifice himself, by Him who is at once the great atonement for our sins, and the great High Priest of our profession. He represented the death of animals as utterly without intrinsic efficacy as a means of expiation, and as utterly abominable in the sight of God, except as a symbolical display of that great sacrifice which Christ offered up once for all upon the Cross. And this is the doctrine of the whole of the Old Testament. It furnishes the only key to those apparent discrepancies which have been observed between the Law and the Prophets, where the latter use the language of indifference, and even of disapprobation, with respect to duties which the former had prescribed and rendered binding by the most tremendous penalties. In Christ these seeming contradictions are all reconciled. That which was pleasing in the sight of God for His sake, was abhorrent when considered without reference to Him. The blood of bulls and goats which, as a sign of his blood, speaketh peace to the perturbed soul, that same blood, in itself considered, speaketh vengeance; for it speaks of cruelty, and murder, and unexpiated guilt. The faith of old believers was the same as ours, only darkened and impeded by the use of symbols from which we have been delivered by the advent of the antitype.

It naturally follows from this difference however, that their ideas of salvation were associated with a class of images quite different from those which in our minds are connected with that great and glorious doctrine. Where we speak of the cross, the ancients spoke of the altar; and where we speak directly of the great atoning sacrifice by which our life is purchased, they would, of course, use expressions borrowed from the rites by which he was to them prefigured, and especially from those appointed animals by whose death his was represented. And among these the one most commonly employed for this end was the lamb; partly because it was more used in sacrifice than any other, partly because of its intrinsic qualities, which made it, more than any other animal, an apt though most imperfect emblem of the Great Redeemer, as an innocent, uncomplaining, unresisting victim. Nor are these two reasons to be looked upon as wholly distinct from one another. The selection of the lamb for the perpetual burnt-offering, besides its frequent use in other sacrifices, is to be explained from its peculiar fitness as an emblem of the Saviour. It was because he was a lamb without blemish, and because he was to suffer as a lamb led to the slaughter; it was therefore that this victim was so prominent an object in the sacrificial system. And because it was so prominent not only in the ordinary rites, but in the solemn yearly service of the passover, it naturally followed that the lamb became the favourite and most familiar symbol of atonement, and of him by whom it was to be effected.

The image which spontaneously arose before the mind of the devout Jew in connexion with his dearest hopes (and) of pardon and salvation, was the image of a lamb, a bleeding lamb, a lamb without blemish and without spot, a lamb slain from the foundation of the world. We have no means of determining how far the doctrine of atonement was maintained without corruption in the age immediately preceding the appearance of our Lord. But we have strong ground for believing that the great mass of the people had lost sight of it, and as a necessary consequence, had ceased to look upon the rites of the Mosaic law as meaning what they did mean. It is not to be supposed, however, that this loss of the true doctrine had become universal. The sense of guilt and of necessity could not be universally destroyed, and while it lasted, it could not fail to lead some whose hearts were burdened with it to a promised Saviour. Some at least who felt their lost and wretched state still looked with a prospective faith to the coming and the dying of the Lamb of God. Some at least, amidst the sorrows which they witnessed or endured, were waiting for the consolation of Israel. Some at least, beneath the chains and yoke of that hard bondage under which they groaned, still looked for redemption in Jerusalem. The hopes of such were naturally stimulated by the appearance of John the Baptist. But he did not satisfy their expectations. He was a preacher of righteousness, but not a sacrifice for sin. He was a prophet and a priest, but not a sacrifice. He taught his disciples, it is true, to look with stronger confidence than ever for the coming of the Great Deliverer; and when their desires had been excited to the utmost he revealed their object; when their sense of guilt and of the need of expiation had been strengthened to the utmost by his preaching of the law, and they were thoroughly convinced that no act of their own could take away their sins, he led them at last to the altar and the sacrifice, and said, "Behold the Lamb of God, which taketh away the sin of the world."

It is worthy of remark, that the two to whom these words were specially addressed, no sooner heard them than they followed Jesus and continued with him; a sufficient proof that they were waiting for him and prepared for his reception. But in what did their preparation consist? Not in personal merit; they were miserable sinners. Not in superior wisdom; they were fishermen. In one point, it is true, they were peculiarly enlightened, and in that consists their peculiar preparation to receive the Saviour. They knew that they were lost, and that he alone could save them: so that when their former master said, "Behold the Lamb of God," they followed him at once. And so it has been ever since. The rich and powerful, the wise and learned, although not excluded from the face of God, are often last in coming to the Saviour, because accidental circumstances blind them to their true condition, while the poor and ignorant, because they feel that they have nothing to be proud of, in their personal character or outward situation, are more easily convinced that they are in a state of spiritual destitution, and more easily persuaded to employ the only means by which their wants can be supplied. But when this conviction and persuasion is effected, in whatever class or condition of society, its causes and effects are still essentially the same; its cause the grace of God, and its effect a believing application to the Lamb of God which taketh away the sin of the world. In all such cases, the same kind of preparation for the Saviour must exist as in the case of John's disciples; a conviction of the sinner's need and of the Saviour's being able to supply it; and where this does exist, no conceivable amount of guilt or ignorance or weakness can disable or disqualify.

My hearers, are not you possessed of this essential requisite? I know that you are sinners, but I know not that you feel it. I know that Christ is a sufficient Saviour, but I do not know that you have seen him to be such. If you have, or if amidst this large assembly there are any upon whom the load of conscious guilt is pressing at this moment with a weight which seems incapable of being longer borne, and whose most urgent want is that of something which will take away their sin; to them I would address myself, and pointing, as the Baptist did, to Christ, say to you, as he said to his two disciples, "Behold the Lamb of God, which taketh away the sin of the world." But why should I restrict the declaration? It admits of universal application. There is no one, from the highest to the lowest in the scale of morals, whom I may not summon to behold the Lamb of God. Have you repented and believed?

If you have, I need not tell you that you are a sinner. The more you are delivered from corruption, the more deeply will you feel the power which it still exerts upon you. Do you never sin? And have the sins of Christians no peculiar aggravation. Is your conscience never stained and never wounded by transgression? And to whom do you resort for reassurance when it is so? To your own religious duties? To your sighs and tears? To the beggarly element of legal righteousness from which you were delivered? "Have ye suffered so many things in vain? if it be yet in vain? Are ye so foolish? having begun in the Spirit, are ye now made perfect by the flesh? This only would I learn of you, received ye the Spirit by the works of the law or by the hearing of faith? Oh foolish souls, who hath bewitched you, that ye should not obey the truth, before whose eyes Jesus Christ hath been evidently set forth, crucified among you." Your first hope and your last hope must be still the same. To you, as well as to the sinner who has never been converted, the same voice is crying: "Behold the Lamb of God, which taketh away the sin of the world;" of the world, not merely of the Jewish nation, not merely of this class or that, but of the world. There is peculiar pregnancy and depth in this expression which means both to take up and to take away. There can be no doubt that, according to the Scriptures Christ did really assume and bear the sins of those for whom he died. "Surely he hath borne our griefs, and carried our sorrows." "He was wounded for our transgressions, he was bruised for our iniquities, the chastisement of our peace was upon him, and with his stripes we are healed. The Lord laid on him the iniquity of us all." "He shall justify many, for he shall bear their iniquity." "He was numbered with the transgressors, and he bare the sin of many." These strong expressions, all contained in one short chapter, do but sum up the Bible doctrine that our Saviour took the sinner's place, paid his debt, bore his burden, and endured his punishment. But it is equally clear that the idea of removing or of taking away, as well as taking up, is really included in the import of the term here used. Indeed the two things go together. It is by bearing sin that Christ removes it. It is by taking it up that he takes it away. It is the Lamb of God which taketh away the sin of the world. While we really recognize the truth that Christ atones for sin by suffering its penalty, we ought not to forget the other meaning of the word used, as implying that he frees the world from sin and from its consequences. This is the end at which philanthropists are aiming. So far as they are really enlightened, they are well aware that all the evils which they try to remedy are caused by sin. And hence their great end is, or ought to be, to take away the sin of the world. But in using secondary means for the accomplishment of this great purpose, they are too apt to forget that which is primary, and from which all the rest derive their efficacy. Even wise and good men in their zealous efforts to extirpate sin and misery for ever from the world, may forget that this can never be effected without some means of atonement; that there never can be reformation where there is no expiation, or in other words, that it is Christ's prerogative to do both parts of this great work; that he is the Lamb of God who in both senses takes away the sin of the world.

But while this view of the matter shows us why some plans for the improvement of mankind have been without success, it ought, at the same time, to encourage us to hope for the success of others, and especially for that of the great means of reformation which has been ordained of God, and without which every other must be ultimately vain, viz., the preaching of the Gospel. Are we painfully affected by the sight of a surrounding world lying in wickedness? And does this view excite us not to lamentation merely, but to active effort for the universal renovation of society? All this is well; but our desires may so far transcend our own capacity and that of other instruments which we employ, that we may sink into despondency. But here we have the antidote to such despair. Behold the Lamb of God, which taketh away the sin of the world.

The same use may be made of this great doctrine in relation to the evils which exist in a particular community. The human heart is everywhere the same, and if abandoned to itself without restraint, would yield in every place, and always, the harvest of corruption and of misery. But even the worst men are under strong restraints imposed by Providence. And these restraints are so diversified and interwoven that they cannot be successfully controlled by man. His wisdom and his power are alike inadequate to such a task. Legal restraints and obligations are indeed within the reach of human governments, and constitute their most important office. But these checks are only one part, and a small part of that vast and complicated system of control, which holds the malignity of human nature under a pressure strong enough to save society from utter dissolution. The external checks of law, moreover, useful as they are, not only constitute a small part of the system of coercion under which we live, but are themselves dependent for their whole effect upon the moral bonds and ligaments of which no laws take cognizance, and which are utterly beyond the reach of all municipal provision. They are in the hands of God, and he relaxes or contracts them at his sovereign pleasure. And it certainly is not to be regarded as a matter of surprise that in this, as in all other parts of his omnipotent and wise administration, his counsels are inscrutable, and even the principles on which they are conducted such, as often to elude our most sagacious observation. Now and then the reins by which he holds the hearts and hands of men in check appear to be relaxed, in order to exhibit human nature as it would be if abandoned to itself. This effect is sometimes answered by individual cases of depravity; by the commission of appalling crimes for which it seems impossible to find a motive. Such cases now and then occur in the heart of the most peaceable communities, where much religious knowledge is enjoyed, and where the providential checks upon depravity appear to be most uniform and powerful. In such states of society, extraordinary instances of crime have sometimes fallen suddenly upon the public ear, like thunder in a cloudless sky. All eyes are riveted, all thoughts absorbed, and for a time the heart of the community appears to beat like that of one man, so coincident and uniform are its pulsations. Out of such events the providence and grace of God may bring the most beneficent effects; but such effects can never be secured by man's sagacity or goodness. Such is the wayward inconsistency of human nature, that the very action which electrifies with horror may incite to imitation, or at least to the commission of analogous offences. Ay, and even among those who are secure from any such extreme effect, there is a dangerous illusion which may easily exist. Among the multitudes who stand aghast at insulated instances of awful crime, there may be many who are not at all aware that they are daily treating with contempt the very motives and restraints which, in the case before them, God has wisely but mysteriously suffered to be powerless. He who despises in his ordinary practice the distinction between moral good and evil, has comparatively little right to wonder even at those acts of hellish malice which might almost seem to indicate an incarnation of the principle of evil in the being who commits them.

But another error which may easily arise in such a case, is the error of supposing that these fearful relaxations of the usual restraint upon men's actions, take place only in the case of individuals. Alas, my hearers, it is frequently exemplified in whole communities, not by the prevalence of such extreme depravity as that referred to, which would be wholly incompatible with any form of social order; but by a general sinking of the tone of public sentiment, a growing insensibility to moral and religious motives, a gradual or sudden dereliction of established rules of order and decorum; a progressive diminution of the popular respect for age and elevated character; a sensible decay of that ingenuous shame which is at once the safeguard and the charm of youth; in creating boldness on the part of crime, and a proportionate increase of timid caution on the part of those whose work is to suppress it; increase of influence in those whose influence is all for evil, and an ominous precocity of vice in youth, portending that without the fear of God preventing it, the next generation will be worse than this. Is this a fancy picture? Have you never seen its counterpart in real life? Have you never even heard of such changes taking place amidst the most unusual advantages, and with an impetus so fearful that the general complexion of society was quickly changed, the seat of order and morality becoming in a few years the abode of wickedness which cannot blush, and, I had almost said, the house of prayer transformed into a den of thieves? Such changes have been and, for aught I know, they may be passing now. The question is not whether they are possible, but whether they can be prevented.

In a community which shows some symptoms of this fatal process, what shall the friends of human happiness attempt in opposition to its progress? Shall they aim their blows at certain special evils, independent of each other, except so far as all sins are committed, and attempt their extirpation? In all such cases there are some specific reformations which must be effected. There are social nuisances which ought to be abated. There are fountains of corruption, some of which are capable of being cleansed by the infusion of divine salt: others set purgation at defiance, and can only be exhausted, choked, or rendered inaccessible. But while these specific remedies may be imperatively needed, they can never be sufficient of themselves. It matters not how many fountains of external vice are dried and stopped, unless a fountain be opened for sin and uncleanness. It matters not how many voices cry aloud in warning to the drunkard and the libertine, the gambler and the thief, exhorting them to put away their sins by righteousness, unless among them some voice cry to all without exception, and without cessation, "Behold the Lamb of God which taketh away the sin of the world." But between these methods there is no contrariety or disagreement. Both are but parts of one harmonious whole. It is only by attempting to divorce them that the one becomes ineffectual if not pernicious; let them be combined, and let the same voice which exhorts men to beware of those sins which most easily beset them, let the same voice continually, earnestly invite them to behold the Lamb of God which taketh away the sin of the world. I know that by many he will be despised; but if this were any reason for withholding the offers of the gospel, its glad sound would long since have been hushed. One of the marks by which he was identified in prophecy is this: "despised and rejected of men," and you will bear me witness that in this point the offence of the cross has not ceased. And let us bear in mind that man's natural condition is a state of illusion, extending to the most important objects, and indeed becoming more profound with the importance of the object; that one of the most natural effects of this illusion is to vitiate his estimate of things and persons, so that he highly esteems that which is abominable in the sight of God, and on the contrary, despises precisely what he ought to love and reverence. Under the influence of this illusion he can despise his own best interest for time and for eternity. He can despise the correct public sentiment by which he is condemned. He can despise the hopes and fears and affectionate solicitude of friends and kindred. He can despise a father's counsels and a mother's tears. He can despise the very fundamental principles of morals both in theory and practice. He can despise the law of God. He can despise the means of grace. He can despise the gospel. So profound is the illusion which produces this contempt, that he can even despise things while he thinks he honours them. The man who pastimes Christ and his religion, who allows the church a place among his sources of amusement, and permits the Bible to alternate sometimes with his play-books and romances, who admits in words that religion is a good thing, and intimates his willingness to show it countenance; the man who does this may imagine that he really respects religion, but, if ever he is brought to see himself as a contemptible worm of the dust, a lost and ruined sinner, whose only hope is in the very gospel which he thus condescends to take under his protection, he will also see that while he thought he did it reverence he really despised it. And to crown the whole, he can despise the cross. He can despise the Saviour. He can despise the groans of Gethsemane and Golgotha. And shall he who thus despises the most glorious and precious of all objects in the universe, be still pursued with invitations to behold the Lamb of God whom he despises? Yes, it must be so. Our Lord himself upon the cross not only prayed for the forgiveness of his murderers, but by his outstretched limbs and streaming wounds said to all who passed by, in tones more audible than language, "Behold the Lamb of God."

His servants dare not be less patient than himself. They must pursue the most inveterate despiser of the gospel with the same importunate and agonizing cry, Behold, behold the Lamb of God. Let that call follow him wherever he may hide himself. Let that call reach him at his table and his fireside, in his closet and his chamber, in his place of business and his haunts of dissipation. Let it mingle with his music and his jovial laughter. Let the rattling of his dice-box and the chink of his dishonest gains be still drowned by the echo of that distant cry, Behold! Behold! And though he still continue to despise it while he lives, let it ring in his ears upon his dying bed, and let the last look of his fading eye be invited to the cross by that same word Behold! Behold! and though he die despising it, he shall not cease to hear it, for that word shall still ring in his ears when his illusions are dispelled forever; when his soul, before it takes its final plunge, shall see the objects which it once despised arrayed in all their excellence and glory, and in spite of its endeavours to avert its gaze, shall be compelled to see them as it would not see them here; then, then shall that despised call be the last sound that strikes upon his failing sense, Behold the Lamb of God that taketh away the sin of the world.

V.

Romans, 1, 25.—They worshipped and served the creature more than the Creator.

There is no fact in the history of the ancient Jews more certain or familiar than their constant propensity to lapse into idolatry. The particular form of the transgression was dependent upon variable circumstances, time, place, foreign associations, special opportunities; but still it was idolatry, the worship of false gods, to which they were continually tempted, and into which they were continually falling, their grand national offence, by which the dark side of their history is uniformly characterized. Their periods of corruption were all periods of idolatry, their worst men were idolaters; this was the standing form in which their national and individual depravity continually showed itself. Their unlawful alliances with foreign powers were almost invariably complicated with participation in their idol-worship. The occult arts which they are charged with practising, were mere appendages of that same worship. In a word, so far as they are said to be corrupt at all, it is in this way more conspicuously and constantly than any other. The sin of ancient Israel was idolatry. The sinners of ancient Israel were idolaters. At every recorded deviation from the service of Jehovah, we come at the first turn to an altar or an image whether of Baal, Ashtoreth, or Moloch.

This fact, however, would be less surprising when taken in connection with the universal prevalence of idolatry around them, were it not for another equally certain and familiar which their history presents as the counterpart of this one. I refer to the fact, that after a certain crisis in their history this stigma is obliterated. Since the return from Babylon, the Jews, as a community, have never been reproached with any tendency to idol worship. Amidst all the corruption which existed in the later periods of their history as a people in their own land, amidst all their persecutions and dispersions since, they have held fast their integrity in this respect. While a large part of the Christian world has resumed the form if not the substance of idolatrous worship, the despised and scattered Jews have still borne witness against their defection. In this the reformed churches now unite them—so, likewise, do the Mohammedans. Among the modern Jews and Moslems, and in Protestant Christendom, the least appearance of idolatry is reckoned a sure symptom of corruption.

This extraordinary contrast very naturally prompts the question, how and why is it so? What has become of the idolatrous propensity which once appeared inseparable from the corruptions of the human heart? How is it that whenever ancient Israel went astray from God, they went astray in this direction, and that now even the most impious never seem to

take it either by accident or choice? If it be said
that the continued existence of the same propensity
appears in the idolatrous corruptions of the Romish
and the Oriental churches, this affords no adequate
solution of the difficulty; first, because the abuses in
question admit of a different explanation, or may at
least be traced to a very different origin, but secondly and chiefly, because it either takes for granted that
the whole amount of human corruption is now shut
up in these churches, or else leaves us still without an
explanation of the fact, that the corruption which
exists among ourselves never takes this form. Leaving entirely out of view the worship of the Virgin
Mary, and of saints and images in other parts of
Christendom, how is it that among ourselves the same
propensity is now extinct, although the general corruption of the heart and of society is still so great? Among
our many crying sins, why is there no idolatry?
Among our flagrant sinners, no idolaters? There
might be less cause to propound this question, if a
corresponding change had taken place among the
heathen; if their false religions had been gradually
passing into new forms, we might then regard the
change among ourselves as part of a great alterative
process, to which the whole race had alike been subjected. But it is not so. The hundreds of millions
of the heathen world are as idolatrous as ever. The
stupendous revolutions which have shaken the whole
structure of their civil constitutions, or resolved society into its elements and wrought them into new combinations, have still left their images and altars standing where they stood before! How is it then, the

question still returns, that in our catalogue of sins we now find no idolatry? Is it because we are too civilized? But if by this we mean a higher degree of intellectual refinement and extreme cultivation of the taste, we have only to remember Greece, to look at Athens, with all the learning and refinement of the world concentrated in her schools and works of art, yet blended, even there, with the insignia of idolatry, her sages teaching wisdom in the portico of idol temples, her artists vying with each other in the decoration of her images and altars. Or is it civil and political wisdom, military force, and practical sagacity, that furnishes the key to this remarkable phenomenon? Then look at Rome, and see how far her arms and laws produced the same effect. Ascend the Capitoline hill, as you before climbed the Acropolis, or enter the Pantheon as you visited the Parthenon. Survey the ruined temples which enclose the area of the ancient Forum, and then separate, if you can, even in imagination, the Roman idolatry from the Roman greatness.

Again, if the difference be ascribed to the moral elevation of our social state above that of the Greeks and Romans even in their palmiest days, the reason is fallacious, as it mistakes the cause for the effect. In cultivation of mere taste and intellect, we certainly have no advantage over those ancients whom we still acknowledge as our models and our oracles; so the moral superiority which constitutes the difference in our favour is itself the fruit of Christianity, and cannot therefore be the reason why Christianity, at least within the chosen sphere of our inquiry, is so free from idolatrous admixtures; why the unrenewed who bear the Christian name, though unacquainted with the power of divine truth, do not fall into idolatry.

Since none of the solutions which have been suggested, seem sufficient to account for this remarkable difference of the forms in which depravity and opposition to the truth have shown themselves at different times; since it seems so hard to explain why idolatry is now so rare or utterly unknown among ourselves, it may not be without its use to look for a moment at the question in another form, and to inquire whether, after all, our religion or our irreligion is so free from the idolatrous element as we have hitherto supposed; and if not, what are the appearances which bear the most resemblance to the false religions of the ancient world. In order to do this without confusion, or with any satisfactory result, it will be necessary to consider and determine what we mean by idolatry. We must, of course, reject the definition founded on the etymology of the word itself, which would restrict it to the worship of material images. Then they who adored the sun and moon, and all the host of heaven, were no idolaters. They who invoked the winds, and bowed down at the fountain-head of streams, and whispered their devotions to the air, and called upon the overhanging mountains to protect them, are excluded from the catalogue. How large a part of the classical mythology would thus be shut out?—nay, how large a part of the idolatry which even now exists among nations less refined and civilized? The idolatry of which we are in search, then, is not simply the external worship of material images, of stocks and stones, though this may be considered its most palpable and grossest exhibition. On the other hand, idolatry is not to be resolved into a purely spiritual act, the preference of some other supreme object of affection to our Maker.

This, though the soul of all idolatry, is not the whole of it. This subtle essence of the sin exists now just as much as in ancient times; just as much in one kind of irreligion as another. Covetousness is idolatry, but idolatry is not covetousness. It is not the mere rejection or neglect of God as the object of our worship, but the religious preference of something else. Of what? What was there common to the false religions of the old world, giving them a common character? Not image worship, in the strict sense which, as we have seen, was far from being universal. Much less the form, or name, or legendary history of the idol, or the attributes ascribed to it; for these were indefinitely various. What then? What was it that imparted to the ancient paganism its distinctive character, not merely as an aberration or apostasy from God, but as an outward realization and embodiment of that apostasy—not merely as a sin, but as a religion? This is a question which has occupied the thoughts and tasked the powers of some of the most learned and profound historical explorers of the present day, and which has led them to a laborious comparison of all that still remains to illustrate or exemplify the false religions of the ancient world; and, whether right or wrong, they are strangely unanimous in the conclusion that the unity of these religions lies in this, that they are all in origin, or tendency, or both, avowedly or covertly, the Worship of nature. However they might differ in their symbols or their rites, in their theology or ethics, they are all reducible to this at last. However far they may have deviated from the first intuition—however far the crowd of worshippers may frequently have been from comprehending the full import of the services in which they were engaged, it is supposed that by a natural historical deduction, this pervading character may still be traced in all of them—the worship of nature.

This view of the matter does not, of course, exclude a vast variety of forms and of gradations in the theory as well as in the practice of idolatry. The lowest stage, above that of mere stupid acquiescence in an arbitrary and unmeaning rite, may be described as the religious worship of particular natural objects or their artificial representatives. Within this limit a diversity might still exist, determined by the nature of the objects worshipped, and their rank in the scale of existence, from the shapeless stone or mass of earth, to plants, to trees—from the meanest brutes to the most noble—from moles and bats to the lion and to the eagle—from the clod to the mountain—from the spring to the ocean—from earth to heaven.

A still more intellectual variety of such worship would be that which, instead of individual sensible objects, paid its adorations to the elements or to the mysterious powers of nature, such as heat, cold, moisture, light and darkness, life and death. By a still higher act of philosophical abstraction, some who were considered most enlightened and exempt from vulgar prejudices, worshipped Nature itself, the material universe, τὸ πᾶν, including all the power and elements and individual objects which have been already mentioned. This was the highest reach of the idolatrous theology, the worship of nature in its last degree of sublimation; but from this down through all the inferior gradations, it was still essentially the same religion—it was still the worship of nature—the highest knowledge was the knowledge of nature—the most sacred mysteries were the secrets of nature—sin was a violation of nature—holiness was conformity to nature—atonement was reconciliation with nature, or restoration to a state of nature. This was the god, or rather the divinity, whom they adored. When regarded as one without personality—when viewed as personal no longer one—a hideous choice between a god without life, and an army of gods with it, between Polytheism with its practical follies, and Pantheism with its abstract horrors.

But amidst all these capricious alternations, and under all these varying disguises, the same unaltered countenance still glares upon us from behind its thousand masks; the same inflamed, yet lifeless eye still follows us wherever we may turn among the altars, and the idols, and the shrines of heathenism. The endless confusion of the voices which ascend in prayer and praise from these polluted sanctuaries, ever and anon are heard in unison, at least in concord. Their gods are many, but their god is one—their worship, after all, is but the worship of nature. Whatever we may think as to the truth or plausibility of these views with respect to the essential character of ancient heathenism, they derive at least some countenance from the solution which they seem to afford of the phenomenon already mentioned—the disappearance of idolatry as one of the most frequent forms in which the corruption of mankind once acted out its opposition to the doctrines and the precepts of the true religion. On this hypothesis, if on no other, it may certainly be said, that, though the impious among ourselves no longer pray to stocks and stones, or beasts and birds, or moon and stars, there is still a strong taint of idolatry perceptible in our religion, science, literature, business,—nay, our very language. Yes, I say our very language; for, to what strange accident can it be owing, that in common parlance and in current literature there should be so constant, so instinctive an aversion to the name of God as a personal distinctive appellation. That the names of Christ and of the Holy Spirit should be shunned, is less surprising, these being so peculiar to the dialect of revelation, not to say of the New Testament. But the same considerations do not serve to explain the almost superstitious care with which our irreligious writers manage to dispense with what would seem to be the most indispensable of all words—the incommunicable name of God. Can it be reverence, religious awe, that prompts this suppression? a feeling near akin to that which led the Jews in early time, and ever since, to hush up, as it were, the tetragrammaton, the dread name of Jehovah, as too sacred even to be whispered in the sanctuary by his own anointed priest, or breathed by the heart-broken suppliant at the altar? Is it this makes our novelists and journalists as much afraid to speak of God as if they thought he would appear before them at the call? Alas, this explanation is precluded by the levity with which the same men often make that venerable name the theme of ribald jests and the burden of blasphemous imprecation. No; the name seems to be shunned because it means too much, suggests too much, concedes too much. Not that they would deny the being of a God, or that they have a settled creed at all about the matter, but they feel, perhaps they know not why, that other modes of speech are more congenial, and the choice of these may throw some light upon the secret motive of the change.

Not only is the grand and simple name of God exchanged for a descriptive title, such as Supreme Being—or an abstract term, the Deity—but still more readily and frequently is God supplanted by a goddess, and her name is Nature. It is nature that endows men with her gifts and graces: it is nature that piles mountains upon mountains in her sportive freaks: it is nature that regulates the seasons and controls the elements. There can be no doubt that this language has a very different sense in different cases, and that it may even be employed by the devoutest Christian without any intentional departure from the truth. There can be no doubt that in some mouths, this definition of nature is only a rhetorical trope or a poetical embellishment—in others a euphemistic substitute for God—in others a collective abstract term, denoting the whole aggregate of second causes and of instrumental agencies, without excluding the immediate presence and efficient action of the First Cause and Prime Mover. But whether these exceptions are enough to cover all the cases, whether these solutions are sufficient to account for the increasing disposition in our popular and fashionable writers, to let nature and her works and her gifts and her graces usurp the place of God and His works and His gifts and His graces, is another question. But even if we give it an affirmative and favourable answer, it is still an odd coincidence that this darling figure of speech or philosophical formula should so exactly tally with the spirit and language of idolatry or paganism considered as the worship of nature.

But this coincidence, though strange, would not be so surprising as it is, if it were limited to literary composition. All but the highest class of writers have their mannerism and their affectations, which, although offensive to a pure taste, must be borne with and forgiven as inevitable. These are sometimes derived from unsuccessful imitation, even of the best models. And the modes of speech in question may, in some, be the effect of classical studies, just as youthful poets often introduce the classical mythology for ornament, without the slightest faith in its reality as matter of belief. It may be said then, that so long as these imaginary traces of the old idolatry are only found in word and phrase they are innocent enough, and that they need excite no serious alarm until they show themselves in deed as well as word, and in the practical realities of life as well as in the fanciful creations of romance or poetry. They who give this challenge might perhaps be surprised to find it readily accepted, and still more to be told that these analogies are traceable in real life and its least romantic and imaginative walks, in the labours of the field and of the shop no less than in those of the study and the library. The compulsory dependence upon seasons, weather, rain, and sunshine, which accompanies the culture of the earth, is a divine appointment, and is therefore perfectly compatible with faith and a devotional spirit. But when divorced from these, it takes the form of an extreme anxiety, a breathless watching of the elements, a superstitious faith in something quite distinct from God, although perhaps below him, and a constant disposition to invest this something with an individual existence and with personal attributes; although it may prove nothing with respect to any formal opinion or belief, it certainly presents another strange approximation to the spirit and the practice of the old idolaters. The besotted fisherman who on our own coast feels himself to be the slave of the winds and tides, without a thought of God as their creator and his own, is not so very far removed as we may imagine from the state of the old Greek or Phenician who sacrificed to Ocean ere he launched his bark. The mariner who spends whole nights in whistling for the wind may do it from habit or may do it in jest; but he may also do it with a secret faith and a feeling of dependence near akin to worship, and by no means wholly different in kind from the emotions of the ancient pagan, as he poured out his libations to Eolus, or his prayers to the particular wind of which he stood in need. The social and domestic superstitions which have lingered in all Christian countries, as to signs of good and evil luck, and the methods of procuring or averting it, are not always mere errors in philosophy or morals, but religious aberrations, the relics and memorials of a heathenism which we sometimes look upon with too much confidence as finally exploded. We often hear, and are compelled to acknowledge, that there is heathenism among us; but it is not merely negative—the ignorance or unbelief of what is true, it has always more or less a positive reality, the actual belief of what is false; and if we should be supposed to relapse as a nation into barbarism and idolatry—perhaps the first steps of the retrocession would be found to have been already taken in the cherishing of petty superstitions, and the practice of devices, which have either been transmitted by tradition from a heathen origin, or sprung directly from the same prolific principle—the natural propensity of fallen man to the worship of nature.

But here again an unfair advantage may appear to be taken of the popular credulity and ignorance, and the same objection may be made to sweeping influences from the errors of the vulgar, as before from the affectations of the literary world. The very fact that the disputed proofs have been derived from quarters so remote and so dissimilar, might seem to give them new and independent weight. But even admitting that the objection is again a valid one—that men in general cannot be philosophers, and that the uninstructed multitude must always embrace errors, some of which may accidentally resemble those of heathenism: let us ascend again into the region of intellectual cultivation, and continue our inquiries there, not as before in reference to modes of speech and styles of composition, but in reference to scientific observation.

Here again we find the furthest reach of speculation and discovery compatible, and actually blended with the simplest faith and the lowliest devotion. But it is not always so. The philosophical explorer does not always "look through nature up to nature's God." He often stops short of that glorious object. He often looks upon God's place as empty, or as filled by another—by another yet the same—for this usurper of the throne and of the worshipper's affections, is still that nature, the appeals to which by other classes have already been explained away as forms of speech or ignorant misapprehensions. No one supposes that astronomers in Christian countries ever formally adore the stars, or that geologists are worshippers of mother earth, or chemists of the elements, or botanists of trees and flowers. But let the evidence that some of all these classes recognize a Nature, quite distinct from God, by whose mysterious virtues these effects are all produced, and whose authoritative laws are independent of his will, I say let the detailed indications of this strange belief be gathered from the language, from the actions, and, as far as may be, from the feelings of these votaries of science; and then weighed against the corresponding proofs of their belief in one Supreme, Infinite, and Personal God, distinct from all his works, and sovereign over them, to whose inspection all things are open, and without whose knowledge and permission not a hair falls or a sparrow dies; but those two testimonies be confronted and compared, and then it will appear whether some who have deservedly been ranked among the prophets and the high priests of material wisdom were in heart and practice worshippers of God, or (like the blinded heathen) worshippers of nature.

The analogies which have been suggested may be fanciful, or even if well founded they may be restricted to the cases specified, and leave untouched a multitude in Christian and in Protestant communities, who in neither of the ways described are worshippers of nature. But of these a large proportion may be comprehended in another category, as romantic and poetical idolaters of nature, who adore her not for her material gifts, nor yet as the object of severe and scientific scrutiny, but as the source of sensible and imaginative pleasure. These are the worshippers of beauty in its widest sense, to whom the beautiful is the chief good, or its highest manifestation. The keenest sensibility of this kind has been found in combination with the strongest faith and most devout affections; nor is there any thing in either to forbid their frequent, their habitual union. But reason and experience alike bear witness that the combination is not necessary; that although the elements may coexist, they may exist apart; they have done, they do still, exist apart. The voice that whispers in the trees or roars in the tornado, may to some ears be the voice of God; and every note of that grand music may be set to words on record here;—but they may also utter other inspirations, and bring responses from another oracle. Instead of calling us to God, they may but call us to themselves, or to the place where nature sits enthroned as God. This form of nature worship far surpasses all the others in the strength of its appeals to human sensibility. The eye, the ear, the memory, the imagination, the affections, may be all enslaved. The spell requires for its effect no scientific lore, no mercenary interest, but only constitutional susceptibility of strong impressions from the grand or beautiful. It requires the aid neither of superstitious fears nor philosophical abstractions. It only asks men to be pleased, excited, awed, subdued. The more delicious the sensations, the more irresistible the spell. It may be, and it is sometimes the case, that this extraordinary power is all used to make God present to the soul. But how much oftener to steep it in oblivion of him, and to bound its views by that stupendous framework which was reared to bring men nearer to their Maker, but when thus employed forever hinders their approach, and even hides him from their view.

This form of idolatry has all the aid that art can yield to nature. The idolater of nature cannot but be an idolater of art. And here the coincidence with heathenism is not one of principle only, but of outward form. The high art of the ancients was a part of their religion. It was not an idle tickling of the sense or fancy. In the perfection of their imitation and the beauty of their original creations they did honour to the god of their idolatry, not indirectly, as the author of their skill, but most directly, as its only object. It was nature that they represented, beautified, and worshipped. The gradual return in modern times to this view of the arts, and the impassioned zeal with which it is pursued, if not among ourselves, in other lands, is one of the most startling analogies to heathenism that can be produced, and promises or threatens, more than any other, to result in an exterior resemblance corresponding to the essential one described already.

It may no doubt be said that this romantic and poetical apotheosis both of art and nature has resulted by reaction from the barbarous neglect and the unscriptural contempt especially of God's material works, as suited to excite the powers and refine the taste, not only without prejudice to faith and piety, but so as to promote them. This is in some sense true, nor is this the only case in which the errors of the church have served to aggravate the errors and abuses of the world. Had Christians always exercised a wise discretion in relation to the love and admiration both of nature and of art, this poetical idolatry might possibly have spared some of its most extravagant displays. But the idolatry itself springs from a deeper and remoter source. As long as man retains the sensibilities which God has given him and yet remains unwilling to retain God in his thoughts, the voice of nature will be louder than the voice of God. If God is not in the wind, the fire, or the earthquake, these will nevertheless sweep the multitude before them, and the still small voice of revelation be heard only by a chosen few. When certain causes now at work have had their full effect, the worshipper of God will again be like Elijah on Mt. Horeb, while the vast mixed multitude are worshippers of nature.

If the agreements which have now been traced between the spirit and practice of the irreligious world and those of the heathen as worshippers of nature, really exist and are what they have been represented, it may reasonably be expected that the principle of this idolatry will not only show itself in art and spread itself as spiritual leaven, but avow itself in doctrine. It has done so already in the pantheistical philosophy of Germany, and in the form which it has given, there and elsewhere, to theology, to science, to romantic fiction, to rhetorical criticism, to the theory and practice of the arts. The taint of this infection may be traced by critical autopsis in places where its name would not be foreseen. It may be found adhering to schemes of doctrine highly evangelical in general form as well as in profession. At the same time it may be detected poisoning the full flow of poetic inspiration, and insinuating its corruption into the enjoyment afforded by the imitative arts in their least offensive and apparently most useful applications. Guided in almost any direction by this phantom, he who sets out as a worshipper of God, may find himself before he is aware, a gross idolater of nature. It would seem then that if we once assume as an established fact that heathenism is in origin and principle the worship of nature, we are not so wholly free from all idolatrous propensities as we might otherwise imagine; and that although Jupiter and Baal have no images or shrines among us, the same spirit which once prompted and controlled their worship, may, at least, be faintly traced not only in our forms of speech, but in the various walks of life and classes of society—in the mercenary, practical, industrial, utilitarian idolatry of worldly, money-making men—in the learned philosophical idolatry of undevout astronomers and men of science—in the poetical, romantic, and æsthetical idolatry of those who worship art and beauty—and in the formal propositions or the indirect insinuations of pantheistical philosophers and theologians.

With respect to the last cases, it is highly important to observe, that they are strongly distinguished from the rest by the religious air which they assume and their appropriation of established forms of speech to new and very different objects. This tone and dialect of piety have aided not a little in the progress of these innovations. Like the child who thought that any book was good in which the name of God occurred, some children of a larger growth appear to be persuaded that the formulas of Christian devotion must be equally significant and equally demonstrative of truth and goodness, whether applied to God and Christ or to the woods and the waves, the lightning, and the flowers. But this tone of deep religious feeling, when divorced from the legitimate objects of such feeling, only shows that this devotion to the works of God or man is truly a religion—that it is not admiration, but worship—that it is not good taste, but rank idolatry. When one of the great founders of this new religion, or rather of this resuscitated paganism, names, as the object of his love and trust, God in his most intimate union with nature, it is easy to perceive that the union he contemplates is a union of identity, that God is still retained as a convenient and familiar name, but that the true divinity, enshrined and chanted, with such exquisite appliances of painting, sculpture, poetry, and music, is not the God of revelation but the goddess of Nature.

From all this it becomes us to take warning, that whatever we do we do with our eyes open, to see to it that we incur not the reproach, "Ye know not what ye worship," and to see to it that we are not led into idolatry by any specious figments or delusions, lest we be constrained to take up the lament of those confessors in the times of heathen persecution, who, though proof against all menace and persuasion, were at last miserably cheated into acts of worship at the altar of an idol, when they thought themselves kneeling at the altar of their God. But against this fearful issue mere precaution avails nothing. To the votaries and victims of these "strong delusions," something definite and positive must be presented, as an object of faith and of affection. To the active mind, excited and half frenzied by the vague but captivating dreams of a disguised idolatry, it is not enough to say—be rational. The surges of that troubled sea, the heart of man, when roused by these impetuous winds of doctrine, can be lulled by no voice but the voice of him, who from the storm-tossed bark upon the waters of Genessaret, cried of old, in tones of irresistible authority, "Peace, be still." And even then the assuaging influence seems to come forth, not so much from the command as from the personality of him who utters it. To some who are already drifting into the exterior circles of this soul-destroying whirlpool, there comes not only a sound but a sight—an unexpected sight. Where all seemed dark and black with tempest, there appears a living form, holding forth to your acceptance, something real, something certain, something living, something lasting, something that may be seen, and felt, and known, and loved, and trusted—a Father—a Saviour—a Redeemer and a Comforter. This, this, is life eternal, to know, &c., falling down at the feet of this revealed, this manifested God, and opening to him your mind, your conscience, and your heart forever. You may turn to the idolaters of every name and say with proud humility, "Ye worship, and we know."

VI.

John 3, 36.—He that believeth on the Son hath everlasting life: and he that believeth not the Son shall not see life, but the wrath of God abideth on him.

This is one of the most evangelical verses in the Bible, that is to say, one of the most strongly marked with the peculiarities of the gospel, not only in sentiment and spirit, but even in phraseology. In order to understand this peculiar quality, we must in imagination change our own position. To us, who are familiar with the Bible from our infancy, its parts, in this respect, seem all alike. With all allowance for the many advantages arising from this long familiarity with Scripture, it cannot be denied that there are also disadvantages connected with it. While the general system of divine truth is impressed upon our understandings with more fulness and distinctness, particular parts of it make less impression on our hearts than if the whole were new. To those who have been trained up in a knowledge of the Scriptures, the method of redemption seems no more surprising than those attributes of God which may be gathered from his works. How different the case of a new convert from idolatry! With him these splendid revelations are as new as they are glorious, and if he believes, he believes with his heart. If he believes, his heaven and earth are new; he inhabits a new world; he is himself a new creature, and he feels it. Our disadvantage, as compared with such a convert, is not wholly irremediable, for although the evil is in some degree inseparable from our situation, and to that degree compensated by immense advantages of another kind, it is unquestionably aggravated by our own remissness and stagnation in the study of the Scriptures.

Who does not feel that in certain states of mind, he sees a freshness and vitality in truth, which at other times are wanting? And that these states of mind are those precisely which he ought to cultivate? Are we not bound then to acquire the habit of thus viewing truth, or rather are we not bound to seek the aid of that quickening and illuminating Spirit whose prerogative it is to give these glimpses of the truth even to sinful mortals? And may we not hope, with his assistance, to approximate, if not to reach, the freshness and the richness of impression made upon the heathen convert by the grand discoveries of the gospel?

How such discoveries affect such minds, may best be imagined by selecting some one passage, and surveying it as if from the position of a heathen for the first time brought to see it. For such a purpose there is not a sentence in the Bible better suited than the text which has been read; for as already mentioned, it is full to overflowing with the gospel. Let us suppose an ancient Greek; entirely unacquainted with the Gospel, or the Jewish system which prepared the way for it, but addicted to reflection and inquiring for the truth, to have been present among John's disciples when these words were uttered. They would have been to him a mere enigma. Interpreted according to his own habitual views and feelings, they would have conveyed ideas; but how strange, how foreign, how fantastic! He that believeth on the Son. Who is the Son? Why used thus absolutely as a title? Who is this Son that must be trusted or believed? and why should he be trusted? or for what? For everlasting life. All heathen nations are believers in a future state, and this expression, therefore, would be less surprising. But how inadequate, how false the meaning, which the stranger must attach to it! How different an endless life in his elysium from the gospel mystery of everlasting life! The wrath of God would also be a significant expression; but here, if possible, the contrast would be greater still between the Christian and the Gentile sense. The God of the Bible, and the gods of Olympus! The wrath of Jehovah, and the wrath of Jove! The calm eternal purpose of a holy God to punish sin, compared with the base malice of an almighty sinner. It is needless to observe how difficult it would be to prepare the mind of such a person for the light of truth. And even if, instead of being a blind polytheist, he were one of those who sought and worshipped the unknown God, how foreign would the doctrines and the terms of this grand sentence be, from his vain speculations. It is plain that it could not be made clear to him without an exposition of the gospel as to all its leading principles. This is apparent from the nature of the truths which it expresses or involves. In order to evince this, the doctrinal and practical substance of the text may be reduced to four propositions or remarks.

The first is, that the highest good to which we can aspire is eternal life. No heathen needs to be informed that life is something more than existence. Their is a sympathetic feeling with what lives, which cannot be excited by a lifeless thing. We cannot feel for a stone or a clod, as we do for a tree or flower which possesses life in its lowest form. Nor have we that community of feeling with a plant which we have with brute existence. We feel that they are nearer to ourselves, and we respect them or the life within them. But what is our sympathy for beasts compared with our regard for human nature? Individual men we may despise or hate even in comparison with lower animals, but no man puts humanity below the brutes. Because he feels that rational life is better than irrational. Even this, however, is not the highest sort of life. For we can conceive of reason without the capacity of moral distinctions, without the perception of moral good or evil. This it is true we possess, and it adds so much to the rank of our nature in the scale of existence. But alas! even heathen know that this moral life, if it may so be called, is quite compatible with spiritual death. We are alive to the perception of moral good, but dead to the enjoyment of it. Is it not plain that a resurrection from this death exalts us to a sort of life still higher? This is spiritual life; *i. e.* not merely the life of our spirits, for in a lower sense they were alive before, but a life produced by the Spirit of God. As this life consists in our being alive to God, to the performance of his will and the enjoyment of his favour, it might seem to be the highest life of which a finite being is capable. In kind it is, but not in degree. Its imperfection results from the remaining power of sin. Lazarus has come forth, but the grave-clothes of spiritual death are still about him. The smell of the sepulchre still stupifies and sickens him. He sees, but with bandaged eyes, the glories that await him. He doubts the reality of his resurrection. There is a conflict between life and death, as if the grave were loth to give him up. Such is the spiritual life of man on earth. From its own nature it is endless and progressive; but from the circumstances of the case, imperfect.

Look back now through the scale which we have been ascending, and observe how each new degree or sort of life towers above that below it. Each might be thought the highest possible, but for that which visibly surpasses it. And now having scaled the heights of spiritual life, what can we desire or expect beyond it, except that the evils which now mar it and obscure it should be done away, and that its duration, which appears to us precarious, should be rendered sure? This is eternal life, but is this all?

There is one stroke necessary to complete the picture. We are too apt in thinking of eternal life, to think of it as an eternal abstraction, or at least as consisting too exclusively in mental acts and exercises. Hence perhaps that want of joyful expectation which is too characteristic of our religious exercises. Even to true Christians, the transition to eternity appears very often like a passage from a wakeful state to sleep. And some whose love for Christ makes them long for any change which will bring them nearer to him, are apt to torment themselves because of th enjoyment they derive from earthly and corporeal things, however pure and innocent. But what if these same sources of enjoyment are to be opened in the other world, and rendered inexhaustible, subordinate to spiritual joys, but not opposed to them. What if all those exquisite delights which we derive from sights and sounds shall be eternal, in a thousandfold degree, and pure from all contamination? Is there any thing unreasonable in the supposition? Are we not still to be complex beings, soul and body, through eternity? Is not the inferior creation adapted to corporeal natures? Is it not subject to vanity and groaning until our redemption? Instead then of striving against God's appointment, and obscuring our own prospect of eternal life, let us make our innocent enjoyments all contribute to our hope of immortality, and when we think of the life to come, think of it as including all that now gives real happiness, refined and sublimated and immortalized. Let us look upon ourselves as sick men in a darkened room, just beginning to be conscious of returning health, and instead of turning away from every sunbeam that steals into our chamber, and turning a deaf ear to every bird that sings without, let us rather feast upon them as ingredients of that exquisite delight which shall attend our final and eternal convalescence.

But as the sick man knows by sad experience that

sights, and sounds, and sensible delights are nothing, nay are torments without health to taste them, so let us remember that these minor sources of enjoyment are dependent upon health of soul, and that they can do nothing more than•pour their tributary streams forever into the ocean of eternal life.

Here again we may look down upon the path we have trodden, and like those who climb the Alps, see diminished in the distance, what appeared stupendous when we saw it near at hand. At every former stage there was something to be added or desired. But now what wait we for? Do we desire life in its highest and its purest form? We have it. Do we ask security from loss? We have it. Do we seek variety and richness of enjoyment? It is here beyond conception; and to crown all it is endless, and not only endless but eternally progressive. The spiritual life which now beats faintly in the heart of the believer, shall beat on with ever-growing vigor of pulsation, till the pulse of eternity itself stands still.

Let us suppose a serious heathen to have formed this conception of eternal life, and to be filled with admiration of its glories. He could not long continue so absorbed in it as to lose sight of its relation to himself. He would soon learn to compare his own experience with this splendid picture, and if at all enlightened by the grace of God, to feel that between himself and this eternal life, there was a great gulf fixed, and that its happiness could only make him miserable; just as we may suppose the sight of Noah's ark affected those who caught a passing glimpse of it before they sunk forever. No man can form any adequate conception of eternal life without some conception of that God in whose favour it consists. No contemplation of the attributes of Jupiter, or Venus, or Apollo, could result in a just idea of eternal life. That life presupposes the idea of a holy God; holy not only in himself, but in his requisitions; the author of a holy law, requiring perfect and perpetual obedience, not in outward action only, but in thought and desire.

The moment the pure light of this conception flashes on the mind of the inquirer, it conjures up an image of himself standing opposite to God, and odious in proportion to God's excellence. Knowing, as he now does, that eternal life is the eternal death of sin, he feels the dagger at his heart, he feels his spiritual death, and he despairs. But he awakes, and arises in the fond hope of escape. As sin has been his death, he now resolves that sin shall die. He will sin no more. Here a new revelation throws its light upon his path. He cannot cease from sin; he is its slave; it dwells within him; his evil thoughts and acts are from his heart, and his heart is dead in sin. Can he give it life? Can his own actions make their own cause pure? Here is a new despair, and it is deepened by perceiving that even if he could cease from sinning, the law already broken would not cease from its demands. His intended reformation is both useless and impossible.

Left to himself, he can conceive but one other method of escape. It is the hope that God will set aside the law, forgive him by a sovereign act, and make him a new creature. As he looks towards the light inaccessible, where God resides, in search of something to confirm this expectation, he is blinded and dazzled, but completely undeceived. He sees no dark spot in that blaze of living light, no shadow of connivance or indifference to sin. He sees, too, that this spotless brightness constitutes the glory of the Godhead, and that the fulfilment of his hopes and wishes would have impaired his reverence for God. He withdraws his dazzled eyes and closes them, as he supposes, in eternal darkness. But on this darkness a new light begins to steal—a ray from the luminous abode of God. He starts up in amazement; he considers for the first time that all his former hopes were centred in himself. His eye now follows the divine light to a point exterior to himself; he conceives the possibility of escape through another; he forms the conception of an intermediate object between God's inexorable justice and himself; and, after many alternations of despair and hope, it flashes on his mind that both the ends which he considered incompatible, may thus be brought about—sin may be punished, and the sinner saved.

But a cloud passes over this celestial light. Are not all men alike? And if no man can make satisfaction for himself, how shall any man make satisfaction for another? The resolution of this doubt is the most astonishing development of all. Though man may not make satisfaction for another, may not God? The thought seems impious that God should pay the penalty of his own law, until the last veil is withdrawn and the astonished soul beholds the great mystery of godliness—God manifest in the flesh. The Mediator is both God and man—the Son of God and the Son of Man, and in both senses called the Son, a name no longer enigmatical—a perfect man without sins to be expiated. Here one difficulty falls away. At the same time he is God, and his divinity gives infinite value to his sufferings and obedience. They are, therefore, available for others also. This resolves the other doubt, the darkness rolls away, and the sun of righteousness, without a spot or cloud,

"Flames in the forehead of the morning sky."

The work demanded of the sinner himself is only hard because it is so easy. It is hard to do little when we think we must do much—hard to do nothing when we think we must do all—hard to believe that we have only to believe, when we expected to achieve our own redemption. When once the soul is brought, however, to believe that this is truly God's plan of redemption; that the Son of God is able and willing to save, and that this salvation is sufficient and secure; and, besides this general belief, accepts of this salvation for himself; the work is done, the man is justified and safe forever. By some such process as that just described, we may suppose a heathen to arrive at the second proposition which the text involves, namely, That eternal life may be attained by simply believing in the Son of God.

From this he would readily infer that the converse must be true, and that the want of faith involves the loss of all that perfect and enduring blessedness called eternal life. But here he would be liable to error. As he himself was destitute of pure and elevated happiness, he might imagine that continued unbelief would leave men in possession of this world's felicity or its equivalent, and merely rob them of that more exceeding and eternal weight of glory which is won by faith. But this is not the doctrine of the Gospel. The loss of heaven, grievous as it is, would not affect the hearts of those who know it not. Their very reason for refusing heaven, is that they love the pleasures of sin. To deprive them, therefore, of that which they despise, and give them that which they delight in, would be rather to reward them than to punish them. The doctrine of the Gospel is, that from him who hath not, shall be taken even that which he hath. He that believes has the promise both of this life and of that which is to come. He that loses heaven loses this world also. In the text it is declared not merely that the unbeliever shall not have eternal life, but also that the wrath of God abideth on him. This obviously means that the effect of unbelief will not be a mere negation, but a positive infliction. The wrath of God is a mysterious phrase full of horror. It is the array of all his attributes against a single soul forever.

Vain as it is to attempt description of things indescribable, there are one or two considerations which may render our conception more determinate. What makes a life of sin tolerable here? Three things:— 1. A participation in the outward advantages of the believer. 2. Positive enjoyment in sin. 3. Ignorance of any thing better which could make the soul dissatisfied with sinful pleasure. Now, these three causes are to be abolished. The wrath of God will separate the lost soul from the saved forever, and from all the advantages of order, comfort, mutual restraint, which now arise from the connection. The pleasures of sin, too, are only for a season; they shall cease, and its native tendency to misery remain unchecked forever. Finally, conscience shall awake, and have sufficient light to plant its daggers with unerring accuracy; and to complete the sum of misery, the sinner shall in some degree know what he has lost. Surely these considerations are enough to give us definite, though painful ideas, of the wrath of God, whatever may be our ideas of the material fires of hell.

It only remains to add, that, as in our estimate of future happiness, we are too apt to preclude those sources of enjoyment which we now know by experience; it is also true, and in a much higher degree, that when we think of future misery, we think of it as something generically different from what we suffer here. But, if we would bring home the matter practically to ourselves, we must suppose the sufferings of this life to be indefinitely aggravated and made eternally progressive. The wretch who commits suicide to shun the shame of public execution or exposure, if he believes in a futurity at all, little imagines that the very pang which he endeavored to escape by this act of daring cowardice, shall wring his soul with everlasting and increasing anguish. Let no unbeliever, in his restless discontent, imagine that his disappointments, losses, or disgraces will be terminated by the end of life; but let him rather look forward to an endless propagation and recurrence of the self-same agonies from which he hopes, by dying, to escape. The dying sinner only exchanges a temporal for an eternal hell—the short-lived wrath of man for the eternal wrath of God, not merely smiting, but abiding on him.

These, then, are the three propositions which must be included in the exposition of the text to one not acquainted with the Gospel:—

I. The highest good to which we can aspire or attain is eternal life.

II. It cannot be merited or purchased by ourselves, but must be secured by simple faith in Christ.

III. Unbelief incurs not merely a privation of the positive enjoyments of eternal life, but the positive infliction of the wrath of God.

IV. To these I add a fourth, which is, that these foregoing truths are of universal application. What they would be to a heathen they are really to us. If to him they involve the whole way of salvation, they involve no less to us. What more, indeed, could we desire? We have here the great end of existence set before us—the glory of God and the enjoyment of his favour, included and summed up in eternal life. Its opposite, eternal death, is also set before us. Here, too, is the *way* of life, by faith and nothing but faith. Not he that worketh, but he that believeth, hath eternal life. Finally, here we have the object of this faith presented as the Son, the Son of God, the Son of Man, God manifest in the flesh, a sacrifice for sin, the Captain of our Salvation, the Author and Finisher of our faith—the end, the way, the guide. What more can we ask? This is all our salvation and all our desire.

By this let each man try himself. What are you

seeking? Immediate gratification or eternal life? And if the latter, do you know what it consists in? Do you know that it includes all forms of happiness not stained with sin, and that the loss of it involves all misery, including such as you experience already?

And now, are you seeking everlasting life? By what law? The law of works, or by the law of faith?

And last, not least, what is the object of your faith? Is it God's uncovenanted mercy?—his mercy as opposed to his justice? Alas! there is no such mercy. It is not he that believeth in a lie shall be saved, but he that believeth in the Son of God. Other foundations can no man lay save that which is laid; for there is no other name given under heaven among men whereby we must be saved. If you have not this faith, with this exclusive object, your prospect is eternal death, and that not merely loss of life, but endless exposure to the wrath of God.

And here may be brought more distinctly into view a remarkable form of expression in the text. The threatening is not that upon the unbeliever wrath shall abide, but it abides already. Here let the procrastinating soul be undeceived. Distance of time and place works strange transformations. Tell one who violates the law of man that he will be condemned for it, and he may laugh the law and you to scorn. But how few laugh when told that they are condemned already. Look at the convict at the bar, and see how different his aspect and demeanour from his aspect and demeanour when at large. Such is your case. You are, perhaps, not yet arrested, the day of formal trial is far distant; but, strange as it may seem, when compared with human process, you are already under sentence. You were born a convict, and your past life has only served to aggravate your condemnation. When you are warned, therefore, to escape the coming wrath, it is not that you can escape conviction as a violater of the law of God. You are condemned already, and reprieve or pardon is your only hope. What if the murderer at the gibbet's foot should prate of his expecting to avoid conviction, and talk of testimony, verdicts, and new trials on his way to execution. Remember, remember, that God's wrath abideth on you.

Here, too, may many an enigma in the life of man receive a full solution. You are rich, perhaps, and prosperous in this world's goods, and seem to the eye of others destitute of nothing. But you yourself know better. In the midst of your abundance there is emptiness; starvation in your feasts, and in your cups undying thirst. You cannot understand how, with all the materials of enjoyment, you are joyless. Hear the reason. It is the wrath of God abiding on you, and distilling wormwood into every drop you swallow.

Or are you poor, but with an unblessed poverty, striving with vain efforts to be rich, or brooding in idleness with spiteful discontent over your neighbour's wealth. Without the advantages of wealth, you have its cares, its load without its strength. You can neither attain the supposed felicity of being rich, nor the more enviable peace of contentment. Do you know the reason? It is the wrath of God abiding on you, from which you must escape before you know tranquillity.

The case is the same if you are sick, without the sanctifying grace of sickness; or in health, without the grace which makes that health a blessing. You have, perhaps, a feeling of perpetual insecurity. You tremble when you hear of death, and turn pale at the slightest pain in any of your members. And alas! you do not know that there is reason for your fears. Look back, the avenger of blood is just behind you, and the wrath of God abides already on you.

There is yet another case, which, though less common in reality than in appearance, must be mentioned. It is that of the man who feels no changes and no fears, and who, by means of a peculiar constitution, or inveterate induration, draws from the materials of worldly happiness their full supply, without admixture. Some of you know, perhaps, how often the appearance of this calmness is an artificial mask, put on to hide the fearful writhings of the countenance. You know what is meant by a life-time of hypocrisy, not hypocrisy in religion, but hypocrisy in sin. We have much of false professions in the church, but we know much of false professions in the world. The profession of indifference, and peace, and courage when ever and anon a gust of passion, or a nausea of the spirit, gives the lie to the profession.

But let the man be what he says he is. Let him neither feel nor believe the pressure of that deadly burden which he bears upon his back. Let him imagine, while he bends beneath it, that he walks erect, and in proportion as it breaks his strength, let him rise in his estimate of human nature, and even when he finally sinks under it, let him sink, believing that he soars, and die in the belief that he can never lose his life. Is this the sinner's consolation? Oh, is this the hope, for which he sold the promise of eternal life? Is this your way of salvation? Oh deceived soul, to escape the present consciousness of wrath only by laying it up in store for your eternity, by treasuring up wrath against the day of wrath, and still not know that the amount of it is growing. Oh what a settling of accounts will that be when the vast accumulations of a life-time are brought out from God's omniscient magazine, and attached to their possessor as a mill-stone to precipitate his everlasting fall. This, and this only, is the hope and consolation of the man who feels no danger, and has no Saviour.

You gain nothing, then, when you gain a transient respite from the sense of present misery. Nay, those who have it, are of all men most miserable, as their insensibility will aggravate their future woe; and even now, in spite of it, the wrath of God abideth on them. Execution is delayed, but they are condemned already.

Instead, then, of aiming at this fatal stupor, strive to feel your burden. Feel that the wrath of God is now abiding on you, and will there abide forever, unless the Saviour soon remove it. No sense of this oppressive burden, how intense soever, can increase your danger. Nay, it will prepare you the better for deliverance. To the careless and insensible the Gospel has no promises. They that are whole, need not a physician. But to the burdened and oppressed our

Saviour uttered one of his most tender invitations. Come unto me all ye that are weary and heavy laden, and I will give you rest. Here is the rest you should seek. The rest, not of stupidity, but penitence. While you continue as you are, the wrath of God abideth on you. But the moment you believe, it is transferred to the great object of your faith, absorbed in the vortex of his meritorious passion, drowned in the many waters of his dying love, and lost forever. Death is then swallowed up in victory, the victory of faith, and life. Everlasting life becomes triumphant. Behold, I have set before you life and death, blessing and cursing. Choose life, therefore, that your souls may live.

VII.

Luke 17, 32.—Remember Lot's wife.

There seems to be a natural and universal disposition to commemorate remarkable characters in history. Not only are monuments erected, and books written to perpetuate their names, but days are set apart for the special purpose of remembrance and of celebration. Where the anniversary of the birth, or of the death can be determined, this is commonly selected as the period of observance. But even when these are no longer ascertainable, the disposition to remember and commemorate must still be gratified, and in the same way by the arbitrary designation of certain times as sacred to the memory of certain persons. This propensity is not confined to civil history, but extends to that of the church, and of religion. Or rather, it is here that it especially displays itself, as in its favourite and chosen field. The civic calendar of patriots and heroes is a meager catalogue, compared with the ecclesiastical calendar of saints and martyrs. Some have usurped a place there whose pretensions it would not be easy to demonstrate; but I do not know that Lot's wife has ever found a place in any calendar. And yet, this is the only case in which a solemn and express divine command can be appealed to. Of patriarchs and prophets, of apostles and martyrs, there is not one, —no, not even Abraham or Moses, not even Paul or Stephen—of whom Christ is recorded to have said what Luke describes him in the text as saying of a nameless sinner in a half-forgotten age, "Remember Lot's wife!"

The singular prominence thus given to an otherwise obscure and unimporant character in sacred history, may serve at least to justify a brief inquiry *how* and *why* the exhortation is to be complied with. In other words, what is there in the case of Lot's wife to be thus remembered; and, of what use can the recollection be to us? These are the two points which I now propose to make the subject of discourse:

I. What is there to remember in the case of Lot's wife?

II. Of what use can the recollection be to us?

I. In considering the first point, we naturally turn to other cases of historical commemoration, and recall the circumstances upon which the attention is usually fastened as the things to be remembered. These are essentially the same in every case, that is to say, there is a limited number of particulars, within which the biography of all men may be circumscribed. But these are indefinitely varied in their combinations and proportions. The entire interest of some lives is concentred in the birth and hereditary honours of the subject. This is notoriously true as to the vulgar herd of kings and queens, and nobles, whose name and titles are their whole biography. In other cases, of a higher order, this element of greatness is entirely wanting. The name is a new name, and the birth obscure. Whatever interest attaches to the person is the fruit of his own doings, whether martial, intellectual, or civil. There are others where the eminence arises neither from position nor achievement, but from character This is the charm of those biographies, in which a historical, and even a poetical—I might perhaps say romantic—interest is thrown around characters who never rose above a private station; who, beyond a little circle of acquaintances, were scarcely known to live until they died, but who now live in the memory and hearts of thousands, and, when every meteor of profane celebrity is quenched in oblivion, shall still shine in the firmament of history " as stars for ever and ever."

These are the customary topics of remembrance and commemoration, illustrious birth, splendid achievement, and surpassing excellence not necessarily exclusive of each other, but alas! too seldom found in combination, that among the "bright particular stars" of human history, there are few constellations, and but one stupendous galaxy. Let us now apply this measure to the solitary case which our Saviour has consigned to everlasting remembrance, and what is the result? In which, or in how many, of these several respects was Lot's wife entitled to be snatched from oblivion? Was it birth, or name, good works, or evil deeds, extraordinary piety or unexampled wickedness that gives her this pre-eminence? Name did I say? Her very name has been forgotten in the record that bears witness to the fact of her existence. Of her birth we know nothing, and can learn nothing, absolutely nothing, from a history distinguished from all others by the fulness and minuteness of its genealogical details. We know who Abraham's wife and Nahor's wife were, not their names only, but their parentage; but Lot's wife, so far as the inspired record goes, is without father and without mother, her birth a secret, and her name a blank!

There are cases, however, in the sacred history, where no small interest attaches to the character and deeds of those whose names are not recorded. Without going beyond the field of female biography, we may cite as examples, the widows of Sarepta and of Shunem, the woman of Samaria, and several others for whom or upon whom our Lord wrought miracles of healing. But in this case the anonymous and unknown subject of commemoration is revealed to us by no description, no characteristic actions, no glimpses of her private and domestic life. She is not even mentioned in the history of Lot's migrations or of his residence in Sodom. She is not included in the question of the angels who were sent to save him: " Hast thou any here besides? son-in-law, or sons, or daughters, or whatsoever thou hast in the city;" unless this last expression be intended to apply to her. She appears for the first and almost for the last time in the brief but vivid picture of that hurried and compulsory escape, when Lot still lingered, and " the men laid hold upon his hand, *and upon the hand of his wife*, and upon the hand of his two daughters, the Lord being merciful unto him, and they brought him forth, and set him without the city, and said, Escape for thy life, *look not behind thee*, neither stay thou in all the plain, escape to the mountain, lest thou be consumed." This is one-half of the history of Lot's wife, and the whole of it contains no hint of her origin or education, course of life, or character, except so far as this may be gathered from her end. It seems, then, that in this case, thus commended to perpetual remembrance by our Lord himself, every one of the accustomed grounds or reasons for remembering is absolutely wanting.

Is this blank, then, to be filled up by indulging the imagination, by investing this anonymous, mysterious figure with fictitious qualities, and making her the centre of poetical associations? Certainly not. We can remember only what we know. The command is not to imagine or invent, but to remember. And in this case we can only know what is recorded. Our Saviour evidently takes for granted that his hearers knew the fact which he commands them to remember. They could know it only from the narrative in Genesis. Had any thing beyond this been required, it would be expressed, as in other cases where our Saviour and his followers reveal something not contained in the Old Testament. Such additions to the history are the names of the Egyptian sorcerers, Jannes and Jambres, not recorded by Moses, but disclosed by Paul to Timothy, and Jude's citation of the prophecy of Enoch, and of Michael's contest with the devil for the body of Moses. But in this case there is no such addition, no completion of the history, but a simple reference to what was already known because it had for ages been on record. It was to some familiar and notorious fact that Christ alluded, when he said to his disciples, "Remember Lot's wife!"

This familiar and notorious fact could not be the one already cited, namely, the angelic intervention and deliverance of Lot's wife, with her husband and her children, from the doomed city, because this was not peculiar or remarkable enough to be appealed to as a great historical example. Thus far, her experience was coincident with that of others more entitled to remembrance. Had miraculous deliverance been all, the wife of Noah might have seemed to have a better claim than Lot's to this distinction. We are therefore under the necessity of going a step further, and considering the other half of her recorded history, as furnishing the lesson which our Lord inculcates in the text. That other half is all comprised in a single verse of Genesis, the twenty-sixth of the nineteenth chapter. "His wife looked back from behind him, and became a pillar of salt." So soon and so sudden is her disappearance from the stage of history. She only appears long enough to disappear again. She is like a spectre, rising from the earth, moving slowly across our field of vision, and then vanishing away. Hence her history is all concentred in a single point, and that the last. It has no beginning and no middle, but an end, a fearful end. Its course is like that of the black and silent train, to which the match is at last applied, and it ends in a flash and an explosion. Our first view of Lot's wife is afforded by the light of the sulphureous flames already bursting from

the battlements and house-tops of the reprobate city;
our last view, the moment after, by the same fires as
they mount to heaven and light up the whole horizon, revealing among many old familiar objects, one
never seen before, a pillar of salt upon the road to
Zoar. That very pillar was the thing which the disciples called to mind when Jesus said, "Remember
Lot's wife."

But, my hearers, there are multitudes of other
cases upon record, where the whole interest of a lifetime is concentred in the hour of death. Some
scarcely seem to live until they come to die. Not
only in the case of soldiers slain in battle, or of martyrs dying at the stake, but on many a lowly and
neglected death-bed, a new character reveals itself,
new powers of mind, new dispositions and affections,
as if a life-time had been needed to mature the character, and death to make it visible. It is not therefore merely in this circumstance that we must seek
the grand peculiarity of that event to which our Lord
directs the thoughts of his disciples. As it was not
her escape from Sodom that made Lot's wife a perpetual lesson and memorial to mankind, so it is not
the extraordinary concentration of her history in one
point, and that point the last, for this, as I have just
said, may be seen in other cases. I proceed directly
therefore to point out the three particulars in which
her end was so peculiar as to render it a fit example
for the purpose which our Saviour had in view when
he told his disciples to remember her. In doing this,
I shall, of course, make no appeal to your imagina-

tion, but confine myself with rigour to the brief and plain terms of the history.

1. The first distinctive feature in the case of Lot's wife is, that she was almost saved. The cases are innumerable, no doubt, in which men have been destroyed when apparently on the very verge of deliverance. But the cases must be few, very few, if any, where the alteration was so rapid and terrific, where the subject passed so quickly through the startling vicissitudes of life from the dead, and death in the midst of life. First entire security; then awful and apparently inevitable danger; then miraculous deliverance; then sudden death. The point to which I would direct your attention first, is the extraordinary, unexpected, and, to all appearance, certain and complete deliverance, which Lot's wife had experienced. In prospect and in expectation she was saved already, and in actual experience she was almost saved. The burning city was behind; she had been thrust out from it by angelic hands; her husband and her children at her side; the chosen refuge not far off, perhaps in sight; the voice of the avenger and deliverer still ringing in her ears, "Escape for thy life, look not behind thee, stay not in all the plain, escape to the mountain, lest thou be consumed." With such facilities and such inducements to escape, with her family on one side, and her saviour on the other, Sodom behind and Zoar in front; my hearers, who would not have thought, as she thought, that Lot's wife was saved. Had she been left behind to perish in the flames, the suicidal victim of her unbelief, her end would have resembled that of thousands, and our Lord would not

have told us to remember her, as if one out of the multitude consumed in that hot furnace were entitled to be any more remembered than the rest. But when actually brought without the gates, perhaps against her will, and by such hands too, and already on her way to the appointed place of refuge, with the cry of the angel and the crackling of the flames both impelling her onwards; surely she was almost saved.

2. But secondly, though almost saved, she perished after all. What I wish you to observe is not the bare fact that she perished; so have millions, both before and since, but that she perished as she did, and *where* she did. Perdition is indeed perdition, come as it may, and there is no need of fathoming the various depths of an abyss, of what is bottomless. But to the eye of the spectator, and it may be to the memory of the lost, there is an awful aggravation even of what seems to be incapable of variation or increase in the preceding and accompanying circumstances of the final plunge. He who sinks in the sea without the hope or opportunity of rescue may be sooner drowned than he who for a moment enjoys both, but to the heart of an observer how much more sickening and appalling is the end of him who disappears with the rope or plank of safety within reach, or in his very hand, or of him who slips into the bubbling waters from the surface of the rock which, with his failing strength, he had just reached, and on which for a moment of delicious illusion he had wept to imgaine himself safe at last! The same essentially, though less affecting, is the case of those who escape one danger only to be swallowed by another, like the sea-

man who had braved all the chances of war and the diseases of a sickly climate, only to be wrecked as he was reaching home; or the case of the soldier who escapes the edge of the sword on many a battle-field, and in many an "imminent deadly breach," only to die a more ignoble death, as the victim of disease or accident. Of all such cases in their infinite variety of circumstances and degrees, the great historical type is that of Lot's wife, of her who was almost saved yet not saved, the article and crisis of whose safety and destruction were almost identical, of her who perished in the moment of deliverance!

3. The third distinctive feature in the case of Lot's wife is, that her destruction was so ordered as to make her a memorial and a warning to all others. You may smile at the credulity of those who imagine that the monumental pillar is still extant, and may yet be identified. Believe, if you will, in the pride of science, or the pride of ignorance, for they are near akin, and often coincide in their conclusions, that this is a strong oriental hyperbole, a metaphorical description either of perpetual remembrance or of a natural transient effect. Even supposing that the pillar of salt had an ideal existence, or, that if real, it bore witness only for a few days to the eyes of all who passed by, God has re-erected it forever in his word. The pillar of salt may have vanished from the shore of the dead sea, but it is standing on the field of sacred history. The Old and New Testaments both give it place, and as it once spoke to the eye of the affrighted Canaanite or Hebrew, who revisited that scene of desolation, so it now speaks to the memory and conscience of the

countless multitudes who read or hear the law and gospel, saying to them, and to us among the number, as our Lord said of old to his disciples, "Remember Lot's wife!" Remember the mysterious and awful end of one who seemed miraculously saved from a miraculous destruction, only to meet it in another form and in another place, the very threshold of deliverance, converting her at once into a pillar of salt, and a perpetual memento of the "goodness and severity of God."

2. This brings us, by a natural transition, to the second point which I proposed for your consideration, namely, the purpose to be answered, or the end to be attained, by our remembering Lot's wife. It is no unreasonable question, if propounded in a proper spirit, free from petulant levity or skeptical presumption, what have we to do with this remote event of patriarchal history, this incident attending the destruction of a place whose very site has been expunged from the surface of the earth?

In the first place, we may rest assured that the narrative was not recorded for its own sake, or to gratify a spirit of historical inquiry; because this would render unaccountable the fewness of the facts recorded, and still more so the emphatic exhortation of our Saviour to remember this particular event. The only satisfactory solution is afforded by assuming that the case of Lot's wife was recorded as a type of God's providential dispensations; or, in other words, that the event may be repeated in the experience of others, not in its outward form and circumstances, but in its essential individuality. This supposition is not only reasonable in itself, and recommended by the reading with which it solves the doubt proposed; but it may be directly proved by the example of our Saviour in applying this historical example to a different case, to wit, the siege and destruction of Jerusalem. After warning his disciples against such security and self-indulgence as prevailed before the flood and the destruction of Sodom, and commanding them "in that day" not to delay their flight for what seemed to be the most necessary purposes, he adds, "Remember Lot's wife!" This can only mean that similar effects may be expected from like causes; that the course of divine providence is governed by fixed laws; and that the same succession of events may therefore reappear; or, as our Lord himself propounds the principle of application, in the conclusion of this same discourse, when the disciples asked him, "Where, Lord? and he said unto them, Wheresoever the body is, there will the eagles be gathered together." It thus appears that, far from being forbidden to apply the text to other cases than the one which our Saviour had immediately in view, we are directly taught, by his precept and example, to consider it as applicable to ourselves and others, and to spiritual no less than to outward dangers. For, if they who were liable to be involved in a great temporal calamity might be warned by the example of Lot's wife against security and rash delay, and taught that men may perish in what seems to be the very moment of deliverance, how much more conclusive is the same example as a warning against fatal security and procrastination with respect to a danger as much more awful than the one in question as the soul is more precious than the body, or eternity than time; and, accordingly, with how much greater emphasis may they who are exposed to this tremendous risk, be counselled and exhorted to "remember Lot's wife."

I proceed, then, in the same order as before, to point out the particular respects in which the strange and fearful end of Lot's wife may be realized in our experience, which, if it can be done, will be the best and most effective application of the text, as an exhortation to remember her and profit by her terrible example.

1. The first point of resemblance is, that we, like Lot's wife, may be almost saved. This is true in a twofold sense. It is true of outward opportunities. It is also true of inward exercises. If a heathen, who has just been made acquainted with the method of salvation, and who sees himself surrounded by innumerable multitudes still strangers to it, could be suddenly transported into this community, and see what you see, hear what you hear, and appreciate your multiplied facilities for knowing what salvation is, and for securing it, he would, of course and of necessity, consider you as almost saved. Regarding heathenism as the Sodom, from which he has just escaped, and from which we have so long been delivered, he would hardly be deterred from looking upon us, not as almost, but as altogether saved. The intellectual and social influence of Christianity, apart from its saving power, the refinement, order, and intelligence produced by it, even in the lowest and the most degraded classes of our people, as compared with heathens, would inevitably lead at first to false conclusions in

the mind of such a stranger, and constrain him to cry out, These people, although not yet in heaven, are already saved; and in reference even to that final consummation, they are almost saved!

We know, my hearers, how mistaken such an inference would be, and how much the fair appearances in question may resemble the smooth surface of that hollow and bituminous soil before its crust was riven and its secret fires enkindled by the lightning of God's wrath. You need not be reminded how far these external advantages, precious as they are in themselves and in their temporal effects, may fall short of securing the salvation of the thousands who enjoy them. In a word, you know, although a heathen convert might be ignorant, that men may have all this and more in actual possession, yet be neither almost nor altogether saved. You know how the deceitful surface may be agitated and convulsed by outbreaks of iniquity long cherished and concealed beneath the refinements and restraints of social discipline, and even where the general decorum remains unimpaired, you know how many individuals may go down from the midst of it, like Korah and his company, if not into the libertine's or drunkard's grave, at least into the death-shade of a hopeless eternity. Yet, even here, and even to ourselves, there is a sense, in which many who are not safe, might seem almost saved. If we could read the hearts of some who hear the Gospel, and amidst the unbelief and opposition to the truth which still prevail there, mark the strong though ineffectual desires for something better, and the nascent resolutions to repent and to believe which are perpetually surging up in the commotions of that sea which cannot rest, we should be tempted to say, surely these struggling souls are almost saved. Yes, if we knew how often childish levity, and stoical indifference, and proud contempt, and even seeming spite, are but the mask of an interior strife which the subject would conceal not only from his neighbors but himself, we should be still more disposed to say of such, that they were almost saved; or, to say to them, in the words of Christ himself, "Thou art not far from the kingdom of heaven."

The grand mistake to which we are exposed in all such cases is the error of regarding this approach to true faith and repentance as peculiarly a state of safety. In itself, it is a state of the highest interest and moment. In itself, it is incomparably better than a state of total opposition or of absolute insensibility. But in reference to the future, it is not a safe state, and the longer it continues the less safe it is. It is not safe, because it is a critical juncture, a transition state, a turning point, on which the future may be finally suspended. It is safe to enter, but not safe to rest in. The sooner we are brought to it the better, and the sooner we escape from it the better, if we only do so in the right direction. For alas, there are two ways in which the doubt may be resolved and the suspense determined,—by advancing or receding, going right or going wrong, escaping to Zoar or turning back to Sodom.

2. For the state described is, after all, like that of Lot's wife, when, against her will, she had been brought out of the city. She seemed to be beyond

the reach of all immediate danger. She was following safe guides, and in the right direction. Yet she looked back, and she perished! So have thousands. So may you. This is a second point of resemblance. Those who are almost saved may perish—fearfully perish—finally perish—perish in reach, in sight of heaven—yes, at the very threshold of salvation. It is vain to quarrel with this fearful possibility and risk. It is vain to say, are we not convinced of our danger? So was Lot's wife. Are we not escaping from it? So was she. Are we not near the place of refuge? So was she. But she looked back—no matter with what motive; she looked back—no matter how long or how short a time, though it were but for a moment; she looked back—whether from curiosity or lingering desire to return, we are not told, we need not care, we only know that she looked back—she violated the divine command—abjured the only hope of safety—and you know the rest. Whatever looking back may have denoted in the type, we know full well what may answer to it in the antitype. Whatever may have tempted Lot's wife to look back, we know the multiplied temptations which lead sinners to do likewise. And this terrible example cries aloud to those who are assailed by lingering desires for enjoyments once abandoned, or by skeptical misgivings, or by evil habits unsubdued, or by disgust at the restraints of a religious life, or by an impious desperation such as sometimes urges us to eat and drink, for to-morrow we die; to all such this terrible example cries aloud, Remember Lot's wife—her escape, and her destruction. However different your outward situation, yet remember her, remember her, for if, like her, you are the destined prey of God's avenging justice, it will find you out, for "wheresoever the body is, thither will the eagles be gathered together."

3. Lastly, they who are, like Lot's wife, almost saved, may not only, like her, be destroyed in the very moment of deliverance, but, like her, so destroyed as to afford a monumental warning to all others, that the patience and long-suffering of God are not eternal. Looking back to the cities of the plain, they may not only be involved in their destruction, but, as "pillars of salt," record it and attest it to succeeding generations. To a certain extent this is true of all who perish. God has made all things for himself, even the wicked for the day of evil. They who will not, as "vessels of mercy," glorify his wisdom and his goodness, must and will "show his wrath and make his power known," as "vessels of wrath fitted to destruction." They who will not consent to glorify him willingly must be content to glorify him by compulsion. This is true of all who perish, and who therefore may be said to become "pillars of salt," standing, like mile-stones, all along the broad road that leadeth to destruction, solemn though speechless monitors of those who throng it, and planted even on the margin of that "great gulf" which is "fixed" forever between heaven and hell. But in another and a more affecting sense, it may be said that they who perish with the very foretaste of salvation on their lips, who make shipwreck in the sight of their desired haven, who are blasted by the thunderbolt of

vengeance after fleeing from the city of destruction, and amidst their very journey towards the place of refuge, become "pillars of salt" to their successors. What a thought is this, my hearers, that of all the tears which some have shed in seasons of awakening, and of all their prayers and vows and resolutions, all their spiritual conflicts and apparent triumphs over self and sin, the only ultimate effect will be to leave them standing by the wayside as "pillars of salt," memorials of man's weakness and corruption, and of God's most righteous retributions. Are you willing to live, and what is more, to die, for such an end as this? To be remembered only as a "pillar of salt," a living, dying, yet enduring proof, that sinners may be almost saved, and yet not saved at all, that they may starve at the threshold of a feast, and die of thirst at the fountain of salvation.

It is not unusual for those who have outlived their first impressions of religion, and successfully resisted the approaches of conviction, to subside into a state of artificial calmness, equally removed from their original insensibility and from the genuine composure of a true faith and repentance. As you feel this new sense of tranquillity creep over your excited senses, assuaging your exasperated conscience, you may secretly congratulate yourself upon a change of feeling so much for the better. But you may not be aware that the relief which you experience is similar to that which often follows long exposure to intense cold, when the sense of acute suffering begins to be succeeded by a grateful numbness, and the faculties, long excited by resistance, to be lulled into a drowsy languor, far from being painful to the sense, but as surely the precursor of paralysis and dissolution, as if the limbs were already stiffened and the process of corruption even visibly begun. Or the change of feeling now in question, may resemble that which came upon Lot's wife as she began to lose her consciousness of pain and pleasure beneath that saline incrustation which enchained her limbs, suppressed her breath, and stopped the circulation of her life's blood. Was that an enviable feeling, think you, even supposing it to be exclusive of all suffering? Or could you consent to purchase such immunity from pain by being turned into a pillar of salt?

It is not the least affecting circumstance about the strange event which has afforded us a theme for meditation, that although Lot's wife was fearfully destroyed, and at the very moment when she seemed to be beyond the reach of danger; we have no intimation that the lightning struck her, or that the fires which they kindled scorched her, or that the waters of the dead sea, as they rushed into their new bed, overwhelmed her, or that any other violence befell her. But we read that she looked back and became a pillar of salt, perhaps without a pang of "corporal sufferance," perhaps without the consciousness of outward change; one moment full of life, the next a white and sparkling, cold and lifeless mass. If this, my hearer, is the death which you would choose to die in soul or body, then look back to Sodom, stretch your hands towards it, and receive the death which comes to meet you in your cold embrace. Turn back, turn back, if you would fain become a pillar of salt. If not, on, on! Escape for your life! Look not behind you! Stay not in all the plain! Escape to the mountain, lest you be consumed! And though you feel a secret drawing towards the scenes which you have left, yield not to it, but let memory do the work of sight. Instead of turning back to perish without hope, let it suffice you to REMEMBER LOT'S WIFE!

VIII.

1 JOHN 3, 2.—It doth not yet appear what we shall be.

THESE words admit of being taken either in a wide and comprehensive, or a more restricted and specific sense, as referring to a blessed immortality beyond the grave, or to futurity in general, including the as yet unknown vicissitudes belonging to the present state of our existence. It is in this larger application of the language, and indeed with special reference to a proximate futurity, that I invite your attention to the fact that "it doth not yet appear what we shall be."

There is nothing, in the actual condition of mankind, or in the method of God's dispensations towards them, more surprising than the fact, that, while the very constitution of the mind impels it to survey the future with intense solicitude, futurity itself is hidden by a veil, which can neither be penetrated nor withdrawn. The light which glimmers through this veil is strong enough to show that something lies beyond it, and the demonstration is completed by the misshapen but gigantic shadows which occasionally flit across its surface; but the size, and shape, and rela tive position of the objects thus beheld in shadow, are completely concealed from view. It is in vain that every artificial aid to the infirmity of sense is brought to bear upon the tantalizing spectacle; the light, the shadows, are still visible and nothing more, except that providential barrier, which at the same time brings the shadows to our view and makes the substances invisible.

This seeming contradiction between Providence and Nature, between human instinct and divine administration, is exemplified with perfect uniformity, in all parts of the world and all the periods of its history. It matters not how little or how much is known as to the present or the past; men everywhere and always long to know the future. The historian in whose memory events are gathered, as in one vast storehouse; the philosopher, who looks into the actual condition of all nature with a view at once minute and comprehensive, can plead no exemption from the restless and solicitous forebodings of the savage, who knows nothing of the past, and but little of the present, but whose darkened and confused mind swarms, as it were, with visions of the future. Not a form of idolatry or false religion has existed which did not undertake to make its votaries acquainted with the future. This has always been regarded as a necessary means of influencing human minds, a strong proof of the universality and strength of the original principle. No pagan altar ever smoked without an oracle of some kind near it. The diviner or the prophet is in all such cases the companion of the priest, if not the priest himself. The occult arts of necromancy, sorcery, and witchcraft, in their infinite variety of form, are integral parts of one great superstitious system, the religion of fear, in which ignorance is indeed the mother of devotion. While the African bows down before his Fetish, and the Indian mutters to his medicine-bag, the Turk wears his talisman, the Egyptian his amulet, and even those who are called Christians sometimes watch the clouds, the flight of birds, or the most trivial domestic incidents, the breaking of a glass, or the upsetting of a vessel, with as much secret dread as ever terrified the most benighted heathen; nay, even educated men and women have been known, amidst the very blaze of scientific and religious light, to steal in secret to the haunts of the conjurer or fortune-teller, not alway in jest, but sometimes with a studied secrecy, indicative at once of shame, fear, misplaced trust, and inexpressible desire to know what God, in wisdom and in mercy, has decreed shall not be known.

The final cause or purpose of this determination appears obvious enough. If sin and misery were wholly foreign from the experience of man, this limitation of his view might be complained of as a hardship or privation. But since man is born to sorrow and temptation, since his heart is deceitful and his understanding fallible, since no foreknowledge could effectually guard him against sin or suffering, without the intervention of a power which can just as well be exercised without his knowledge and consent as with it; since the pains to be endured would in multitudes of cases be immeasurably aggravated by anticipation, and the most important duties often shrunk from in despair, if all the preceding and accompanying circumstances could be seen at once, whenever the contrary effect results from the gradual development in slow succession, urging only one step in advance, and at the same time cutting off retreat as either shameful or impossible; for these, and other reasons like these, the concealment of futurity is on the whole to be regarded not as a privation, but a priceless mercy.

We have only to look back upon our progress hitherto, and some of us, alas, not far, to see experimental evidence, which we at least must own to be conclusive, that in hiding from us that which was before us, God has dealt with us not as an austere master but a tender parent, knowing well how his children can endure, and in the exercise of that omniscience determining not only how much they shall actually suffer, but how much of what they are to suffer shall be known to them before their day of visitation comes.

But this part of God's providential government, though eminently merciful, is not designed exclusively to spare men a part of the suffering which sin has caused. It has a higher end. By the partial disclosure and concealment of futurity, continually acting on the native disposition to pry into it, the soul is still led onward, kept in an attitude of expectation, and in spite of its native disposition to look downward, to go backward, or to lie stagnant, is perpetually stimulated to look up, to exert itself, and make advances in the right direction. The immense advantage of the impulse thus imparted may indeed be lost, and even made to aggravate the guilt and wretchedness of those who disregard it; but considered in itself and its legitimate effects, it is one of the most striking proofs of God's benevolence to man, that when the soul through sin has acquired a fatal tendency to sink forever and forever lower, or to rest where even rest is ruin, instead of suffering this tendency to operate without obstruction as he justly might, he has created a new counteracting influence and brought it to bear mightily, not only on the conscience and the understanding, but upon instinctive fears, and the natural desire of man to know what is before them.

This view, partial and imperfect as it may be, of the divine purpose is abundantly sufficient to vindicate His wisdom and His goodness, in making men so curious of the future and yet utterly unable to discover it except so far as he is pleased to make it known. For I need hardly say that this concealment of the future, is not, and cannot be, from the nature of the case, absolute and total. In making us rational, in giving us the power of comparison and judgment, and in teaching us by the constitution of our nature to infer effect from cause and cause from effect, God has rendered us incapable of looking at the present or remembering the past, without at the same time, or as a necessary consequence, anticipating that which is to come, and to a great extent with perfect accuracy, so that all the knowledge of the future which is needed for the ordinary purposes of human life is amply provided and infallibly secured; while far beyond the limits of this ordinary foresight, he has granted to some gifted minds a keener vision and a more enlarged horizon, so that objects, which to others seem to lie behind the veil of providential concealment, are detected and revealed by the far reaching ken of their sagacity.

Nor is this all, for even with respect to things which neither ordinary reasoning from analogy, nor extraordinary powers of forecast can avail to bring within the reach of human prescience, God has himself been pleased to make them known by special revelation. Experience and reason are enough to teach us that all men must die. Professional or personal sagacity may see the signs of speedy death in one, whom others look upon as firm in health, and sure, to all appearance, of long life. But neither reason, nor experience, nor sagacity, could ever teach us that the body now dead shall again live; that the soul now living shall yet die, the death, not of annihilation, but, of perdition; that this second death is, by nature, the inevitable doom of all mankind, and yet that it may be escaped, but only in one way. Much less can that one way be distinguished or revealed by the exercise of any unassisted human power. These are things which neither eye can see, nor ear hear, nor heart conceive, until the Spirit of God makes them known. The light which shines upon the ordinary duties and events of life, is that which glimmers through the curtain of futurity; the more extraordinary sights which are occasionally seen by some minds in the exercise of an extraordinary power, are the vague and dubious shadows which appear and disappear upon the curtain which conceals their cause;

but the view which man obtains of heaven and hell, of everlasting life and of the second death, can only be obtained through some opening which the hand of God himself has made in that mysterious curtain, or at some favoured spot where he has gathered up its folds, and given man a clear, though partial glimpse beyond it, free from all obstruction.

Revelations thus imparted do not change or modify the operation of that great law of concealment under which God's dispensations are conducted. He has indeed made known the way of life, the necessity and method of salvation, but the personal futurity of every man is still hidden from the view both of himself and others. And even with respect to that which is revealed, there is reserve and limitation, so that while men may rejoice in those discoveries which through divine grace now belong to them and their children, they are still constrained to say with Moses of old, "Secret things belong unto the Lord our God."

Through one such opening into Futurity as I have been describing, God has permanently brought within the view of all, who have his Word in their possession, a long line of light, reaching like Jacob's ladder from the earth to heaven, a path for the descent of ministering angels, and the ascent of such as shall be saved. The points where it begins and ends are clearly marked; and all along its intervening course, the line of its direction is identified by landmarks, by the altar erected at the gate of Paradise, the ark of Noah, and the ark of the covenant, the tabernacle, the temple, the manger at Bethlehem, the garden of Gethsemane, the cross on Calvary, the tomb of Joseph, the ascent from Olivet, the throne of God, and the seat at his right hand. Along this pathway, from the depths of sin and sorrow, thousands have made their way through fire and flood, through the blood of martyrdom and that of atonement, out of much tribulation, and with fear and trembling, to that world where there is no night, neither light of the sun, where the wicked cease from troubling and the weary are at rest.

That there is such a way and such an end, no one can doubt who will use the light which God has given him. Behold, oh soul, behold it for thyself. Withdraw thy curious gaze from vain endeavours to discover that which is concealed, or from the useless sight of visionary phantoms; let the veil still hide the secret things of God until his hand shall rend it; but behold that luminous and dazzling point, that ray of light illumining futurity, an aperture through which you may behold the life that is to come. See that narrow pathway with its difficult approach, and straitened entrance, scaling one mountain—then another and another and another—till it seems to disappear among the clouds; and then again to be seen through them, indistinct, but still unchanged in its direction—still ascending, still surmounting every intervening object, till the aching sense toils after it in vain, or the view which was afforded you is suddenly cut off. For here is an example of that limitation and reserve which I have mentioned as acompanying even the clearest revelations of futurity. If any thing is certain it is this, that they who do escape perdition, and by faith in the omnipotence of grace, pursue this upward course, shall still continue to ascend without cessation, rising higher, growing better, and becoming more and more like God throughout eternity. I say that this is sure—sure as the oath and promise of a God who cannot lie can make it; and it is a glorious certainty indeed; but when we task our powers to distinguish the successive steps of this transcendent change, to compute specifically the effects which certain causes will produce, and to anticipate the actual results of the whole process, we are lost, we are bewildered; this is not yet revealed to us; it could not be without confounding all distinctions, and making the present and the future one. Hence the Apostle, who is speaking in the text, although inspired to reveal the general fact that true believers are the sons of God, and joint-heirs with the Saviour of a glorious inheritance, even he stops short before attempting to describe in its details what glorified believers are to be hereafter, even his tongue falters, even his eye quails, he turns away dazzled from the light which no man can approach unto, and which even inspiration did not enable him to penetrate, saying, "it doth not yet appear what we shall be,"—we shall be something, something great and glorious, something which we are not, and never have been, something of which we cannot form an adequate conception; this we shall be, this we must be; but beyond this, as to the mode of our existence, or the circumstances of our new condition, "it doth not yet appear what we shall be." So that with respect to that which is most certain as a general truth, many at least of the particulars included in it, may be still beneath the veil of providential concealment.

This vagueness and uncertainty, although at first sight it may seem to be a serious disadvantage, is nevertheless not without important and beneficent effects upon the subjects of salvation. It may seem, indeed, that as a means of arousing and arresting the attention, an indefinite assurance of transcendent blessedness hereafter is less likely to be efficacious than a distinct and vivid exhibition of the elements which are to constitute that blessedness; but let it be remembered that no possible amount, and no conceivable array of such particulars, would have the least effect in originating serious reflection or desire in the unconverted heart. This can be wrought by nothing short of a divine power, and when it is thus wrought, when the thoughts and the affections are once turned in the right direction, the less detailed and more indefinite description of the glory which is yet to be experienced, seems often best adapted to excite and stimulate the soul and lead it onwards, by still presenting something that is yet to be discovered or attained, and thus experimentally accustoming the soul to act upon the vital principle of its new-born nature, forgetting that which is behind, and reaching forth to that which is before.

The same thing may be said of the indefinite manner in which the doom of the impenitent and unbelieving is set forth in Scripture. The general truth that they shall perish, that their ruin shall be total, final, and irrevocable, and that their condition shall be growing worse and worse and worse forever; this is

taught too clearly to be rendered dubious by any
natural or rational interpretation of the Word of God.
And in the truth thus clearly taught there is a fathomless depth of solemn and terrific import, rendered
more impressive by the vagueness and reserve of the
description, when the mind has once been awakened
to the serious contemplation of futurity; but until
this is the case, the general threatenings of perdition
fall without effect upon the heavy ear and the obdurate conscience. No attempt, however, has been
made in Scripture to increase their efficacy by an accumulation of appalling circumstances. There are
fearful glimpses of the world of woe, but they are
merely glimpses, abundantly sufficient to assure us
that there is a future state of punishment, but not to
feed or stimulate a morbid curiosity. In this, as in
the corresponding case before described, if the mind
is awakened, such details are needless, and if not
awakened, they are unavailing. Tell a poor man that
he has suddenly been made rich by the bequest of
some unknown kinsman or a stranger, and so long as
he regards it as a jest or an imposition, you gain
nothing by the fullest and most accurate detail of the
possessions which have thus devolved upon him; nay,
the very minuteness of your description seems to confirm him in his incredulity. But let him by some
other means be thoroughly persuaded of the fact that
he has undergone this change of fortune, and he listens even to the most indefinite and vague assurance
with avidity, and now, instead of slighting the particulars of which before he took no notice, he is eager
to obtain them, and pursues his importunate inquiries

until on fact after another has been fully ascertained. So too in the case of warnings against some impending danger. Tell a solitary traveller, that in the forest which is just before him there are wild beasts, robbers, pitfalls, precipices, labyrinths, or any other perils, and if he believes you not, it is in vain that you exaggerate the evil, or depict it in the most impressive and alarming colours. Every stroke that you add to your description seems to make it less effective than the indefinite assurance which preceded it. But if a sudden panic should take hold of him, or, instead of being fearless and self-confident, he be naturally timid and accustomed to shun danger, even the first vague intimation of that danger is sufficient to unman him, and he either turns around, without waiting for a more detailed description of the case, or else he hears it with the eagerness of unaffected terror.

These familiar illustrations may suffice to show that in the wise reserve with which the Scriptures speak of the details of future blessedness and misery, there is no sacrifice of any salutary influence upon the minds of men; and that it does not in the least impair the majesty, benevolence, and justice of God's dealings with the souls of men—that while the certainty, eternity, and endless progression, both of future blessedness and future misery, are clearly set forth in the word of God, the minute particulars of neither state and neither process are detailed, nor any attempt made to describe things indescribable; but both are left to be made known by a glorious or terrible experience, with the solemn premonition, clothed in various forms, that in reference, as well to our destruction if we perish, or to our blessedness if saved, "it doth not yet appear what we shall be."

In thus extending what the text says of God's adopted children, to the misery of those whom he shall finally cast off, I have merely held up to your view the same great truth in two of its important aspects. It is the same pillar that is light to Israel and dark to the Egyptians. It was not, however, my design to dwell upon the mere doctrinal proposition, though unquestionably true and inconceivably important, that neither reason nor experience nor imagination can, in this life, furnish us with any adequate conception either of the joys of heaven or the pains of hell; nor can I be satisfied with simply pointing to the one and to the other, and in reference to both, assuring those who now hear me, in the accents of encouragement and warning, that "it doth not yet appear what we shall be." I desire rather to bring this interesting fact of the text to bear with all its rightful power on the character, interests, and duties of my hearers. To effect this purpose, I have no need to resort to any forced accommodation or arbitrary application of the text, which I have chosen with direct view to the use which I now propose to make of it. All that is necessary for my present purpose, under God's blessing, is to lead your minds a little further in the same direction which we have been hitherto pursuing, and if possible, to show you the effect which the doctrine of the text, if rightly understood and heartily embraced, must have upon our views of human life, and more particularly of its earlier periods.

If, my hearer, it be true, as I believe, and you believe, and as God's word assures us, that in reference even to the case of those who shall assuredly be saved or as assuredly be lost, "it doth not yet appear what they shall be;" if it be true that even those who are already saved, not merely in God's purpose, but in fact, beyond the reach of all disturbing and retarding causes, even they who are rejoicing at this moment in God's presence as the spirits of just men made perfect, if even they are unable to enclose in their conceptions that illimitable ocean into which they have been plunged but for a moment; if it be true that even those who are disembodied spirits are now drinking of the cup of divine wrath, can, in the anguish of their torment, frame no definite idea of the volume and duration of that stream of fire which forever and forever fills their cup to overflowing; if both these souls, however different their actual condition and their prospects for eternity, are forced alike to cry out in a triumphant burst of grateful joy and a convulsion of blaspheming horror, "it doth not yet appear what we shall be!" Oh, with what multiplied intensity of emphasis may those whose future state is still unsettled, who are still upon the isthmus between hell and heaven, wavering, vacillating, hanging in terrible suspense between the two, unable or unwilling to decide their fate, and waiting, it would almost seem, until some heaving of the ocean of eternity should sweep them from the earth they know not, think not, care not whither, Oh! with what emphasis might such exclaim, as they hang over the dizzy verge of two unchanging, everlasting states, "it doth not yet appear what we shall be."

But is it, can it be, a fact, that rational, spiritual beings, godlike in their origin, and made for immortality, with faculties susceptible of endless elevation and enlargement and activity, can hesitate to choose life rather than death, and good in preference to evil? Yes, it may be so; it is so; such neutrality is possible, so far as a decisive formal action of the will goes. The performance of that last act may be long deferred, and in deferring it, the dying soul may cherish the belief that all is still at its disposal, and that by one independent act of will, the whole work of salvation or perdition is to be begun and finished. Oh, what a delusion! when the cup, by long-continued droppings, has been filled up to the brim, to imagine that the last and almost imperceptible infusion which produces its final overflow is all that it contains; or, that the withholding of that one drop, leaves it empty and removes all danger of its ever overflowing. How preposterous a hope! and yet in no respect less rational than his, who lets his life not only run to waste, but run to ruin, in the expectation that by some one energetic act at last, the countless acts which have preceded it, shall all be cancelled and their effect neutralized. It is the crying sin and the stupendous folly of our race, that while they own their need of expiation, and repentance, and conversion, and acknowledge, yea, insist upon God's sovereign right to give them or withhold them, they not only make no efforts to obtain them at his hands, but, as it were, take pains to make the work which they acknowledge to be necessary, harder, and the grace which they prefer to wait for, more and more hopeless. Does the man who looks to God for the productions of that which he has buried in the earth, demonstrate his dependence by introducing tares among his wheat, by laboriously cultivating noxious weeds, or by violently tearing from the earth the very seed on which he is depending for a harvest? Does the man who looks to God for the recovery of health, presume on that ground to drink poison, to court exposure, and to plunge into the most insane and ruinous excesses? Does the mariner who looks to God for a successful issue to his voyage, throw his cargo and provisions overboard, dismantle his own vessel, pierce its bottom, or deliberately drive it upon fatal rocks? Is such madness possible? or, if it were, would it be in the least extenuated by the calm profession of a purpose to do otherwise and better, at some future time, when all the evil may have been accomplished, and amendment irretrievably too late?

Of all reliances, the weakest and the worst is a reliance on the permanence of present motives, which now have no effect, and may one day gather overwhelming strength, and those which now seem all-sufficient, and may be powerless. Because you now wish to repent, and to believe, and to be saved hereafter, you imagine yourselves safe in your impenitence, and unbelief and condemnation. Why, the very disposition which is now made the pretext for procrastination, may forsake you. The respect you now feel for the truth, for God's law, for the gospel, may be changed into a cold indifference, contemptuous incredulity, or malignant hatred. The faint gleams of conviction which occasionally light up the habitual darkness of the mind, may be extinguished. The compunctious visitings which now preserve your conscience from unbroken stupor, may become less frequent, till they cease forever, or give place to the agonizing throbs of an incurable remorse. In short, the very feelings and intuitions upon which you vainly build your hopes of future reformation, may themselves be as evanescent as the outward circumstances which produce them; and when these have passed away, the others may soon follow; so that, even though your judgment may be now correct, your feelings tender, and your plans of future action all that could be wished, "it doth not yet appear what you shall be."

How often, oh, how often, has some real or imaginary sorrow touched the secret springs of your affection with a sympathy so exquisite that change appeared impossible, and you imagined, aye, perhaps, declared, that you would never smile again! Has that pledge been redeemed? In other cases, how your heart has swelled with gratitude for some deliverance or surprising mercy, which you fondly dreamed could never be forgotten? Were you right in so believing? Oh, my hearers, where are the delights of infancy, the sports of childhood, and the hopes of youth, the joys and sorrows which absorbed your thoughts and governed your affections but a few years back? Are they not all gone? Have not their very objects and occasions in many cases been forgotten? And has not this process been repeated more than once, it may be often, till you find it hard to look back a few years or even months, without a passing doubt of your identity, so changed are your opinions, inclinations, habits, purposes and hopes? Recall that wish, and then consider whether its fulfilment now would make you happy as it promised to do then; nay, does it even seem desirable, or worthy of an effort to secure it? No, the appetite has sickened and so died. The object is the same, but you are not; your mind, your heart, your will, are changed; and do you, can you, dare you think, that you are now unchangeable, or capable of changing for the better only, so that what you now approve, and wish, and purpose, will still continue to be thus approved, desired, and purposed, and at last performed. Alas, my hearer, if, when you look at what you are, you can scarcely recognize what you have been, surely "it doth not yet appear what you shall be."

To some of you the period of childhood is so recent that memory has not yet wholly lost its old impressions. You can easily remember objects upon which you then looked with a solemn awe, perhaps with terror. Do they still command your reverence? There were others upon which you looked with infantile contempt, as far less interesting than your childish sports; and yet these objects have been rising and expanding in the view with every moment of your life and every handsbreadth of your stature. And now, I ask you, what is the change owing to? to lapse of time? to change of circumstances? to the growth of all your faculties? And are you not soon to be still older than you are? Must not your circumstances undergo still further change? Can you imagine that the development and cultivation of your powers are already finished? Is it not then possible, at least, that your future views and feelings may as widely differ from your present views and feelings, as the present from the past. And is it rational or right to seal up your own destiny and character?

Turn not away, then, from the gracious invitations of the gospel, merely because you do not now feel the need of its protection, consolations, and rewards. Life is not only short but full of change. If you could now look back and see some golden opportunity of wealth and greatness lost forever, through a freak of childish levity, you would scarcely be consoled by the reflection that you thereby gained another hour of amusement. But, oh, how inadequate is this to give the least idea of your feelings in that awful hour, when you shall see eternal life forever lost for the mere playthings of this passing scene. Try then to antedate experience, to anticipate as possible feelings the most remote from those which you are now indulging. For example, when I speak of consolation, there are some perhaps among you who could smile at the idea as entirely foreign from your present feelings. And when you look before you and imagine scenes of sorrow, they are mere fantastic images, on which your stronger feelings rest but for a moment. This may not be the case with all. There may be some here whose experience has made them prematurely old. There may be hearts among you whose deep fountains have been broken up and taught to gush already. Such need no admonition upon this point. The heart knoweth its own bitterness, and the stranger intermeddleth not with its joys. But you who are without experience of real and deep-seated sorrow, look afar off at that strange phantasmagoria of darkened chambers, desolated houses, beds of pain, dying struggles, funeral rites, and broken hearts—and amidst all these behold that human form, and tell me whether you can realize yourself. Now, as to outward things, you may be far beyond the reach of such considerations as a motive to repentance, but you know not what an hour may bring forth. Whatever you are now, "it doth not yet appear what you shall be."

But your danger lies not merely in disregarding motives which you are to feel hereafter, but in blindly trusting to the performance of those which you acknowledge now. I might go farther and excite your incredulity and even your contempt, by holding up, as possible, a total change not only in your feelings and your principles, but even in your outward lives, a change which you would look upon as utterly impossible, a change no less humbling to your pride than blasting to your hopes. I might startle you by holding up a mirror which, instead of giving back the smiling aspect that you now wear, the countenance of health and buoyant spirits, should confront you with a ghastly likeness of your present self, under the strange and hideous disguise of an exhausted gamester, a decaying libertine, a bloated drunkard, a detected cheat, a conscience-stricken murderer. I might present you to yourself, surrounded by the wreck of fortune, family and character, seated amidst the ashes of deserted hearths and their extinguished fires, gazing unmoved upon peaceful homes made desolate and fond hearts broken—the wreck, the refuse, the unquiet ghost of all that you are now. I might present all this, but you would shrink with indignation from the foul aspersion. You may be unfortunate, you may be changed, but this, but this you can never be, never! My heart's desire and prayer to God is that you never may; but what is your security? The mere intentions which you cherish now, to be fulfilled hereafter? Ah, my hearer, go to yonder silent dwelling-place of crime, and learn how many good intentions have been cherished in those now degraded and perhaps now despairing bosoms. Go to some one haunt of vice, and trace the miserable victims who assemble there, back through their melancholy progress to the time when their intentions were as good as yours, their external circumstances no less promising. Go to the gibbet, to the yard-arm, to the horrid scene of horrid vengeance wreaked by man upon himself, and learn that even there the deadly fruit has often sprung up into a rank vegetation, from the seed of good but ineffectual intentions.

It is high time for our youth to be aware that they who die upon scaffolds, and pine away in prisons, are not seldom such as once scornfully smiled at the suggestion of their ever being worse than they were then; and as they looked upon the kind friends and the multiplied advantages by which they were surrounded, and then in upon the purposes of future good they were intending, would have blushed at their own cowardice or self distrust if they could have been brought to say, "It doth not yet appear what we shall be."

When I recall to mind the countenances, persons, manners, talents, attainments, hopes, and purposes of some whom I knew in early life, and then consider what they now are, my heart sickens at the sight of early promise, not because it is not infinitely lovely, but because the possibility of fatal change looms with a ghastly speculation through the eyes of these encouraging appearances, as evil spirits may have glared upon spectators from the bodies of the men whom they possessed of old.

From such anticipations, rendered more distressing by the growing frequency of such deterioration and of awful crime, the heart is forced to turn away in search of something to reanimate its hopes, and this is only to be found in the immovable belief that God's grace is omnipotent, and Christ's blood efficacious. To this the true philanthropist must cling, not only as the ground of his own hope, but as the only source of safety to the young around him; and when they earnestly inquire, as they sometimes do, how these fearful perils are to be avoided, instead of mocking them with prudential maxims of mere worldly policy or selfish cunning, let us lead them at once to the only secure refuge, to the only Saviour, to the cross and to the throne of Jesus Christ. Turn ye to the strongholds, ye prisoners of hope! Press into yonder gateway! Cleave to those massive pillars! Bind yourselves with cords to the horns of yonder altar! And at every fresh heave of the ocean and the earth, take the faster hold of Christ's cross and throne, and you are safe. Whatever trials may await you here, a glorious compensation is reserved for you hereafter;

final and eternal deliverance "from the bondage of corruption into the glorious liberty of the children of God." "Behold what manner of love the Father hath bestowed upon us, that we should be called the sons of God!"

But strange as the exaltation is, it is a real one. "Beloved, now are we the sons of God, and it doth not yet appear what we shall be; but we know that when he shall appear we shall be like him, for we shall see him as he is!" Oh blessed sight! Oh glorious assimilation! We shall not only see him as he is, but shall be like him! Let this bright anticipation stimulate and cheer us! Let Christ be in us the hope of glory! But let every one that hath this hope in him, purify himself even as He is pure!

IX.

LUKE 11, 26.—The last state of that man is worse than the first.

SOME of the most remarkable inventions and discoveries, by which the present age has been distinguished, are of such a nature as to realize ideas which were once regarded as peculiarly visionary and absurd. The steam-engine, the daguerreotype, and the electric telegraph, are all of this description. To our fathers, these results would not only have appeared improbable or impossible, but as belonging to that class of impossibilities which most resemble mere imaginative fictions. That man should be conveyed upon his journey by the vapour of boiling water; that the sun should be constrained to do the painter's work; and that words should be communicated instantaneously to any distance by a wire; are facts which, if predicted a few centuries ago, would not merely have been disbelieved as philosophically false, but laughed at as fabulous inventions, or the dreams of a disordered fancy. And yet these realized impossibilities are now so familiar to our every-day experience, that we scarcely think it necessary to distinguish between them and the most ordinary processes of nature and of art, to which the world has been accustomed for a course of ages. The power of steam, however highly valued, is now seldom thought of as more wonderful than that of water, wind, or animal strength. The instantaneous operation of the light in delineating forms, seems scarcely more surprising than the tedious process of the chisel; and an instantaneous message from the ends of the earth may one day seem as natural and common-place an incident as oral communication with our nearest neighbours.

The use which I would make of this extraordinary change from a contemptuous incredulity to a faith so unhesitating as even to exclude surprise, is to illustrate the position that a corresponding revolution may perhaps take place in morals and religion; that the time may be at hand when some of those religious doctrines, which are now rejected by the mass of men, not merely as unscriptural or unphilosophical, but as fanciful and visionary, shall begin to take their place among realities too certain and familiar to be even wondered at as something strange. If such a revolution of opinion and of feeling should indeed take place, there is no subject with respect to which we could expect its effects to be more striking than the subject of evil spirits; their existence and their influence on human conduct and condition. The predominant feeling with which these are now regarded, even by multitudes who hear the gospel, and profess to be believers in the Bible, is a feeling of tolerant contempt or compassionate indulgence, such as we all entertain with respect to navigation through the air, or the schemes of universal language, and such as our fathers entertained with respect to those familiar facts of our experience already mentioned. If to this suggestion of a like change in men's feelings and associations with respect to demoniacal agency, it should be objected that religious truth affords no room for new discovery, being already fully made known in a complete and authoritative revelation, it may be replied that this is true of every thing essential to salvation or even to the full development of Christian character, but not of all things partially disclosed in Scripture. As the intimations which we find there of the origin and structure of the universe do not preclude physical investigation and discovery as useless, or forbid them as unlawful, because there are only incidental and subordinate subjects of Divine revelation; so the knowledge, or at least the faith, of men as to the fearful doctrine of a devil and his angels, may, for the same reason, be regarded as susceptible of vast increase. At all events, the very possibility of such a change should lead us to receive with any thing but levity or supercilious indifference, the faint but solemn intimations of the Bible upon this mysterious subject. There is something sublime in the reserve with which it is thus treated. The views presented are mere glimpses rendered necessary by the context. Sometimes the light is allowed to rest longer on the object than at other times, as in the history of Job's temptations. Even there, however, the unusual distinctness of the view afforded, is counterbalanced by the doubt which overhangs the question whether the statement is literal or figurative, poetical, or historical. Between the two testaments there is a great difference of clearness and minuteness in the statements on this subject. Even in those of the New Testament, however, there is still the same appearance of reserve, the same entire absence of a disposition to indulge mere curiosity, by limiting the statement to such facts as seem required for some specific purpose. To the attentive reader there will everywhere be visible a marked peculiarity of tone and manner in the treatment of these matters which is well adapted and no doubt designed to keep the reader in perpetual recollection of the awful nature of the things referred to, and of the fact that their complete development is yet to come. Some have inferred from this reserve, that expressions so obscure could not have been intended to convey important matters of belief, and that they ought therefore to be looked upon as strong oriental tropes or mere poetical embellishments. This may seem plausible enough when looked at in the general; but it is not susceptible of a continued and consistent application in detail. The further we pursue it, the more clearly shall we see what may be mentioned as a second characteristic of the teachings of the Bible on the subject.

It is this, that while the revelation is reserved and partial, it is so made as to convey an irresistible impression of the literal reality of that which is revealed. Whatever different conclusion might be drawn from the language or the spirit of particular passages, it is impossible to view them all in a connected series without a strong conviction that these imperfect and obscure disclosures of an unseen world of evil spirits were intended to be strictly understood; that the

Bible does distinctly teach the agency of such a spirit in the great original apostacy and fall of our first parents, and his continued influence on fallen man, an influence which, although it exists at all times, was permitted while our Saviour was on earth, to manifest itself with extraordinary violence and clearness, in the form of demoniacal possessions, which affected both the minds and bodies of the victims, and afforded the subjects and occasions of some of Christ's most signal miracles, designed not merely to relieve the sufferer, nor merely to display his superhuman power, but to signalize his triumph, as the seed of the woman, over the adverse party represented in the first promise of a Saviour, as the seed of the serpent, whose last desperate struggles, not for existence but for victory, were witnessed in those fearful cases of disease and madness which the gospel narrative ascribes expressly to the personal agency of demons, the history of whose dispossession and expulsion is so prominent a feature in the life of Christ.

There are here two errors to be avoided, that of denying the reality of these possessions, and that of supposing that the influence of evil spirits upon men was restricted to the time of our Lord's personal presence upon earth. It existed before. It continues still. Its nature and extent are undefinable at present and by us. We only know that it is not a coercive power, destroying personal responsibility, but a moral influence extending to the thoughts and dispositions. The true view of the matter seems to be, that from the time of Eve's temptation to the present hour a mysterious connection has existed between fallen man and fallen angels, the latter acting as the tempters and seducers of the former, the influence exerted being mental and insensible, or, so far as it is corporeal, inscrutable by us; but that at the time of Christ's appearance, the physical effects were suffered to display themselves in an extraordinary manner, for the purpose of manifesting his superiority to the powers of darkness, and showing forth his glory as the conqueror of the conqueror of mankind. If he were now to re-appear, the same effect might be again produced. The latent adversary might be forced to show himself, and manifest at once his fear and hatred, not only by the paroxysms of his victim, by his unearthly shrieks, and spasms, and foaming at the mouth, but by the repetition of that cry, so often heard of old, "what have I to do with thee, thou holy one of God? art thou come to torment me before the time?" Or if the veil which hides the spiritual world could now be lifted even for a moment, we might stand aghast to see how large a portion of the moral history of sinners is determined by satanic influence; not such as to extenuate the sinner's guilt, but rather to aggravate it by disclosing that his sins are committed in obedience to the dictates of such a master, and in compliance with the suggestions of such a counsellor. The drunkard and the libertine, and every other class of sinners, might be then seen attended by their evil genius, smoothing the way to ruin and averting every better influence. The moral changes now experienced, might be then seen to have more than an ideal connection with the presence and absence of these hellish visitants. The apparent reformation of the sinner might then be found to coincide with their departure, and his relapse with their return. Yes, and in many cases, the experience of such might be found to correspond, not merely in a figure, but in literal truth, with the fearful picture set before us in the text. By means of a vision supernaturally strengthened, we might actually see the evil spirit going out of this man and that man, now regarded as mere ordinary cases of reformation or conversion, and then returning with seven others worse than himself, so that the last state of that man is worse than the first.

There is something fearful in the thought that such a process may be literally going on among us and around us; that from one and another of these very hearts the evil spirit may have recently departed, and may be wandering in desert places, seeking rest, and finding none, until, despairing of another habitation, he shall come back to his old house and find it swept and garnished, rendered more desirable by partial and temporary reformation, and taking with him seven others, he may even now be knocking for admission, and woe to him who opens, for the last state of that man is worse than the first.

But even granting what to some may seem too clear to be denied, that there is no such process literally going on, and that our Saviour's words contain a mere comparison drawn from a real or ideal case of demoniacal possession, and intended to illustrate a familiar fact in morals, that relapses into sin are always dangerous, and often fatal; we may still gather very much the same instruction from the parable as if it were a literal description. Whatever horrors the imagination may associate with the personal invasion and inhabitation of an evil spirit, is it really more dreadful, to the eye of reason and awakened conscience, than the constant presence of an evil principle, not as a mere visitant, but as a part of the man himself? Is it not this, after all, which makes the other seem so terrible? The coming and going of good angels has no such effect on the imagination; nor would that of neutral spirits, neither good nor evil. Apart from their moral effects, their presence or absence is a matter of indifference. And if the effects are wrought, it matters little whether they are literally brought about, in whole or in part, by the influence of demons, or only metaphorically so described. It matters little whether our Saviour meant to represent the fluctuations of man's spiritual state as actually caused by the departure and return of these invisible seducers, or only to describe their fearful import and result by mysterious figures borrowed from the world of spirits.

The primary application of the words, as made by Christ himself, was to his own contemporaries—the Jewish nation—who for ages had been separated from the Gentiles; and from whom the demon of idolatry had been cast out at the Babylonish exile; but who now, in their malignant persecution and rejection of their born Messiah, seemed to be repossessed by devils far more numerous and spiteful than those by which they had been actuated in the worst days of their earlier history, or even those which they believed themselves to be the gods of the heathen. Of such a people—so peculiarly distinguished, and yet so unfaithful, who had proved untrue to a vocation so extraordinary; and, while boasting of their vast superiority to the heathen, had outdone the heathen themselves in crime, and were yet to sink as far below them in punishment—of such a people it might well be said, that their last state was worse than their first.

The same thing is no less true of other communities, distinguished by extraordinary providential favours, and by flagrant abuse of their advantages. If we could watch the tide of national prosperity, in such a case, until it ebbed, it would require no great stretch of imagination to perceive the evil spirit, who had seemed to forsake a people so enlightened and so highly favored, coming back under the cloak of the returning darkness, from his wandering in the desert, not alone, but followed by a shadowy train, overleaping the defences which appeared impregnable to human foes, or mysteriously gliding through the very crevices of fast-barred doors, and unexpectedly appearing in their ancient haunts, which all the intervening glory and prosperity have only seemed to sweep and garnish for its repossession by its ancient master and his new confederates, under whose united usurpation and oppression the last state of that race, or society, or nation, must be worse than the first.

But it is not merely to the rise and fall of whole communities that these terrific images were meant to be applied. The same law of reaction and relapse controls the personal experience of the individual. This is, indeed, its most instructive and affecting application. The vicissitudes of nations, or of other aggregate bodies, however imposing to the eye of the spectator, and however sweeping in their ultimate effects, do not, and cannot so excite our sympathies as those which take place in a single soul, and by which the experience of communities and nations, after all, must be determined. It is not as the invaders of a country or besiegers of a city, that the evil spirit, with his sevenfold reinforcement, rises up before the mind's eye in terrific grandeur. It is when we see him knocking at the solitary door from which he was once driven in disgrace and anguish. The scene, though an impressive one, is easily called up. A lonely dwelling on the margin of a wilderness, cheerfully lighted as the night approaches, carefully swept and garnished, and apparently the home of plenty, peace, and comfort. The winds that sweep across the desert pass it by unheeded. But, as the darkness thickens, something more than wind approaches from that quarter. What are the shadowy forms that seem to come forth from the dry places of the wilderness, and stealthily draw near the dwelling? One of the number guides the rest, and now they reach the threshold. Hark! he knocks; but only to assure himself that there is no resistance. Through the opened door we catch a glimpse of the interior, swept and garnished—swept and garnished; but for whose use?—its rightful owner? Alas! no; for he is absent; and already has that happy home begun to ring with fiendish laughter, and to glare with hellish flames; and, if the weal or woe of any man be centred in it, the last state of that man is worse than the first.

Do you look upon this as a mere fancy scene?

Alas! my hearers, just such fancy scenes are passing every day within you or around you, rendered only more terrific by the absence of all sensible indications, just as we shrink with a peculiar dread from unseen dangers if considered real, and are less affected by the destruction that wastes at noon-day, than by the pestilence that walks in darkness. Come with me and let me show you one or two examples of familiar spiritual changes which, if not the work of evil spirits, may at least be aptly represented by the images presented in the text and context. To the eye of memory or imagination, there rises up the form of one who was the slave of a particular iniquity, which gave complexion to his character and life. It was, perhaps, an open and notorious vice, which directly lowered him in public estimation. Or, it may have been a secret and insidious habit, long successfully concealed or never generally known. But its effects were seen. Even those who were strangers to his habits could perceive that there was something wrong, and they suspected and distrusted him. He felt it, and in desperation waxed worse and worse. But, in the course of Providence, a change takes place. Without any real change of principle or heart, he finds that his besetting sin is ruining his health, his reputation, or his fortune. Strange as the power of temptation, appetite, and habit is, some form of selfishness is stranger still. The man reforms. The change is recognized at once. He is another man. After the first painful acts of self-denial, the change appears delightful to himself. He seems once more to walk erect. A new direction has been given to his hopes and his desires, and, like Saul, he rejoices that the evil spirit has departed from him. At first he is afraid of its return, and keeps strict watch against the inroads of the enemy. By degrees he grows secure, and his vigils are relaxed. The temptation presents itself in some form, so contemptible and little to be feared, that he would blush not to encounter it. He does encounter it. He fights it. He appears to triumph for a moment, but is ultimately overcome. The next victory is easier. The next is easier still. He tries to recall the feelings which preceded and produced his reformation; but the spell is over. He knows that they have once proved ineffectual to save him, and he trusts in them no longer. Even the checks which once controlled him in his former course of sin are now relaxed; he is tired of opposition, and seeks refuge from his self-contempt in desperate indulgence. Do you believe a change like this to be unusual in real life, or too unimportant to be fairly represented by our Saviour's fearful image of the dispossessed and discontented demon coming back to the emancipated soul, and reasserting his dominion, till "the last state of that man is worse than the first?"

Another man passes through the very same process of reformation, but with different results. His watch against the inroads of his once besetting sin is still maintained. His jealousy and dread of it continue unabated. The appetite seems to sicken and to die. He is indeed a new man, as to that one sin, and rejoices with good reason that the fiend has left him. As the habit of forbearance gathers strength, he learns to trust in his own power of resistance. He naturally measures his morality by that sin which once so easily beset him. Freedom from that sin is to him a state of purity, and he flatters himself that he is daily growing better. But, alas! in his anxiety to bar one door against the enemy, he has left the rest all open. A successful breach is made in his defences by an unexpected foe; perhaps by one whom he had harbored and regarded as a friend. Before he is aware, he finds himself a new man in another sense. The evil spirit has returned, but in a different shape, and taking unopposed possession, is again his master. The reformed drunkard has become a gamester; the reformed prodigal a miser; the reformed cheat a voluptuary. Such conversions are by no means rare—conversion wrought without the troublesome appliances of prayer, or preaching, or the Holy Spirit. In all such cases the dominion of the new vice will probably be stronger than the dominion of the old one. The reaction and relapse from a state of self-denial is attended by an impetus which makes itself to be perceived. The man, as it were, makes amends to himself for giving up his former sin by larger measures of indulgence in the new one. The limits which impeded his indulgence in the one are perhaps inapplicable to the other; and, from one or the other of these causes, or from both, "the last state of that man is worse than the first."

I have said, that in this case the anxiety to shut one door leaves the others open. Hence, it often happens that the soul is invaded, not by one new spirit, out by many. Imagining that abstinence from one sin is morality, the man, of course, falls into others; and the conquest of the citadel is frequently effected by the *combined* force of the enemy. If you ask the evil spirit which at first has possession: What is thy name? you may receive for answer: Drunkenness, or Avarice, or Lust. But ask the same after the relapse, and the response must be: My name is Legion. Have you not seen in real life this terrible exchange of one besetting sin for several? Have you not known men, who once seemed vulnerable only at a single point, begin to appear vulnerable, as it were, at all points, perhaps with the exception of the one first mentioned? Now, when this is the case, besides the power exerted by each appetite and passion on the soul distinctly, there is a debasing and debilitating influence arising from the conflict which exists between them. Let the reformed libertine become at once ambitious, avaricious, and revengeful, and let these hungry serpents gnaw his soul, and it will soon be seen by others, if not felt by the miserable victim, that the evil spirit which had left him for a season has returned with seven others worse than himself; and, as we see them in imagination enter the dwelling swept and garnished for their use, we may read, inscribed above the portal that shuts after them, "the last state of that man is worse than the first."

Let us now leave the regions of gross vice, with the seeming reformations and their terrible conversions from one sin to another, or from one to many, and breathe for a while the atmosphere of decent morals, under the influence of Christian institutions. Let me show you one who never was the slave of any vice, and whose character has never been subjected to suspicion. Such are always to be found among those who have enjoyed a religious education and the means of grace. Yet, so long as these advantages are unattended by a change of heart, the evil spirit still maintains possession. Methinks I see one who has long held a high place in the public estimation as a moral and conscientious person, but whose views are bounded by the sensible horizon, who sees nothing serious in religion, or deserving of profound regard. All is sunshine. Even death, while distant, has no horrors, and the world beyond is blank. The past, the present, and the future are alike themes of jest and laughter. But the scene is changed. A sudden shadow falls across the countenance and heart. The laugher becomes grave. He indulges for the first time in serious reflection. Without knowing whence his change of feeling comes, he yields to it, and it increases. The realities of life are seen in a new aspect. What mere trifles seem momentous. Sin is no longer mocked at, and the grave looks dull and dreary. The question of salvation and the necessary means to it, begins to be considered, and the world begins to see that he who once was so light-hearted, has become, as they correctly term it, serious. The duration of this state of mind is indefinitely variable. Most men experience it for moments or for hours, many for days or weeks, and some for months, or even years. In many cases it becomes habitual; the feelings are adjusted to it; it proceeds no further, and is equivalent to a simple change of temperament. Nay, in some cases, while the appearance lasts, the feeling itself wears away. The shadows cast by some mysterious object on the soul are gradually mitigated and reduced in depth, until the sun breaks through the intervening obstacle, and broad daylight returns. The sensation of this change is naturally pleasant. It is welcomed, it is cherished, till the ancient habits of the mind are reinstated in their full dominion. Even supposing that the change is unaccompanied by any moral renovation, and is merely an alternation or vicissitude of gaiety and sadness, the return to the former state is not precisely what continuance in that state would have been. There is now a sensitive shrinking from all gloomy thoughts, a dread of solitude, an instinctive shunning of the ordinary means by which serious reflection is produced. In itself this state may be a pleasing one; but with respect to its effects, it is worse than the first.

But some go further. Having passed through the change which I have just described—the change from levity to serious reflection—they reach a new stage of experience. Sin, which was heretofore a mere abstraction, or at most the name of certain gross enormities, is seen in its true nature. The law of God is seen to be what it is. The conscience is awakened to a sense of guilt, a dread of wrath, and a consciousness of deserving it. Every act is now seen to have a moral quality. The man grows scrupulous. He who was once bold to commit known sin, is now afraid to perform even innocent actions. The burden of unexpiated guilt becomes oppressive, nay, intolerable. An undefined anxiety torments him. He feels that some great crisis is approaching. Earthly pleasures grow insipid. The cares of life are child's play. He becomes indifferent to life or death, except in reference to the great absorbing question of salvation or perdition. The intensity with which he seeks relief exhausts him. He begins to grow languid. His alarm subsides into a stupid desperation. As this new sensation creeps upon him, he is conscious of relief from the poignant anguish of his former state. The soothing apathy is cherished. Strong emotion is excluded. Sin seems no longer so repulsive as it once did. Words begin to have their ancient meanings, and to awaken only old associations. One strong impression is effaced after another. Conscience slumbers. Hope revives. The noise of the world again rings in the ears. The dream is past; the spell is broken; and the once convicted sinner is himself again. He has recovered his reason; his false friends assure him— for they see not that the spirit of delusion which had left him for a season has returned and found his habitation swept and garnished, and shall dwell therein forever. Ah, sirs, whatever may have been the first condition of the man who has passed through all these changes, there is little risk of error or exaggeration in saying that "the last state of that man is worse than the first."

But the evil spirit does not measure the duration of his absence by any settled rule. He may return before the truth has made the least impression. He may wait until a serious state of mind has been induced, but come back before the soul has been convinced of sin. Or he may stay until a lively sense of guilt and danger has been wrought upon the mind, whether the views entertained be false or true; and the anguish of distress, having reached its extreme point, instead of gradually sinking into cold insensibility, is suddenly succeeded by its opposite—delight, joy, happy wonder. At this most critical and interesting juncture, when the soul seems ready to embrace and rest upon the truth of God, the enemy returns, and substitutes a false hope for the true one; he encourages the false joy of a spurious conversion. In the rapture of the moment, all suspicion and all vigilance appear to be precluded, and the soul feeds upon its apples of Sodom till they turn to ashes. Then succeeds misgiving, unbelief, displeasure, shame, despondency, temptation, a new thirst for sinful pleasure, weak resistance to the enemy, an easy conquest, stronger chains, a deeper dungeon, and eternal bondage. He who once had his periodical returns of sensibility, and his convulsive efforts to be free, now lies passive, without moving hand or foot. But out of the deep dungeon where he thus lies motionless, an unearthly voice may be heard proclaiming, with a fiendish satisfaction, that "the last state of that man is worse than the first."

Even this, however, does not seem to be the farthest length to which the soul, forsaken by the evil spirit, may be suffered to proceed. The man, from being gay, may not only become serious, and from being serious, convinced of guilt and danger, and desirous of salvation, and from this state pass into a joyful sense of safety; but he may long remain there, and without suspecting where his error lies, may openly acknowledge his experience and his hopes, and pass the bound which divides professing Christians from the world. Methinks I see one who has thus been forsaken by the evil spirit, not only brought into the church, but made conspicuous in it, set in its high places, drunk with its flatteries; but in the hour of his intoxicating triumph, as he lies unarmed and unprotected, in imaginary safety, the tramp of armed men is heard without, the sacred precincts of the church itself are suddenly invaded, his old master is upon him—has returned to his old home—he smiles to see it swept and garnished for his use. He takes possession with his fellows, never more to be cast out. Even such are not beyond the reach of divine mercy, but it is not ordinarily extended to them, as appears from the images by which the state of such is represented in the text. The oil is spent and the lamp extinct. The axe is laid at the root of the tree. Its fruit is withered, nay, it is without fruit, twice dead, plucked up by the roots. Twice dead!—oh, fearful reflection; dead by nature—then apparently alive—and now dead by relapse and by apostasy. Twice dead and plucked up by the roots. Surely such a catastrophe is terrible enough to be the work of one or even many devils, or whatever we may think as to their literal agency in bringing it about, it is terrible enough to be described by the figure which our Lord here uses, and emphatically summed up in those fearful words "the last state of that man is worse than the first."

There is but one more view that I can take or give you of this painful subject. Looking back to the nonentity from which we all have sprung, and on to the eternity which awaits us all; tracing the downward progress of the lost, from bad to worse, from worse to worst, marking the aggravated guilt of each relapse into iniquity, after a seeming reformation and conversion, and remembering by whom and of whom it was said, "it were better for that man if he had never been born,"—we may take our stand between the gulf of non-existence and the gulf of damnation, and comparing the negative horrors of the one with the positive horrors of the other, may exclaim, as we see the sinner pass, through so short an interval, from nothing, into hell, "the last state of that man is worse than the first!"

If what I have been telling you is true, true to nature, scripture, and experience, there is one application or improvement of the truth, which ought to be self-evident. I mean its application to the young, to the young of every class, and character, and station, but especially to such as are peculiarly environed by temptation, and yet prone to imagine, as a vast proportion of the young do really imagine, that the wisest course, is to secure the pleasures of the passing moment, and reserve repentance for a distant future, thus contriving, by what seems to be a master-stroke of policy, to serve God and Mammon in succession.

Instead of arguing against this resolution as irrational and sinful, let me hold up before you the conclusion to which reason, scripture, and experience, with a fearful unanimity, bear witness that the only spiritual safety, is in present and immediate action; that a purpose or a promise to repent hereafter, is among the most successful arts by which the evil spirit drowns his victims in the deadly sleep of false security; that previous indulgence in a life of sin, so far from making reformation easy, is almost sure to make it utterly impossible. You who are, even at this moment, on the verge of the appalling precipice beneath which millions have been dashed to pieces, stop, if it be but for a moment, and consider. The comparative innocence of childhood, the restraints of a religious education, the very resolutions you are forming for the future, may all be looked upon as indications that the evil spirit to whom you are by nature a hereditary slave, has, for the time, relaxed his hold upon you; his chain, though still unbroken, may be lengthened, but beware how you imagine that, without divine grace, you can ever break it. It may be that the unclean spirit has but left you for a time, and is even now wandering through dry places, seeking rest and finding none—roaming in search of a repose which is impossible, and gaining in malignity and craft at every moment—mustering new strength of purpose, virulence of hatred, and capacity of torment and corruption, to accelerate your fall, embitter your remorse, and deepen your damnation. At every access of temptation from without, and every movement of corruption from within, imagine that you hear the foul fiend knocking for admission; and distrusting the strength of your defenses, fly to Christ for aid. Without it you are lost. Without it your best efforts, in your own strength, are unavailing.

X.

ROMANS 16, 27.—To God only wise, be glory through Jesus Christ forever. Amen.

AMONG the peculiar features of the sacred writings are its numerous benedictions and doxologies. The former are expressions of devout desire that man may be blessed of God; the latter, that God may be honored of man. They are the strongest verbal expressions of that love to God and love to man, which are together the fulfilling of the law. Doxologies are frequent in both Testaments, benedictions chiefly in the New, because so large a part of it is in the epistolary form, affording frequent opportunities for the expression of benevolent wishes. A solemn benediction, however, formed a part of the solemnities of public worship under the old economy. The form prescribed is still on record in the sixth chapter of Numbers (v. 22),—"The Lord spake unto Moses, saying, Speak unto Adam and unto his sons, saying, On this wise ye shall bless the children of Israel saying unto them, The Lord bless thee and keep thee: The Lord make his face shine upon thee and be gracious unto thee: The Lord lift up his countenance upon thee and give thee peace."

The use of the doxology in public worship is apparent from the inspired liturgy of the ancient church, the Book of Psalms. This book has long been divided into five large portions, the close of each being indicated by a doxology. Thus the 41st psalm ends with these words: "Blessed be the Lord God of Israel from everlasting to everlasting. Amen and amen." The 72d psalm: "Blessed be the Lord God, the God of Israel, who only doeth wondrous things; and blessed be his glorious name forever, and let the whole earth be filled with his glory. Amen and amen. The 89th: Blessed be the Lord for evermore. Amen and amen. The 106th: Blessed be the Lord God of Israel from everlasting to everlasting: and let all the people say Amen—Praise ye the Lord! The 150th: Let every thing that hath breath praise the Lord: praise ye the Lord! Whether this fivefold division of the Psalter is of ancient date, and these doxologies were originally intended to mark the conclusion of the several parts; or whether the division was itself suggested to the rabbins, from whom we have received it, by the fortuitous recurrence of these formulas at tolerably regular intervals, may be disputed; but, in either case, the familiar use of the doxology in worship by the ancient saints is evident.

But in the New Testament there is this peculiar circumstance, that the doxologies, though still more numerous than in the Old, occur in such connections, and, as already hinted, in such kinds of composition as to be not merely formulas for common use, but spontaneous ebullitions of devout affection. As such, they show more clearly than any other form of speech could, the habitual bent of the affections, on the part of the inspired writers, the favorite subject of their thoughts, the points to which their minds instinctively reverted, not only as the customary theme of usual meditation, but as the great object of desire and hope. As they never forgot, in care for self, the interest of others, so they never forgot, in care for others, that God was to be honored; that of him, and through him, and to him, are all things; that to him must be glory forever.

Of the twenty-one epistles contained in the New Testament, seventeen begin with a solemn benediction, and sixteen close with one. Two others close with a doxology, instead of a benediction, while one concludes and two begin with a benediction and doxology together; and another substitutes a malediction for the latter. But it is not merely in these solemn openings and closings of the canonical epistles that the doxology occurs. It is sometimes interposed between the links of a concatenated argument, or in the midst of a detailed description. This is especially the case when something has been said which seems to savour of irreverence towards God, in order to express the writer's protestation against any such construction of his language, or to disavow his concurrence in such language used by others, or his approbation of their wicked conduct. Thus, in the first chapter (v. 25) of this epistle, Paul describes the heathen as having "changed the truth of God into a lie, and worshipped and served the creature more than the Creator who is blessed forever, amen." And again, in the eleventh chapter, after indignantly repelling the suggestion that man can add any thing to God, and argumentatively showing its absurdity, he winds up his argument by an adoring exclamation, a triumphant interrogation, and a devout doxology. "Oh, the depth of the riches both of the wisdom and knowledge of God! How unsearchable are his judgments, and his ways past finding out! For who hath known the mind of the Lord, or who hath been his counsellor? Or who hath first given to him, and it shall be recompensed to him again? For of him, and through him, and to him are all things, to whom be glory, forever, amen." It is by these apparently misplaced ascriptions of all honor to God, that is occurring where the ordinary usages of composition lead us to expect them least, it is by these that the habitual bent of the Apostle's thoughts and feelings is most clearly manifested. Such ejaculations, in the midst of ordinary speech, may indeed be the mere effect of sanctimonious habit, and have often been so; but, where inspiration sets the seal of authenticity on all the emotions and desires expressed, there could not be a more unerring symptom of a heart overflowing with devout affections.

There are two things included in a doxology—the expression of a wish and the performance of a duty. The writer gives utterance to his desire that God may be glorified, and at the same time actually glorifies him, and is the occasion of his being glorified by all who read or hear his words, with understanding and with cordial acquiescence in the sentiment expressed; for God himself has said, "Whoso offereth praise glorifieth me." By these interruptions of their doctrinal discussions, therefore, the inspired writers have not only manifested their own dispositions, and actually glorified God themselves, but led to the performance of the same act by innumerable readers and hearers. There is something truly ennobling and exciting in the Christian doctrine that, although God is infinitely blessed in himself, and man incapable of adding to his essential excellence, there is yet a sense in which he may be glorified or rendered glorious even by the humblest of his creatures. To render God thus glorious by manifesting and according his perfections, is the very end of our existence, the pursuit of which sets before us a boundless field of exertion and enjoyment. The prominence given to this motive in the Christian system, is one of the marks by which it is most clearly distinguished from all others, and, at the same time, of the strongest proofs of its divinity.

The constituent parts of a Christian doxology have already been described. As another essential feature may be mentioned that they are always and exclusively addressed to God. The jealousy of the inspired writer, as to this point, is remarkable. Their doxologies not only include the name of God as their great subject, but they always occur in connections where he has already been the subject of discourse. To him the glory is ascribed, to the exclusion of false gods and of men, but especially of self. The spirit of these doxologies is everywhere the same—"Not unto us, oh Lord, not unto us, but to thy name give glory." The very design of the doxologies of Scripture is to turn away the thoughts from man to God, from the creature to " the Creator who is blessed forever, amen." When they occur at the beginning of a passage or a book, they seem to remind the reader that, in order to go right, he must set out from God. When at the close, they teach him to remember the great end of his existence. When they interrupt the tenor of discourse, they answer the salutary purpose of checking the tendency to lose sight of God in the contemplation of other objects. Thus, according to their relative positions, they continually teach us or remind us that "of him, and to him, and through him, are all things, to whom be glory forever, amen." It is not, therefore, a mere incidental circumstance, but an essential feature of the scriptural doxologies, that they have reference to God and God alone.

The only seeming exception to this general statement, really confirms it. There are doxologies to Jesus Christ, but as a divine person. It is because he is God that glory is ascribed to him. In the present instance, there is a singular ambiguity of construction in the original. The literal translation of the words is this: "To the only wise God, through Jesus Christ, to whom be glory forever." In the common version the ambiguity is removed by the omission of the relative. The true construction may be this: "Glory be to the only wise God, through Jesus Christ, to whom be glory likewise forever, amen." As it stands, however, it seems doubtful whether Christ is expressly mentioned merely as a means or also as an end, whether merely as an instrument of glorifying God, or also as an object to be glorified himself. This very dubity of phrase, however, seems to justify us in embracing both ideas in our explication of the terms. It is highly probable, indeed, as already suggested, that both were designed to be expressed; that Christ was meant to be exhibited, at one view, as, in some sense, the medium by which God is or may be glorified; and, as himself, entitled to that glory which belongs to God; and the anomalous construction may have arisen, not from inadvertence or excited feeling, but from a desire to suggest these two ideas simultaneously. The latter, it is true, might be considered doubtful if this were the only case in which he is the subject of a doxology. But this is far from being true. When Jude, in the close of his epistle, says, "To the only wise God, our Saviour, be glory and majesty, dominion and power, both now and ever, amen," it may be plausibly alleged that he is speaking only of God in his character of Saviour or Deliverer, without express allusion to the incarnation, and that the cases, therefore, are not parallel. Even admitting this to be the fact, the same thing cannot be alleged of Paul's wish, that the God of peace would make the Hebrew Christians perfect in every good work to do his will, working in them that which is well pleasing in His sight, through Jesus Christ, to whom be glory forever and ever, amen. Or, if it should be said that, even here, although Christ is the immediate antecedent, the God of Peace is the main subject of the sentence, and to him the doxology must be referred, there is still a case in which no such grammatical refinement will avail to make the reference to Christ uncertain. I mean the doxology which closes the second epistle of Peter, where there is no double subject to confuse the sense, or render the interpretation doubtful. The

Apostle closes with a simple exhortation to "grow in grace and in the knowledge of our Lord and Saviour Jesus Christ. To him be glory both now and forever, amen." This text is not only unambiguous itself, but serves to throw light upon those which are more doubtful. If Christ, in this case, is the evident and only subject of the doxology, there is no longer any reason in explaining the one quoted from Hebrews, for overleaping the immediate antecedent; and, with respect to that in Jude, there is at least some ground for regarding "God our Saviour" as descriptive of the same blessed person. While it remains true, therefore, that the Scriptural doxologies never have reference to any subject less than God, it is equally true that Jesus Christ is a partaker in these exclusive divine honors. We need feel no hesitation, therefore, in adopting such an explanation of the text as will exhibit Christ not only in the character of a revealer and a glorifier, but in that of a glorified being; not only of creature but Creator; not only man but God; God over all, blessed forever.

There is another circumstance to be attended to in the doxologies of Scripture. Being ascriptions of glory to God exclusively of all mere creatures, they might seem to require nothing more than a bare mention of his name, or the most general description of his nature. And in some cases nothing more is given. But in others, the mind of the doxologist appears to have been fastened specially on some one aspect of the divine character, some attribute, or group of attributes, as the foundation of his claim to universal and perpetual praise. Thus, in the case before us, while the text embraces the doxology itself, the two preceding verses contain the preamble, or explanatory preface, setting forth the grounds on which the doxology is made to rest. The first of these is the omnipotence of God, or rather the omnipotence of his grace; for the allusion is not merely to the creative and sustaining power of God, but to his infinite ability to perfect what he had begun in all believers—the new creation of a spiritual nature on the ruins of that righteousness which man had lost. "Now, to him that is of power to stablish you according to my gospel, &c., to God only wise be glory through Jesus Christ forever, amen." A more general, but equally emphatic, declaration of the same kind may be found in the third chapter of Ephesians, where the Apostle, after expressing an importunate desire for the spiritual progress and perfection of the Christians whom he was addressing, adds: "Now unto him that is able to do exceeding abundantly above all that we ask or think, according to the power that worketh in us—unto him be glory in the church by Jesus Christ throughout all ages, world without end, amen."

Another attribute thus singled out to be the ground of a doxology, is wisdom, the intellectual omnipotence of God in working out his purposes by chosen means. In rational beings, this view of the divine perfections is peculiarly adapted to excite astonishment and admiration. The universal presence and activity of mind throughout the vast frame of nature and machinery of Providence, the triumph of that all-pervading mind over matter, over other minds, over apparent difficulties springing from the natural relations of one being to another; the wonderful results evolved from causes and by means apparently least fitted to produce them; the indisputable evidence contained in such facts of one harmonious design and one controlling power, through a series of events which, as they happened, seemed fortuitous and unconnected, independent of each other, and of any higher principle than this—this divine wisdom is indeed an ample and satisfying reason for ascribing glory to the being who possesses it, not only as considered in himself, but as compared with others; not merely as wise, but as only wise, alone entitled to be so considered, since the wisdom of all other beings is not only infinitely less than His, but derived directly from him—the gift of his bounty, the creature of his power, a drop trickling from the ocean, a spark kindled at the sun. The only true wisdom upon earth is "wisdom that cometh from above." The wisdom that sets itself in opposition to the wisdom of God, is earthly, sensual, and devilish—is folly in the lowest and worst sense. The admiration thus expressed in Scripture for God's wisdom, is an admiration which implies contempt of all opposing claims—an admiration which belittles, nay, annihilates all other in comparison. God is not merely wise, but only wise; not merely wiser than all other gods—which would be saying nothing, since we know that an idol is nothing in the world—not only wiser than the brutes, than man, than devils, than angels, but so far exalted above them, each individually, and all collectively, that when confronted with the aggregate intelligence of all ages and all worlds, HE ALONE IS WISE.

This sublime description of Jehovah as "the only wise God," is not peculiar to the text. It occurs not only in other places, but in other doxologies, as an appropriate and ample ground for the ascription of eternal praise. The same apostle, writing to Timothy, after speaking in the most affecting terms of his own character before conversion, and expressing his gratitude that he should have been honoured with permission to preach Christ, adds, in the manner which has been described already, as characteristic of his writings and his spirit—"Now unto the King eternal, immortal, invisible, THE ONLY WISE GOD, be honour and glory forever and ever, Amen." (1 Tim. 1, 17.) And another apostle, in a doxology already quoted, connects an appeal to the power of God in his preamble with a reference to his wisdom in the doxology itself— "Now unto him that is able to keep you from falling, and to present you faultless before the presence of his glory with exceeding joy—to the only wise God our Saviour be glory and majesty, dominion and power, both now and ever, Amen."

We have seen that the doxologies of Scripture, though they sometimes speak of God in general terms merely, often specify some attribute as giving him a peculiar claim to the adoring admiration of his creatures. We have also seen that the attribute of *wisdom* is repeatedly thus singled out and rendered prominent. It may now be added that it is not merely the wisdom of God in general that is thus held up to view. There is a certain manifestation of his wisdom which is placed above all others—not the wisdom displayed in the creation of the universe, or in its sustentation; not the wisdom displayed in the common dispensations of his providence, or even in those extraordinary methods which he sometimes uses to effect his purpose. These are all recognized and represented as becoming subjects of our praise and meditation. But none of them is set forth as the great, peculiar, and decisive evidence that God alone is wise. That evidence is sought in the system of redemption, in the means devised for the deliverance of man from the inevitable consequences of his own transgressions. And this selection is entirely justified, even at the bar of human reason, by several obvious considerations. The first of these is the magnitude of the end to be accomplished. The second is the difficulty of effecting it —a difficulty springing, not from fortuitous or outward circumstances, but from essential principles, from the nature of sin, from the nature of God himself. To the extent of this difficulty, justice never can be done by our conceptions. Its existence may be recognized, its reality admitted, but its magnitude cannot be adequately measured. The hypothesis of infinite holiness and justice, as essential to God's nature, seems to render the pardon of sin, if once committed, and the salvation of the sinner so impossible, that unassisted reason reels and staggers under the attempt to reconcile apparent contradictions. But this reconciliation God has effected; he has solved the problem; he has practically shown us how he can be just and yet justify the ungodly. Reason approves of this solution when presented, but could never have discovered it. No created skill or strength could have surmounted difficulties so appalling.

This, then, is a second reason for regarding the method of salvation as the greatest and most glorious display of divine wisdom. A third is the absolute success of the experiment, if such it may be called. Where the end is so important, and difficulties so great, a partial attainment of the end might be regarded as a great achievement. Failure, in some respect, in some degree, might be forgiven, for the sake of what is really accomplished. But, when all is done that was attempted, and when all that is done is completely done, the means being perfectly adapted to the end, and the magnitude of the difficulties fairly matched, nay, far surpassed, by that of the provision made to meet them, this is indeed a triumph of wisdom—such a triumph as created wisdom never could achieve—such a triumph as could only be achieved by Him who claims and is entitled to the glorious distinction of THE ONLY WISE GOD.

It is not surprising, therefore, that in those doxologies which make the divine wisdom their great subject, this pre-eminent display of it in the system of redemption, in the person and the cross of Jesus Christ, as the great centre of that system, should be brought distinctly into view. It is not surprising that in such connexions, the gospel should be represented as a stupendous revelation of God's wisdom, as disclosing what the wisdom of man could neither have invented nor discovered; that the doctrine of salvation should be called a mystery, a truth beyond the reach of unassisted reason, until made known by a special revelation; a demonstration, therefore, both of human folly and of divine wisdom, a proof of what man cannot do, and what God can do. Thus in writing to Timothy, when Paul breaks out into that grand doxology already quoted, "now unto the King eternal, immortal, invisible, the only wise God, be honour and glory, for ever and ever, Amen," it is immediately preceded, with the exception of a parenthetical allusion to the final cause of the apostle's own conversion, by that memorable summary of the gospel, "this is a faithful saying and worthy of all acceptation, that Jesus Christ came into the world to save sinners." It was this appearance of the Son of God for such a purpose that presents itself to the apostle's mind as the masterstroke of wisdom, and affords a ground for the doxology that follows, TO THE ONLY WISE GOD. And even where the name of Christ does not appear, as in the closing words of Jude's epistle, the same idea is suggested by the epithet connected with the name of God himself. It is not to God our creator, our preserver, or our providential benefactor; it is not to God our sovereign, our lawgiver, or our judge, that supremacy in wisdom is directly ascribed, but TO THE ONLY WISE GOD OUR SAVIOUR, be glory and honour, dominion and power, both now and ever, Amen." The doxology which closes the third chapter of Ephesians, is merely the winding up of one long sentence coextensive with the chapter, in which the apostle repeatedly mentions the preaching of the gospel, and especially its open proclamation to the Gentiles, as the revelation of a mystery, concealed for ages from mankind in general, but made known by the Holy Ghost to Prophets and Apostles, a mystery which from the beginning of the world was hid in God; a mystery, *i. e.* a truth which human wisdom could not have discovered, the disclosure of which, therefore, tends to illustrate and magnify the wisdom of God. Precisely the same reference to Christ and the gospel of Salvation, as the master-piece of wisdom, no less than of mercy, may be found in the preamble to the text before us, where the ascription of glory to God is founded on his wisdom, and his wisdom argued from the manifestation, in the gospel, of a method of salvation, which the human mind could never have discovered, and which is therefore called a mystery, a secret brought to light by no exertion of mere reason, but by direct communication from above, from Him whose wisdom was alone sufficient to devise and to reveal it. "Now to him that is of power to stablish you according to my gospel, and the preaching of Jesus Christ, according to the revelation of the mystery which was kept secret since the world began, but now is made manifest, and by the Scriptures of the prophets according to the commandment of the everlasting God, made known to all nations for the obedience of faith, to God only wise, be glory, through Jesus Christ, for ever, Amen.

From a comparison of all these passages, it is is evident that while the sacred writers no doubt recognized the proofs of divine wisdom, furnished by the works of nature, and the movements of providence, their minds were habitually fastened on the method of salvation taught in Scripture, as the grand decisive proof by which all others are surpassed and superseded. It was *through Christ*, not only as the brightness of God's glory and the image of his person, but as a saviour, a propitiation set forth by God himself, a means devised and provided by him for the accomplishment of what appeared impossible; it was through Christ, considered in this light, that the lustre of God's wisdom shone with dazzling brightness upon Paul and Jude and Peter. Hence there is no absurdity in holding, as some have done, that the words "through Jesus Christ," in the text, are to be construed, not with "glory," but with "the only wise God," by which, in the Greek, they are immediately preceded. As if he had said: "to him, who in the person, work, and sufferings of his Son, has revealed himself to us as the only wise God, to him be glory for ever, Amen." At the same time, the unusual collocation of the words, and the irregular construction of the sentence, seem to authorize, if not to require, that Jesus Christ himself should be included in the description of the object to which glory is ascribed. "To God only wise, made known as such by Jesus Christ, and to Jesus Christ himself as God, be glory forever." Nor is this the only sense which may be put upon the pregnant phrase *through Jesus Christ*. The simplest and most obvious, and indeed the only one expressed by the sentence in the common version is, that Christ is the medium through which the divine wisdom is and must be glorified. Not only does he share, by right of his divinity, in all the divine honours. Not only, by his mediation and atoning passion, does he furnish the most luminous display of divine wisdom. But as head of the Church, and as the father of a spiritual seed, to whom that wisdom is, and ever will be, an object of adoring admiration, and as their ever-living and prevailing intercessor with the Father, he is the means, the instrument, the channel through which everlasting glory shall be given *to the only wise God*, who has established a church, and caused the gospel to be preached for this very purpose, " to the intent that now unto the principalities and powers in heavenly places might be known by the church the manifold wisdom of God; unto Him be glory, in the church, by Jesus Christ, through all ages, world without end, Amen." (Eph. 3, 10. 21.)

To this doxology, as well as to the others which the word of God contains, the pious in all ages have been wont to say *Amen*. This ancient expression of assent to prayer and praise is, from its very nature, full of meaning. He who says Amen to the doxology before us, must be understood as giving the assent of his judgment to the propositions, that there is a God; that he is infinitely wise; that his wisdom has been specially displayed in the provision made for saving sinners, without the sacrifice of justice, through the incarnation and atonement of his Son, that mystery of godliness, the disclosure of which, by the Spirit, through the prophets, in the preaching of the gospel, is the most transcendent demonstration of God's wisdom ever given to his creatures; that the being thus proved to be the only wise God is deserving, in reason and in justice, of eternal praise; that of this honour, though exclusively divine, Jesus Christ is infinitely worthy to partake; and that it is only through him, and by virtue of his mediation, intercession, and spiritual oneness with his people, that their obligation to give glory to God can, in any sort or measure, be discharged. All this may be considered as involved in the doxology, as interpreted by the context and comparison with others. Let no one who refuses to acknowledge and embrace all this as true dare to re-echo the apostle's words; but whosoever does believe and hold these precious doctrines, let him say *Amen*.

This act, however, is expressive of far more than a mere intellectual assent to the righteousness and reasonableness of ascribing everlasting glory to the only wise God. It implies, moreover, an assent of will, nay it expresses a desire that what reason and a sense of right thus recognize as due to God, should be actually given to him. This has already been described as entering essentially into the structure of a scriptural doxology. It is not the dry statement of an abstract truth. It is the language of emotion, of affection, of desire, of an earnest, an engrossing, a supreme desire, that God, to use the prophet's strong expression, may not be robbed by his ungrateful creatures. It is an actual rendering to God the things that are God's, by actually giving him the praise that is his due, not by constraint or grudgingly, not from a mere intellectual conviction, or through stress of conscience, but with hearty acquiescence, with affectionate delight, with joy, with triumph, with a sympathetic sense of personal interest, of individual participation in the glory thus ascribed and given to another, not because the giver counts himself as any thing in the comparison, but for a reason diametrically opposite, because he counts himself as nothing, out of God, out of Christ, and as being something only so far as he is united and attached to Him, so that the more God is glorified, the more the humble worshipper is really exalted, as the drop, which by itself would have been lost, may rise to heaven in the heaving of the ocean. This is the secret of the only exaltation which to man is safe or even possible. God resisteth the proud, and giveth grace to the humble; they humble themselves under the mighty hand of God, that he may exalt them in due time. Not only then to those who disbelieve the truths involved, is this doxology a riddle or a profanation, but to those who embrace the doctrines merely with the understanding, and with no such enlargement of the heart, and going out of the affections as the great apostle evidently felt in writing it. Let all such hold their peace, and let only such as can thus enter into the full meaning of his language say *Amen*.

But there is more than this required to a full participation in the spirit of the passage. Not only is the mere admission of the truth that God is worthy to be glorified forever insufficient, without a sincere willingness, or rather an importunate desire, that he may receive the glory which belongs to him. Even this is not enough. Such a belief and such a wish as have been just described, either presuppose or lead to the reception of the great truth that "the Lord has made all things for himself," that his rational creatures, especially, have been created capable of serving and of glorifying him; and for the very purpose of so doing, that they are consequently bound not only to acknowledge his just claims, and to desire that they may be satisfied, but to spend and be spent, to do and to suffer, to live and to die, to live and move and have their being for this end, not only passively, but actively, remembering it, hoping for it, longing for it, looking towards it, hastening towards it, making every thought, and word, and act, so far as possible, contribute to it. We who have not yet reached the height from which such views are possible, have reason to lament that we are still unprepared to give a full assent to Paul's doxology; but if, through God's grace, any have obtained, not only passing glimpses, but a clear and steady view of the great end of their existence as revealed in Scripture, and have turned their faces thitherward for life, forever, with a fixed and hearty resolution to forget what is behind, and reach forth to that which is before, with all the heart and mind and soul and strength—let all such say Amen.

The word *forever* I have not supplied. It is included in the terms of the doxology; and as it is a word of vast and deep and awful import, it becomes us to consider it before we undertake to say Amen to the apostle. For by so doing, in addition to all that has been said already, we acknowledge that God's glory is not only the great end to which we now look forward, but an end to which we must look forward through eternity; not only an object which ought now to fill, and animate, and rule the soul, with all its powers and affections, but an object which can never cease to do so. If we are still unwilling thus to take God as the portion of our souls, and to seek our happiness forever in his glory, our assent to Paul's doxology is still imperfect, if not insincere; but let him who knows already what it is to have made God his all in all, forever, say Amen and Amen. And as this absolute assent can be produced in us by no strength or wisdom of our own, let our hopes be founded upon nothing in ourselves, but on the encouragement which the apostle's benediction and doxology afford us: "The grace of our Lord Jesus Christ be with you all." "And to him that is of power to stablish you according to my gospel and the preaching of Jesus Christ, to God only wise, be glory through Jesus Christ forever, Amen."

XI.

LUKE 14, 17.—" Come, for all things are now ready."

WE have here, as in many other passages of Scripture, a most precious invitation, and a reason for accepting it. An invitation—" come ;" a reason— " all things are now ready." The first of these requires no explanation. In the spiritual sense or application of the parable from which the text is taken, " come" means, of course, come to the gospel feast, to the provision of God's bounty, to the fountain, to the cross, to Christ himself. It is equivalent to saying, Be ye saved, and includes the exhortation to repent, believe, submit to the righteousness of God, and accept of the salvation that he offers. It is therefore the same call that is continually ringing in the ears of those who hear the gospel, and which needs not so much to be explained as to be enforced. For this very purpose, it is added, because all things are now ready. To this reason for yielding to the call of mercy I invite your attention. " Come, for all things are now ready." In the parable, it obviously means that the precise time of enjoyment was now come, that the provision was complete and the arrangements perfect. A little earlier might have been too early. A little later was too late forever. Such a time there is and must be in all human invitations. Such a time there is in every invitation of the gospel. But between the cases there is this momentous difference: In the one it may be equally amiss to come too early or too late. In the other we need only fear to come too late. It is impossible to come too early; because the provision is already and completely made for those who will receive it, and needs not to be constantly renewed, as in the other case. Oh, if our eyes could be unsealed, or these surrounding mists dispelled so as no longer to obstruct our view of the divine compassions, we might behold the banquet hall of mercy rise before us "like an exhalation," with its flashing lights, its music, and its odours,— making the outer darkness more profound by contrast, and the cold and hunger of the gazing crowd more keen and pinching! Before such displays of human splendour and festivity, the poor and wretched often stand in envious admiration. For to them that threshold is impassable. And even those who are allowed to feed there because full already, must await the appointed moment. But how different this feast of mercy. Those who do not enter will not hear the call or cannot see the bounties spread before them. If, when their eyes and ears are opened, they still linger, it is only for a moment, in the first feeling of incredulous surprise that this provision can be meant for them, and that they need no preparation or delay, but may partake of it at once. While they stand amazed at the sights and sounds so suddenly presented to their senses, as at something quite beyond their reach, their hopes, and almost their desires, the doors fly open, a fresh flood of light, new waves of melody, new gales of odour, stream forth upon them, and loud yet gentle voices cry to them—not merely to others—but to them: Come and see; eat and drink, oh beloved; come, for all things are now ready. And from age to age the call is still the same. As one generation sweeps another off the stage,—some heeding, some despising, some not even hearing the benignant invitation,—it is still repeated: all things are now ready. Yes, at whatever moment the poor sin-sick, starved, exhausted sinner first begins to feel his want and turns his dim and haggard eyes towards that scene of splendour and festivity before unknown or madly disregarded—however untimely the appeal may seem—though the prayer be breathed at midnight, in the dark—from the beggar's hovel, the field of battle, or the dungeon, or the scaffold,—the response is still the same: come, for all things are now ready.

The resort to this supply can never be too early; it should never be too late. It can never be too early; for the soul is never without consciousness of want—a restless craving for enjoyments better than the best it has experienced. It should never be too late—as it is, alas! too late for thousands—because all things are now ready; and when all things are now ready, and the opportunity afforded of securing them but transient, it is self-destruction to refuse acceptance;—it is folly, it is madness, even to postpone it. Let us then consider the readiness of all things as a reason for coming to Christ now. And as the simplest way of doing this, let us consider what it is that hinders us from coming. I speak not to those who are still utterly insensible—unconscious of their danger, or unwilling to confess it—for with such it is impossible to reason, and they must be left to the fearful consolation of that solemn irony: they that are whole need not a physician. But to you who own yourself a sinner, and in need of mercy, and expect to find it one day in the Saviour, to you I put the question—and would pray you to put it yourselves:—what prevents your coming now? what invisible hand drags you back when you are almost on the threshold?—holds your eyes fast shut when you begin to see light; stifles your very cries for mercy; and chokes down the throbbings of your bursting heart;—what is it? No external force; you act freely in refusing to come. What inward cause, then,—why do you not come? what keeps you still away? Alas! I need not ask; for in the way of every sinner who knows what it is to think, there always rises up one barrier which effectually stops his course till God removes it; it is guilt—the paralyzing and benumbing sense of guilt. The very same thing that creates the necessity of coming, seems to render it impossible. God is a holy God, a just God, and a Sovereign. His law is broken; we ourselves have broken it: He cannot but condemn us,—nay, we are condemned already. The conviction of this truth is like an iron yoke upon our necks, and chains around our limbs; we feel the pressure, and we would be delivered,—but we cannot move. We cannot willingly appear before the presence of our enemy—our judge—our executioner. As long as this relation still subsists, or seems to do so, we will not, cannot, dare not come, whatever may be ready. Oh, my hearers, is there none among you before whom this conviction has shot up into a massive wall which you can neither scale, nor penetrate, nor go round,—and at the foot of which you are now lying, neither able to go further, nor yet willing to go back? Would to God this might be the experience of some who have not yet been brought so far, for they might then expect deliverance. All that you need is ready—even now ready. If you cannot look up, you can listen. What is that sound which comes forth from the darkness or the light inaccessible where God resides? Is it the muttering of distant thunder, or the premonition of a coming storm? It is indeed a voice like the voice of thunderings,—sweet yet solemn to the ear—but it speaks of mercy, not of wrath; it is a voice like the voice of many waters, saying: Come and see! Look up! Above, beyond these barriers, see the throne and Him who sits upon it; the cloud in which He wraps himself is not charged with tempest,—it is radiant with light; his diadem is not vindictive lightning, but the peaceful rainbow. He desireth not the death of the sinner, but that all should turn and live. He permits, he commands, he entreats you to be saved,—the strongest possible expression of his willingness. Oh, my hearers, if you are deterred by a sense of alienation and estrangement from your God, or by a doubt of his benignity, his willingness to pardon and be reconciled,—if this is what deters you, come, oh come without delay, for all things are now ready.

But, perhaps your way is not yet open; your obstacles are not yet all removed. Whatever you may think of the benevolence of God, you cannot lose sight of his justice. However his compassion might consent, his holiness, his truth, his righteousness, still stop the way. He cannot lie. His threatenings must be executed. He cannot deny himself. The soul that sinneth, it shall die. The law is broken, and its awful penalty must be discharged. Whatever else is ready matters not while this vast debt remains unpaid. All these are certain and appalling truths. There is no danger of exaggerating their reality or fearful import. You can never gain relief from this discouragement by learning to extenuate the claims of the divine law, or the turpitude of sin, or the necessity of punishment, or the tremendous nature of the penalty annexed to all transgression, or your utter incapacity to evade it or to heal the vast breach of the violated law. You may tamper as you will with your understanding and your conscience, but the only fruit of such attempts, when most successful, is delusion or despair. The dream of self-deception must be followed soon or late by a fearful waking; and however often or however long you may forget yourself in sleep, the awful truth will still rush back upon your waking thoughts, only rendered more intolerable by the brief oblivion which preceded. If the pressure of pecuniary debt can rob men of their sleep, embitter their enjoyments, mar their peace, make life a burden, drive them mad, and even arm them with the weapon of self-murder, so that cowards against others become brave against themselves, and they who shrink from the sufferings of this life rashly venture on the next—if these are but familiar consequences of the agony produced by consciousness of mere pecuniary debt beyond the man's ability to pay, oh, what would be the issue, if the vast account-books between us and God should be completely opened and made fully legible? by what arithmetic could we compute, or in what terms express the terrible result? It is impossible; and partly for the reason that it is impossible, we shut our eyes, and stop our ears, and turn away our thoughts from this confounding theme; and even when we do attempt to scan it, and to plead the greatness of our debt as an excuse for not accepting Christ, it is not because we have, but because we have not, any adequate conception of that debt, which, if we saw it as it is, instead of filling our mouth with arguments against God, would strike us dumb, and strike us blind, and strike us dead before him. In this direction you are right in seeing no escape; there is none; you are right in denying that this debt must be discharged—it must; and that you cannot pay it, for you never, never can. If you are only partially and superficially convinced of this, you will remain where I now leave you, and continue to excuse yourself by pleading that your sins are inexcusable. But if you are really and thoroughly persuaded that you must and cannot pay this awful debt, the very darkness of your self-despair may give you light or serve to make it visible; at first a dim spark,—then a faint gleam,—then a glow—a flame—a blaze—and in the focus of that blaze you may behold,—as the ancient persecutor saw amidst the white heat of his own devouring furnace, a form like that of the Son of God, standing erect beside the way which leads you to the throne of mercy. You must pass by him, or you cannot reach the footstool. Who is he that thus awaits you? his eye moist with pity, but his features pallid, as one risen from the dead. And in his outstretched hand the eye of faith can discern something shining; something precious; something priceless; not the glare of gold or silver, or the sparkle of invaluable gems, but something wet with tears and stained with blood; the blood still oozing from that stricken heart. It is the purchase of your life; it is the ransom of your soul; it is the price which you could never pay; which men and angels could not have paid for you; in default of which you had resigned yourself to perish. See, he holds it out; he presses it upon you; and the turning point is—can you reject it? If you can, oh let your lips be sealed forever from all mention of the penalty of God's law, as deterring you from mercy; for, as you plunge into the gulf of self-destruction, the last sound from above that reaches you, may be the dripping of that blood, one touch of which would have sufficed to cancel your vast debt forever. Oh, if this alone is wanting to embolden your approach to God, I say again, my hearer, "come, for all things are now ready."

But now, perhaps, you feel another hinderance; one of which you took but little note before. Though God be ready to forgive you for the sake of Christ's atoning sacrifice, you find a hinderance in yourself, in your heart, in your very dispositions and affections. Besides being guilty, righteously condemned, justly exposed to punishment, unable to atone for your transgressions; you are polluted, your very nature is corrupt, averse from good, disposed to evil. How can you come into the presence of a holy God? How can you fail to be an object of abhorrence to him? How can you love what you detest, or find your happiness in that which is directly contradictory to all your nature? Here again the fact alleged is true and awful beyond your worst conceptions. There are depths,—there are abysses of defilement, which you need not undertake to fathom; into which you cannot even look without bewilderment and sickness of spirit. If God should lift the veil which hides them, and permit the light to shine directly on them, you would be unable to endure it. Oh, look away from that heart-rending spectacle. Here is another object to contemplate. Over against that blood-stained form which proffers ransom, what is this? A gushing spring, a flowing stream, a flood, a sea, of purifying virtue. Plunge into it, and you are cleansed already. You come up out of its waters changed, and yet the same. Coercion is no longer needed; for your very dispositions and desires are revolutionized. Old things are passed away; all things are become new; new without and new within; new heavens and a new earth; a clean heart and a right spirit; this is indeed a new creation, a new creature, a new birth, born again, born from above, born of God; the washing of regeneration, the renewing of the Holy Ghost. Be not deterred then by the sense of what you are, any more than by the sense of what you cannot do, or what you have already done.

The provision of God's mercy includes this as well as every other want. A new heart is as much his gift as expiation and forgiveness. Come, then, and receive what he vouchsafes to offer. Come without reserve, without delay, for all things are now ready.

But I hear you say you cannot come alone, you cannot struggle by yourself, you cannot brave alone the thunderings and lightnings of Mount Sinai, you cannot stand with Moses on the smoking and the quaking summit, you must mingle with the multitude below. You are not even willing to be saved alone. Having followed a multitude so long to do evil, you still feel the need of communion and example, of mutual incitement and restraint. And you shall have it. You shall have it in perfection if you will but come. For ye are come unto Mount Zion, and unto the city of the living God, to the general assembly and church of the first-born, which are written in heaven. The Church of Christ stands open to receive you, to protect you, and to nourish you. Her institutions, her examples, her worship, her ordinances, her communion, all, all are ready for you. This is a want for which the grace that rescues you has specially provided. You are not asked to be saved alone, though that were surely better than to perish. You may bring as many with you as you will, and you will find many entered in before you. When we bid you *come*, you are invited to a feast, of which many, thanks be to God, are after all partakers, and though many that are bidden make excuse or even venture to make light of it, the giver of the banquet shall be still supplied with guests; for while the broad way that leadeth to destruction remains crowded with infatuated victims, another concourse is seen streaming from the bye-ways and the hedges to the table of the Lord, where they shall sit down, clothed and in their right minds, washed and beautified, ennobled and refined, while many who appeared to be hereditary children of the kingdom, are excluded or exclude themselves from all participation in the banquet. Of the company thus gathered and transformed you are to form a part. The doors stand open, open to receive you, and yet there is room. If all obstructions have now vanished from without and from within, if atonement, and forgiveness, and renewal are accessible, and if the Church is ready to receive you into its communion of saints, what remaining pretext for delay can be imagined? Come, for all things are now ready.

Do you still object that these are only temporary institutions? that they do not reach as far as your necessities and fears? Do you ask, When these fail, whither shall I go, and who shall then receive me unto everlasting habitations? I still reply, but in a higher sense, that ye are come unto Mount Zion, to the heavenly Jerusalem, to an innumerable company of angels, and to the spirits of the just made perfect. Heaven is ready to receive you, and in that assurance all is comprehended. Whatever local and material associations you may have with heaven, they are but the veil, the hull, the casket. We use heaven to denote a state, in which place other circumstances may be comprehended, but oh how much more! All goodness and all blessedness. All wrong and suffering shut out forever. Let memory and imagination do their worst in multiplying images of evil, and in calling up before the mind the forms and the occasion of distress; then add that all these will be wanting. Give indulgence to your boldest flights and wildest dreams of happiness, apart from sin, then add that all, and infinitely more than all you can imagine, will be yours and yours forever, without the fear or possibility of change, or loss, or diminution. Every pure wish gratified, all lofty aspirations more than realized, and what is past or present still as nothing in comparison with what is yet to come. All attempts to heighten such an object, only lower it, and leave our apprehensions of it less defined and satisfactory than at first. But if this ineffable condition, this negation of all evil, this perpetual fruition of the highest good awaits you, stands prepared for you; then surely it may well be said to you, Come, oh come, for all things are now ready. Expiation, pardon, renovation, the grace of the Father, the merit of the Son, the influence of the Spirit, the Church on earth, and the Church in heaven, safety in life, peace in death, and glory through eternity; a good hope here, and an ineffable reality hereafter; all things, all things, are now ready.

Will you come? If not, you must turn back, you must retrace your steps, and take another view of this momentous invitation. Higher we cannot rise in the conception or the presentation of inducements. If you must have others, they must be sought in a lower region. Let us then descend from this exalted point of observation whence you have surveyed the glorious things now ready to receive you, and surveyed them, it may be, without emotion or effect; let us descend, and from a different position, take a momentary view of certain other preparations no less real in themselves, and no less everlasting in their issues. I have already mentioned one important difference between the ideal feast and others, namely, that at these we may arrive too early, while at that, the only fear is, we may be too late. Another striking difference is this, that the refusal of an earthly feast involves at most the loss of some enjoyment, or at most the alienation of the giver. But in those parables of Christ, where this is the predominant image, the refusal of the feast is represented as a crime, and they who would not partake of the supper are cast into outer darkness, where is weeping, and wailing, and gnashing of teeth. The reason is obvious. The feast is a figure for salvation or deliverance from ruin. To refuse it, therefore, is to choose destruction. This must be taken into view, if we would estimate the motives here presented. All things are ready, and in all is included more perhaps than you imagine. There are other things ready besides pardon, expiation, renovation, the communion of saints, and the joys of heaven. I shall mention only two.

Such is the brevity of life, and such the transitory nature of the offer of salvation, that even the youngest who decides this question, may be said to decide it in the prospect of death, and on the confines of eternity. However numerous and long the years that stretch before you may appear when viewed in comparison with this world's trifling interests, they vanish into nothing when confronted with eternity. I say then to you, who even now are balancing the reasons for consenting and refusing to obey the exhortation of the text, that you are really so balancing with death immediately before you, that among the things now ready and awaiting your decision, this is one. Of some this is doubtless true, even according to your customary method of computing time. An eye endowed with supernatural perception, might detect among those youthful forms and beautiful countenances, some for whom the grave, almost without a figure, may be said to be already open. But of all, of all without exception, for the reason before given, the same thing may be affirmed, because the space which intervenes between the fatal resolution, to reject this gracious invitation either finally, or till a more convenient season, and the actual close of your probation, will hereafter seem, and ought now to seem, so short and evanescent, and contemptible, that he who now rejects Christ may be fairly represented as rejecting him with one foot in the grave, or with the body half submerged in the cold waters of the river of death. Whoever you may be, then, whether young or old, in sickness or in health, I tell you plainly, that among the things "now ready," and awaiting your decision, is the grave, the grave; the cold, damp earth, is ready to receive you. If you impatiently repel this suggestion, as untimely or irrelevant, this only shows how unprepared you are to meet the fearful spectre that it raises. Even true believers may be all their lifetime subject to bondage, through fear of death, even in this restricted sense; how much more natural and rational is such a fear in you who are unwilling to obey the invitations of the gospel. Death is the king of terrors, and however we may hate his presence, it is better to encounter it, when such encounter may be possibly of use to us, than when all hope of victory or rescue is extinguished.

Look then, my hearer, with as steady and as bold an eye as your philosophy can furnish, look into those shadowy recesses which even poetry describes to you as overhung by the funeral cypress, tenanted only by the dead, and vocal only with the dirge, the voice of weeping, and the solemn noises which accompany the rites of burial. Look at that silent shadow or the earth which it enshrouds, as your appointed place, your long home, and at that narrow chasm as the very bed in which your limbs are to repose perhaps for ages. Claim it as your own, assert your right to it, and give it place among the things now ready for you and awaiting your decision. Do you say that all this is as true of one as of another, and that die you must, whether you accept or refuse the invitation of the text? This is indeed theoretically true, but it is practically false. Go tell the prisoner, as he enters his dark dungeon for the last night of repose before he mounts the scaffold, that his cell is no whit darker, or his couch harder, or his chains heavier than those of his next neighbour, whose captivity expires on the morrow. Go read the countenances of the two men as they enter the same comfortless abode of crime, each knowing that the morrow is to break his chains. To both, the filth, and darkness, and confinement may be now as nothing, but how different the reason. To the one the filth seems splendour, and the darkness light, and the confinement freedom, in the rapturous anticipation of deliverance, and as he falls asleep, he hugs the very chains that bind him, in the certainty that he shall never lie down chained again; while to the other, all these same things are absorbed and annihilated in the prospect of a doom compared with which captivity itself seems perfect freedom. Go persuade yourself that when those two men enter their dark dungeons and lie down to sleep, they are alike in their condition; then come back, and we will hear you say death comes alike to all, and deny that the grave's being ready to receive you is a reason which should govern your decision. Death comes alike to all; but know, O vain man, the sting of death is sin, and the strength of sin is the law. It *is* appointed unto *all men* once to die, and after that the judgment; but oh how different the case of those who can abide that judgment, and of those who cannot; of those who die but once, and of those who die self-doomed and self-predestined to the second death. It is appointed unto all men *once* to die, but some die twice, some die again, some die forever, and if this is your doom, you may well shrink back and shudder at the grave before you, as the vestibule, the entrance to another. For, after all, it is not the terrestrial sepulchre considered in itself that I would set before you, any further than as shutting the door forever on all choice. I look not merely into it, but through and beyond it, into that mysterious world which seems to yawn beneath it. There with the eye of fancy or of faith, you may see a deeper, darker, ghastlier grave, ready for your soul, and for your soul and body when again united. You may turn from this as a diseased imagination, but imagination as it is, the day is coming when to some it will seem poor and weak indeed contrasted with the dread reality. The grave is ready both for body and for soul. I do not ask you to look into it, or listen to the wailings that come up from it, or breathe its sulphurous vapours. I only ask you to believe, and to remember that the grave and the abyss are as truly ready if you will not come, as pardon, and redemption, and sanctification, and the church, and heaven, are ready if you will come. On both sides, therefore, all things are ready. The world of bliss and the world of woe spread out their motives in your sight. If you will die, death is easy, for the grave is ready both for soul and body; it is hollowed for you both in time and in eternity. The earth, to which you must return, is open, and the narrow house already yawning to receive you, while beneath—far off in yonder shadowy world—a funeral pile begins to send up its thick smoke, and to project its lurid flames into the air. On that pile there is room enough for you, beneath it, fire enough for your destruction. Tophet is ordained of old, he hath made it deep and large, the pile thereof is fire and much wood; the breath of the Lord, like a stream of brimstone, doth kindle it. These are strong figures, but if such be the figures, what must be the reality? Whatever it be, know that it is ready for you if you will not come, and if you choose death rather than life. Are you willing to live? Life is no less attainable. Your guilt, your weakness, your corruption, the justice, truth, and holiness of God, are all against you where you stand. But come, and all things that you need are ready for you. Come, oh come, and expiation, pardon, renovation, the church on earth, and the church in heaven; all things are *ready*, all things are *yours*, whether Paul, or Apollos, or Cephas, or the world, or life, or death, or things present, or things to come, all are yours, and ye are Christ's, and Christ is God's.

XII.

PROVERBS 22, 2.—The rich and poor meet together; the Lord is the maker of them all.

THIS is a proverb, and must be explained according to the principles and usages of proverbial language. An essential characteristic of this language is its condensation, and the pregnancy of its expressions, which often imply more than the same word would in continuous composition, where there is not the same effort to concentrate much thought in a few words. This peculiarity is common, however, to the popular or practical proverb and the scientific aphorism. The difference between them is, that while the latter affects abstract and generic terms, the former shuns them, and delights to clothe its lessons of wisdom in the dialect of common life, from which its substance is in fact derived—the genuine proverb being a summary expression of the result of long experience. The same extent and fulness of meaning, which is given to the philosophical maxim by the use of comprehensive terms, is no less certainly secured in the case of the popular maxim by a means directly opposite, viz., the exhibition of particular examples to represent whole classes. The specific terms employed in this way are sometimes figurative, and even symbolical; but in a multitude of cases, they are to be literally understood, with due regard, however, to their representative design as specimens or samples.

Of this kind of expression, we have two instances in the case before us, both clauses of the verse being highly specific in their strict immediate import, yet both generic in the whole sense which they were intended to convey. "Rich" and "poor" are terms properly descriptive of a single and familiar difference of external condition. Yet here, as in common parlance, there can be no doubt that they are put for social inequalities in general. And this interpretation is the more admissible, because the distinction which the words immediately denote is not only one of the most universal and most palpable, but also one which, to a great extent, determines all the rest. Knowledge and ignorance, grossness and refinement, power and weakness, are, as a general fact, dependent upon wealth or poverty; *i. e.* upon the want or the possession of the comforts and necessities of life without the necessity of constant and engrossing labour to obtain them.

It is true that the advantage of refinement and of knowledge may be often found upon the side of poverty. It is also true, not only in the case of individual exceptions but as a general fact, that they who become suddenly possessed of wealth, or who acquire it slowly by their own exertions, may be signally destitute of that elevation and improvement which is often found accompanying scanty means and humble station. But these are only apparent exceptions to a general rule, which they really illustrate and confirm. In all such cases, wealth and poverty have not had time to operate the change which they naturally tend to produce, and what appears to be concomitant of either, is in fact the fruit of an opposite condition which vicissitude has not yet succeeded in destroying. The vulgarity and ignorance of some who have recently become rich, are not the effects of their new condition, but the exuviæ of their old one; and the opposite qualities of some who are struggling for subsistence, bear witness to the previous possession of advantages now lost. And even in the case of those who have obtained an education and experienced its refining influence, without any such vicissitude of fortune, it is plain that this could only be made possible by something, whether it be personal exertion or the aid of others, which exempted them so far and so long from the usual disadvantages of poverty, as to put them in possession of advantages naturally belonging to an opposite condition. There is nothing arbitrary or capricious, therefore, in the usage both of common parlance and proverbial diction, which puts "rich" and "poor," or "poverty and wealth," for all the inequalities of social condition.

Another example of the same thing is presented in the other clause, which, in its strictest sense, appears to relate only to the fact of creation, or the character of God as the creator of all men without exception. But the analogy of the first clause, and the general usage of proverbial language, fully justify us in supposing that this one relation between God and man is put for all the rest, the rather as in this case the related things are really inseparable, and not merely similar, as in the other. The various distinctions among men, as we have seen, are not necessarily or invariably coincident. Riches and knowledge, poverty and rudeness, do not always go together. But the being who created us must of necessity be also our preserver, our sovereign, our legislator, our judge, and, if we are redeemed, our Saviour. The possession of creative power implies the rest. To say that "the Lord is the maker of them all," is therefore equivalent to saying that "they have one God," or sustain a common relation to him, with all the fulness and variety of meaning, which the clearness of the gospel revelation now enables us to put upon these otherwise indefinite expressions.

The affirmation of the first clause, that the classes there described "meet together," may be best explained by reference to another characteristic feature of proverbial language; namely, its antithetic form. Besides the parallel construction so familiar to the Hebrew writers generally, there is a pointed opposition, both of thoughts and words, particularly frequent in the Book of Proverbs. Of this usage we have also more than one example in the case before us. Besides the obvious antithesis between the "rich" and "poor," there are two others not less real, because residing rather in the thought than the expression. In the first place, there is an implied comparison or contrast between human and Divine, or temporal and eternal relations; between those which men sustain to one another, and those which they sustain to God.

In the first point of view, they are described as rich and poor, but in the second, as the creatures of one maker. Under one of these aspects, there is variety, under the other sameness. As members of human society, men are unequal; as creatures of God, they are alike. This, though really a mere variation of the one already stated, may with critical precision be regarded as a third antithesis; viz., that between the inequality of men in one respect, and their equality in another.

This view of the structure of the sentence, will assist us in determining the sense of the expression, that "the rich and poor *meet together*," by showing that it does not mean, as some suppose, that both are mingled in society, that they oppose or encounter one another, or as others understand it, they ought to have more intercourse, for neither of these perfects the antithesis; but rather that they are alike, that with all their differences there is still something common to both, that with all their alienation and remoteness as to some points, there is one, after all, in which they "meet together."

But what is this common ground, this point of contact and agreement? Not the bare fact of a common origin, for in this way all things may be equalized, and therefore the assertion of equality would be unmeaning. Not the fact that God has made men to be absolutely equal, for in this sense the assertion, although not unmeaning, would be false, and proved so both by reason and experience. We know that men are made extremely unlike in their capacities and susceptibilities, we know still more certainly that their condition is diversified by providence, beyond all variations for which they are held responsible; and we have reason to believe that there will be as great a difference in heaven and in hell as upon earth, not, indeed, with respect to essential moral qualities, but as to the degree in which the same essential qualities will be possessed, and the amount of suffering and enjoyment by which they will be punished or rewarded. The point of contact and assimilation, then, is not an absolute identity of character or sameness of condition, but participation in a certain good common to both, and independent of external qualities. And as these latter are commonly regarded, at least by one part of mankind, as evils, and are recognized as such by the word of God itself, the substance of the whole when stripped of its proverbial form, may be thus stated: that the true corrective of all social inequalities, so far as they are evil, must be furnished, not by human institutions and arrangements, but derived from a higher and an independent source. In other words, the only practicable efficacious remedy for social evils of the kind in question, is and must be, a religious one, *i. e.*, one founded not in mere prudential changes of man's mutual relations, but in their common relation to their common God, whether considered as their master and preserver, as their sovereign and their judge, or as their Saviour and Redeemer.

In further prosecution of the subject, it may not be unprofitable to consider how and why the religion of the Bible is adapted to exert this influence; and that inquiry, in its turn, will be facilitated by a brief enumeration of some other means, to which men have confidently looked, and are still looking, for the practical solution of the same great problem. These may, with reference to our present purpose, be reduced to three. The first is the idea of obliterating social inequalities by a coercive distribution of all property. This method is condemned by its violent injustice, by its doing evil that good may come. It is condemned by the unworthiness and meanness of its aims, by its assuming as the most essential element of human happiness, the very thing which may most easily be dispensed with, if the other conditions of well-being are fulfilled.

It is further condemned by the hypocrisy of its professions, as betrayed in every case where there has been an opportunity of trial, by the tendency then manifested, not to extirpate social inequalities, but simply to reverse them; not to substitute universal competence and comfort for the actual extremes of poverty and wealth, but by revolutionary and revengeful process, to make the poor rich by making the rich poor. And even if it were exempt from all these fatal errors and defects, it would still be condemned, as a practical expedient for removing evils actually felt, by the proved impossibility of carrying it into execution without sacrificing the very ends which it engages to accomplish. No municipal contrivances or constitutional provisions can repeal or thwart the providential law, by which variety of outward condition no less than of character, is recognized not only as an incidental evil, but as a necessary means to the attainment of the divine purpose, as with respect to man's condition in the present life, or at least in the present state of things.

The remarkable provisions of the law of Moses, for the relief and sustentation of the poor, are accompanied by the no less remarkable declaration that the poor shall not cease out of the land. If this providential arrangement was intended for the moral discipline of God's ancient people, it is hard to perceive why it should be discontinued now, when every reason for it still exists in full force in the human heart, and in the structure of society; and when we see, around us, most conclusive evidence that neither Christianity, nor civilization, nor political contrivance has succeeded in abolishing the old distinction upon which the Mosaic institutions rest. In what sense the community of goods prevailing in the apostolic church is to be understood, and how far in the sense which is often put upon it, it affords a type of the future condition of society in this world, when the power of injustice and of selfishness shall yield to that of equity and kindness, as the governing motives in the mass of men, may be still regarded as unsettled questions. But judging the future by the past, and by the probable design for which the world still stands, we have certainly strong reason to regard it as a prophecy still valid, that the poor shall not cease out of the land.

Another remedy, less violent, irrational, and chimerical, but still inadequate, is that which aims at the removal of the evil, by securing an equality of civil rights, in spite of personal and social disadvantages. So far as this means has the negative effect of hindering oppression, and delivering the weak from the encroachments of the strong, it is a priceless blessing and a noble contribution to the sum of human happiness. But when it is considered as a positive means of rendering men actually equal, and correcting the effects of providential inequalities, it is as worthless as the other. The poor man's right to vote, or in any other way to control the power under which he lives, on equal terms with his rich neighbour, may be preventive of a thousand other evils, but it no more suffices of itself to put him on a level with his neighbour, as to knowledge, or refinement, or intelligence, or character, than an agrarian division of all property. It may be said indeed, and said with truth, that this political equality permits the poor man to aspire to the possession of advantages from which he would be utterly shut out if living under an arbitrary or despotic system.

But here again the advantage is not positive but negative, consisting in the removal of obstructions and impediments, but not of itself, and necessarily, affording either strength or stimulus, to positive improvement. The difference is like that between a starving prisoner and one who starves at liberty for want of work, or want of strength, or want of inclination to employ it. In the absence of these personal disqualifications, freedom from all restraint is certainly a vast advantage, but of what use is it when these other difficulties all exist? of no more than the negative security afforded by political equality, when those enjoying it are endlessly distinguished from each other in capacity, improvement, character, and disposition. They are safe from the oppression of their neighbours, but it may be only to oppress themselves.

Far superior to either of these schemes is that which seeks to remedy the evil by means of intellectual increase of knowledge and refinement of taste. Unlike the first, its aim is nobler, good in itself and wholesome in its influence, and this end it seeks to reach without injustice, without violence. Unlike the second, its effect, when realized, is not merely negative, but positive. It not only makes improvement possible, but actually produces it. The objection to this intellectual remedy, when applied alone, is that its influence, though positive and real, is not necessarily or wholly good. It strengthens, but the strength which it imparts may be used for evil as well as good. It gives a capacity for higher enjoyments than those of sense, but it may create the desire without affording any thing to feed it; it may render lower objects distasteful, without really exchanging them for higher. Mere cultivation of the understanding, taste, and sensibilities, may be carried so far as entirely to disqualify the subject for his actual condition without opening before him any other. If the existence of the mass of men were limited to this life, such refinement would be still more undesirable, because it would unfit them for the only world in which they are to live. It would be like the laborious and expensive education of a man for professional or literary labour, who is doomed for life to the drudgery of mechanical employment. The same expense and intellectual exertion would be nothing if it were preparatory to a corresponding period and field of labour, but extreme intellectual refinement is not only useless as a preparation for hard labour, but positively hurtful, by directly tending to unfit the person for the sphere in which he is compelled to move. Now instruction, such as social reformers commonly rely upon to revolutionize society, restricts its views and those of its disciples to the present life, while at the same time it directly tends to make its actual duties and enjoyments more or less distasteful. So far then as it operates at all on social inequalities, it aggravates instead of healing them, by tending to make all, as far as possible, alike in taste and capacity, but leaving them as unlike as ever with respect to their actual condition and enjoyment. If some men after all must be rich, and others poor, some laborious and some idle, is it not better upon mere utilitarian and worldly principles, that their habits and their tastes should correspond to these diversities, than that all should desire and relish the same objects, while the objects are attainable by only some?

Even this imperfect view of the principal attempts which have been made to remedy the real or imaginary evils of external inequality, may aid us in our subsequent inquiry, how religion, or the Christian system, undertakes to accomplish the same end, or what advantages experience has shown it to possess over every supplementary or rival system. This, as being the immediate subject of consideration, must of course be exhibited in more detail than either of the methods which have been described already.

The first particular to which I would invite your

attention, is the fact that Christianity distinctly recognizes the existence and necessity of some providential inequalities in the external situation of mankind. It is characteristic of the Bible that it does not address itself to an ideal class of readers, but has reference throughout to the world as it is, and to the actual condition of mankind. This is the more remarkable because its standard of moral perfection is so high, and its demands upon the race so large. It neither keeps out of view the corruption of our nature on the one hand, nor consigns us to it without hope upon the other. It neither exalts earth to heaven, nor debases heaven to earth. It places us in sight of the one, but in the midst of the other. In short, the Bible is as far as possible from that cheap and expeditious mode of remedying social evils which begins by denying their existence. The picture which it gives of human character and condition, is one drawn from the life with terrible exactness, and may be recognized in any country and in any age. The evils which it represents as calling for a remedy, are not ideal, but precisely those which all men feel and know in their experience to be real. This creates a strong presumption that the remedies themselves will be adapted to their end, and that a book which so faithfully describes a thing to be done, may be safely relied on when it tells us how to do it. Let it also be observed, that the Bible differs from human systems of reform, by recognizing not only the existence of these inequalities, but their injurious effects, so far as they are real; yet far from representing them as irremediable, it provides, as we shall see, the only practicable and effective remedy, consisting not in any one specific nostrum, but in a series and combination of corrective influences, each of which gives power and effect to all the rest, and none of which can therefore either be dispensed with or relied upon exclusively.

The first of these remedial effects, is the direct mitigation of the evils in question by the change wrought in the tempers and affections of the parties, so far as they are brought under the influence of gospel truth. In this way the tendency of wealth to foster pride, and of privation to breed discontent, is counteracted and controlled, and thus the chasm which divides the two conditions, meets with a double diminution. The hardships of the poor are greatly aggravated in their apprehension, by the luxurious abuse of wealth which they are forced to witness, or too ready to imagine; while on the other hand, the proud contempt of the rich and prosperous is embittered by the real or imputed thanklessness and insubordination of the humbler classes. So far is a mere equality of civil rights from rectifying these unhappy mutual relations, that it rather seems to render them still more unfriendly, as appears from the unquestionable fact that under our free institutions, wherever these distinctions have a well-defined existence, and are brought into collision, it is with a deeper feeling of inveterate hostility than in those countries where there is actual experience of oppression, but less intelligence or less freedom of utterance on the part of those who suffer wrong. The consciousness of independence and of equal rights, instead of soothing the repugnance to distinctions of another kind, beyond the reach of constitutions and the ballot-box, necessarily exasperates it where it is already felt, and may perhaps tend to produce it where it is not.

Now the gospel operates upon the same materials in a very different manner and with very different results; instead of reconciling men to one kind of inferiority or disadvantage by abolishing another which has no connection with it, Christianity applies its alterative remedies directly to the part diseased, subdues the pride from which revenge and discontent invariably flow, creates a general and habitual disposition to forbearance, and a modest estimate of self. How? not by philosophical abstractions, but by convincing men of sin and prompting them to accept of a gratuitous salvation. However imperfect these effects may be, they *are* produced and just so far as they are realized in any man's experience, just so far do they tend to heal the breaches in society produced by providential inequalities. He who heartily believes himself to be a miserable sinner justly condemned, and entirely dependent upon sovereign mercy for salvation, must and will, in some direct proportion to the strength of these convictions, lower his demands upon his fellow-men, and rise in his demands upon himself. If rich, he will, to some extent, grow liberal; if poor, contented; and if either, thankful.

For another thing observable in this whole process of correcting social evils by the positive influence of true religion, not of orthodoxy merely, but of enlightened spiritual piety, is this: that while it recognizes these invidious distinctions as existing, and in some degree inseparable from the mixed condition of society in this world, it attaches to the various degrees of wealth, refinement, knowledge, influence, and leisure, their corresponding measures of responsibility. The gospel, when it operates upon the rich man's heart, does not force him to impoverish himself, but it constrains him to discharge the obligations by which wealth is accompanied. It does not necessarily make the rich man poor, but so far as it operates at all, it always makes him do the duties of a rich man just as in the other case, it often leaves the poor man poor, or makes him poorer, but it never fails to make him feel that God requires of poverty contentment, and submission, and frugality, as truly as he calls the rich to Christian liberality. And so of ignorance and knowledge, public station and obscurity, and all the other contrasts and antitheses of our social condition.

It is not, however, by mere stress of conscience, or a painful sense of obligation, much less by a slavish dread of punishment, that true religion exercises this corrective influence. Such a conviction by itself would only make the evil fester in concealment, while the conscience thus enlightened, makes the way of duty plain, the renewed affections move spontaneously along it, so that the rich and poor, the strong and weak, not only own it to be right that they should severally bear and forbear, and sustain each other's burdens, but are inclined to do it by as natural a movement as they were once inclined to reciprocal envy and contempt.

This is the first step in the grand remedial process, which the Christian religion is even now applying to the evils of social inequality. It makes each party, at least to some extent, contented with his actual condition, aware of its peculiar obligations, and spontaneously disposed to discharge them, while by thus removing or diminishing on each side what is chiefly provocative of envy or contempt upon the other, it not only makes each better in itself, but draws them nearer to each other. Now all this—and it is much—might be experienced, though all the original difference in point of wealth, or knowledge, or refinement, still subsisted in full force; because the salutary change is in the moral sensibilities, disposing them to overlook disparities of culture and condition, and does not consist in the removal or material diminution of the disparities themselves.

But in the next place Christianity contributes to this great change in the very way which I have just excluded from the first stage of the process. That is to say, after making men willing to regard with charity and even complacency those far above or below themselves upon the scale of intellectual improvement and of social cultivation, the gospel brings them nearer to each other upon that scale too—first disposes them to mutual benevolence while far apart, and then diminishes the interval between them, not by equalizing property or bringing all parts of society to one dead level, but by giving to each rank or class, or whatever else you please to call it, a high degree of relative refinement, *i. e.*, of refinement suited to the actual position, and conducive to the right discharge of its peculiar duties. Here is a grand mistake of every other system for the elevation of what must be called, even among us, the lower classes of society, that they aim at an absolute and uniform amount of cultivation, having reference to some arbitrary standard, whereas Christianity gives each class what is best for it and most conducive to its harmony with every other. The kind of cultivation which some would bestow upon the poor, could only serve to render them ridiculous, while that which Christianity really imparts to them, tends, on the contrary, to dignify and elevate. However it may be explained, the fact is certain that the gospel has in some parts of the world, given even to the peasantry a species of refinement which no other means has been able to effect without it, even under the most favourable circumstances. Compare what the arts and the artistical attractions of the Romish faith have done for Italy—with what an austere Calvinism has done both for the Celtic and the Saxon race of Scotland. While in the one case the eye and the ear may have been trained, and picturesque attitudes and costumes rendered almost universal even among beggars, in the other case a poor laborious population has been raised to a pitch of intelligence and real cultivation, which the best advantages of education often fail to produce among ourselves.

This is the other part of the great creative and healing process by which the gospel is continually bringing the discordant elements of society together, and correcting the evils which would otherwise result from providential inequalities. By a process of *moral* elevation, men are first taught to surmount the disadvantages arising from this cause, and then by one of *intellectual* elevation, the operation of the cause itself, is circumscribed and weakened, till in some cases it appears to be destroyed, and in all cases the result of this twofold influence exerted on the mind and heart directly by religion, is a manifest reduction of the difference between the various classes of society arising from diversity of outward circumstances and position. That diversity may still continue and be formally as great as ever, but the evils flowing from it will be neutralized exactly in proportion to the action of the cause described.

If, in what has now been said, too much should seem to be ascribed to religion in the abstract or the general, without regard to precise forms and systems of belief, this has arisen from two causes—one of which is, that even the most diluted form of Christianity on one hand, or its most corrupted form upon the other, will be found more efficacious for the cure of social maladies, and more especially the healing of these alienations which we are considering, than any system of means which philosophers or politicians can devise without involving the assistance of religion. The other reason is, that general terms have been used for brevity, where more specific ones would really have made the case still stronger. For it is not more certain or susceptible of proof, that religion is more potent in this matter than any other principle, and Christianity more efficacious than all other systems of religion put together, than it is that among the various forms of Christianity itself. The highest influence of this kind has been ever exerted by the doctrines of grace, or what we are accustomed to distinguish by the name of evangelical religion.

This is no vain boast in behalf of what we hold to be the present form of Christianity. The fact itself is a matter of history, and its causes easily explained. If a graduated scale could be constructed, showing the degrees in which the national intelligence and character have been visibly affected by the direct influence of religion on the masses of the people, and the evils of social inequality thereby corrected, there can be no doubt that while the weakest influence of this kind would be found to have proceeded from the Romish and oriental forms of Christianity, or from the most diluted systems of Socinian or deistical neology, where these have been allowed to act, not merely on the educated classes, or on very small communities, but on a large extent of population, the highest measures of the same effect must be ascribed to what its enemies delight to brand as Calvinism, even where it has been mingled and diluted, as in Holland or New England, and the highest of all, precisely where its purity and vigour have been least abated, as in Scotland.

If a direct comparison is wanted, let it be furnished by the Scotch and Irish peasantry—the two most signal instances in history of whole nations brought almost entirely under the control of certain systems of belief and certain spiritual leaders, yet, how different the moral, intellectual, and social fruits of these contiguous experiments! The very evils which in one case have almost disappeared from the surface, if not from the interior of society, are even now menacing the other with terrific revolution. I have said too that the cause of this notorious difference is easily assigned, I mean a cause residing in the very nature of the several systems. It is the combination of the doctrines of individual responsibility and private judgment with those of human corruption and gratuitous salvation, that has produced the grand elixir to which Scotland owes her healthful social state; and as the lower degrees of the same influence are found to correspond to less degrees of purity and reform in the maintenance of these same doctrines, it may safely be affirmed, as a lesson even of experience, that this system of belief is demonstrably the best adapted to exert a purifying, healing influence on human society, and thereby to correct the evils flowing from the unavoidable diversities and outward situation and degrees of intellectual improvement, or, in other words, that it affords the safest and the best ground upon which "the rich and poor" may "meet together" and acknowledge that "the Lord is the maker of them all."

If these views be correct, they throw a welcome light on a subject of great practical importance—I mean the necessity of popular religious education, not only as a means of personal improvement and salvation, but also as the grand corrective and perhaps the sovereign cure of the disorders which now prey upon society and "eat as doth a canker." It is not enough to believe that religious knowledge is a good thing for religious purposes, and that it even may supply the want of other knowledge and of general cultivation, where these last are unattainable. We are bound to believe, because experience leaves no room to doubt, that religious education has a social and a secular as well as an exclusively religious use; and that it is not merely a good thing, but the good thing, the very thing, the only thing, by which the masses of mankind can be extensively and healthfully affected, so that if, with reference to them, we were allowed to choose between a general intellectual refinement and complete religious training, considered simply as two rival means of social improvement and conciliation, we should still be bound to choose the latter, and to send it rolling as a mighty flood throughout the earth " for the healing of the nations."

The other point which these considerations serve to set in a clear light, is the importance of the ministerial office, in its relation to society at large, as the administrator of this reconciling, elevating, purifying system. It has been said of the English clergy, that they belong to all ranks in society, enjoying free access to each, without thereby forfeiting the confidence of any. Of ministers, even among us, the same thing may be said, or rather, that they properly belong to no class, because their authority and influence are not dependent upon human usages or institutions, but on God's appointment and God's blessing. Let those who seek the office bear in mind, then, that, in more than one sense, they are called or will be called to dispense "the word of reconciliation," first, by reconciling men to God, and then by reconciling man to man—healing the breaches and divisions of society, and rendering the evils which they generate, as few and harmless as they can. This noble end is not to be promoted by a partial and exclusive self-devotion, either to the higher or the lower ranks, by making common cause, as some do, either with the rich against the poor or with the poor against the rich, but by endeavouring to bring the truth and power of God to bear upon the adverse parties with a moderating, elevating, and uniting influence, and thus preparing all, by mutual forbearance and assimilation, for that better country and those better times when these invidious distinctions shall no longer be remembered, but "the rich and poor" shall finally and forever meet together in the presence of that God who " is the maker of them all."

XIII.

Romans 11, 22.—Behold therefore the goodness and severity of God; on them which fell, severity; but toward thee, goodness, if thou continue in his goodness; otherwise, thou also shalt be cut off.

There is something sublime in the constancy of nature. We derive thence our strongest impressions of stability and uniformity. This association has become proverbial in many languages. It is also recognized in Scripture, and in the dialect of common life. But there is another side to this grand picture. The changes of nature are sublime too. Some of these are rare and even recondite. Such as occultations and eclipses. Some are familiar to men in certain situations. Such are the ebb and flow of tides; still more the changes in the surface of the ocean. When calm, it seems immovable; when roused, incapable of rest. Thus it furnishes the most vivid types of life and death. He who sees it in both states, might almost question the identity of the object. But these sights multitudes have never seen. There are other instances of change more universal. Who has not seen the cloudless sky? Who has not seen it overcast? What contrast can be more complete than that between a bright and lowering day? What more unlike than their effect upon the senses, the imagination, and the nervous sensibilities? But this is an occasional and fitful alternation, which cannot be computed or foreseen, at least in our climate. There are others, and these the most familiar, which are absolutely uniform, and from which our ideas of regularity and constancy are chiefly borrowed. Such are the vicissitudes of day and night, and the stated revolution of the seasons.

As to all these, our earliest impressions may be those of different objects. To the child perhaps, the dark and clear sky may have no identity; the smooth and rough sea may be different oceans; the world by day, and the world by night, distinct parts of the universe. Then when we learn to speculate and reason, we may verge towards the opposite extreme. We may suspect ourselves of some illusion, and conclude not only that the object is the same, but that its changes are imaginary. The truth lies between these two extremes.

All this may be used to illustrate spiritual things. Whoever seriously contemplates God, is startled by apparent inconsistencies. While we gaze at the clear sky it is overcast; or at the serene ocean it begins to lash itself; or at the sunset, it merges into twilight, and that into darkness. We fasten upon some view of the divine nature and become absorbed in it, till it is intercepted by another in a kind of occultation or eclipse. The first effect may be like that of natural changes on the child: we refuse to identify the object. This is perhaps the source of polytheism. Unable to reconcile the various phases of the divine nature, men regard them as appearances of different objects. Philosophical abstraction goes to the opposite extreme, and identifies the attributes as well as the subject in which they inhere. Thus we are told that wrath and love, justice and mercy, are the same thing. But from this, common sense and natural feeling alike revolt. We rest at last in the conclusion that what we behold, are consistent because co-existent manifestations of one and the same substance.

When Israel first saw the cloudy pillar growing luminous at night, he might have thought it was another; when convinced of his mistake, he might have suspected some illusion of his senses; but a little experience must have satisfied him that both these conclusions were erroneous; that the Lord his God was one Lord, and that this one Lord did go before him in a pillar of cloud by day, and a pillar of fire by night. Especially must they have been convinced of this in that night, long to be remembered, when the Lord looked out in the morning-watch upon the host of the Egyptians, through the pillar of fire and of cloud, and troubled the host of the Egyptians (Exodus 14, 24); when the angel of the Lord which went before the camp of Israel, removed and went behind them, and the pillar of cloud went from before their face and stood behind them, and came between the camp of the Egyptians and the camp of Israel, and was a cloud of darkness to them, and gave light by night to these. Some—however we may speculate at ordinary times—may be brought into circumstances where it is equally impossible to doubt, that the wrath of God is something very different from his love, and yet that the justice which we dread, and the mercy we invoke, are co-existent and harmonious characters of one and the same God, " glorious in holiness, fearful in praises, doing wonders." (Exodus 15, 11.)

This is still more striking when historically viewed in the actual exercise of those great attributes which seemed at first to be in conflict. To one such example Paul has reference in the text. The Jews had been chosen from among the nations, and made the depository of an exclusive revelation, not forever but a time ; not for their own sakes, but for that of men in general. But as a race they proved unfaithful to their trust. The honour which belonged to God, they arrogated to themselves. The salvation given to the world, they desired and hoped to monopolize. Hence they were cut off from the church and deprived of their national pre-eminence, while the despised Gentiles, whom they looked upon as hopelessly rejected took their place. This the apostle finely embodies in the figure of an olive tree deprived of its own branches, while those of a wild olive tree are grafted in. In reference to this stupendous change, he exhorts the favoured Gentiles both to thankfulness and fear. "Behold the goodness and severity of God, on them &c. ;" plainly implying that still further change was possible, and that they who had so strangely exchanged places might again be restored to their original position, and so gave occasion to a new application of the same solemn words, "Behold therefore the goodness and severity of God."

In fact, this formula admits of an extensive application to the history of God's dispensations towards his rational and moral creatures, and it is in this wide view of it that I have selected it as the subject of discourse. We may even go back to the age before the world began, and view the relation of Jews and Gentiles as a mere type of that between men and fallen angels. It is a fearful truth of which we have mere glimpses in the Bible that a portion of those unhappy spirits who surrounded the Divine throne in the highest heavens, fell by their own sin to the lowest hell, and that the same God whose goodness crowned their first estate with glory, stamped the last with the indelible impress of his wrath. As his goodness had been boundless, so his justice was inflexible. What a lesson to those who kept their first estate; how plainly does this dispensation say to them, "Behold therefore the goodness and severity of God."

But the same contrast soon presents itself again. Man is created, made a little lower than the angels, in the image of God, with dominion over the inferior creation, holy and happy, yet capable of falling. What a spectacle to angels both in heaven and hell. What an object to the malignant ambition of the latter to destroy man too; thus dishonouring God, and extending the reign of sin and death: they are allowed access to the new creature, in the paradise where danger seemed unknown and sin impossible; yet God had warned them by a prohibition of the possibility of evil. That possibility is too soon realized. Seduced by one already fallen, man falls too. It might have been imagined that a divine fondness for this new creation would have stayed the exercise of justice. Higher intelligences may be conceived as waiting in suspense for the decision of this question; half-hoping that the sky would still remain serene, the ocean of Divine love still at rest, the garden of Eden in the bloom of a perpetual spring. But see, no sooner is the sin committed, than the spotless purity of God is vindicated; the heavens become black, and seem to meet the ocean as it rises in its wrath, and mingles its tempestuous murmurs with the thunderings from above while every flower in Paradise seems blighted in a moment; all its verdure withers and a dreary winter overspreads the earth. The change is fearful, but it teaches us a glorious truth, that God is holy, just, and true; that he is not mocked, and that he cannot deny himself. To the spirits yet unfallen, this new demonstration seems to say again, "Behold therefore the goodness and severity of God."

In the first of these cases there is no vicissitude to be expected. "The angels who kept not their first estate, but left their own habitation, he hath reserved in everlasting chains, under darkness unto the judgment of the great day." (Jude 6.) There is no re-grafting of excinded boughs into the heavenly olive tree; they are not only "withered and without fruit," but "twice dead, plucked up by the roots," (Jude 12,) whose end, whose only end, is to be burned.

From this hopeless prospect, let us turn to that of our own race, and consider the illustration of the same great truth afforded by its history, or rather that of God's most gracious dispensations towards it; seeking the necessary contrast, not in the comparative condition of men and devils, but in the vicissitudes presented by the case of man alone. There could not be a stronger exhibition of God's goodness, than in man's creation and original condition. He was made not only happy, but holy. His physical, intellectual, and moral state were all exalted, and yet all susceptible of further exaltation; he was in immediate contact and communion with the source and sum of all conceivable perfection. Beyond this, our conceptions of God's goodness could not rise, but for the new disclosures which we meet with afterwards. True, man was put upon his trial, and that not only for himself, but for his children. But how could this detract from the divine goodness in the case of one created holy, and with nothing to complain of or desire, as wanting to his happiness? The very test prescribed, illustrates the divine goodness. What seems to be its arbitrary character was all in favour of obedience, and therefore illustrative of the divine goodness; while in the same proportion it must vindicate the justice which inexorably punished the transgression.

Every stroke in the picture of man's pristine happiness sets out in more prominent relief God's subsequent severity, not as conflicting opposites, but as the lights and shades of the same picture. Whatever selfish or morbid feeling might desire in an ideal case, the severity of the divine dispensations, when man fell, is as perfectly accordant with our highest conceptions of the divine nature, as the previous exhibition of transcendent goodness. We might not be able to obtain this view by any unassisted use of our own faculties, but when presented, it approves itself to reason, conscience, and affection; we not only feel that such severity towards sin is reconcilable with what we know of God, but that without it, we could not now be satisfied; the very goodness which confounded sin with holiness in indiscriminate indulgence, would no longer seem to be goodness, or at best the goodness of inferior natures, not the perfect goodness of a perfect God. The subsequent severity, instead of marring what precedes, throws back a new and glorious light upon it. Once convinced that the severity and goodness are the attributes of one and the same substance, we are forced to admit that they enhance each other, and even if the history of man stopped here, we should be forced to own that in its darkened mirror the divine perfections were resplendent, and to cry out in the language, not of cavil or complaint, but of profound adoration, "Behold the goodness and severity of God!"

But thanks be to God, the history of man does not stop here. The dismal scene which we have just surveyed is but the entrance to a new and strange spectacle. As we gaze upon the darkness into which our race was plunged by the great original apostacy, like men who gaze by night upon the troubled sea, beneath which some great fleet has just gone down, the day begins to dawn, light breaks upon the surface of those heaving waters, and reveals to us, at first the yawning gulf still open, into which the victims have descended, but the next moment, by a strange departure from the laws of nature, we behold them reappear, or at least some of them, many of them; the abyss disgorges its devoured prey, and the ascending sun illuminates the unexpected spectacle of life from the dead; mercy triumphant over justice. Yes, the scene has again been shifted, or to use a figure worthier of the subject, the unchanging orb of the Divine perfections has again revolved, and as we watch its revolutions, we recognize with joy the phase of mercy, the same pure light which shone on Paradise, but heightened by the contrast of the intervening wrath, and mellowed by the memory of sin and sorrow, lately born into this lower world.

This reappearance of the divine goodness, when it seemed to have been swallowed up in wrath forever, may be likened to the rising of the sun in the west, still dyed with crimson by his setting, to the substitution of a fresh dawn for an evening twilight, and the prospect of a new day, when a long night seemed inevitable. As such a change in the order would affect our senses and habitual associations, so our hearts and consciences would be affected by a clear, full view of this astonishing vicissitude. That God, after all his lavish kindness to the first man, should requite his first offence with such severity, might seem surprising, till explained by a correct view of the divine holiness and justice as essential to his very being, but that surprise, even in its first unrectified indulgence, could be nothing to the fresh surprise of men and angels at the first announcement of deliverance; salvation, not from suffering only, but from sin itself; not temporary, but eternal; not capriciously or arbitrarily bestowed, but rendered possible, and actually purchased, by the humiliation of the Deity himself, the incarnation of the co-essential and co-equal Son; his subjection and obedience to the law which man had broken, his endurance of the penalty which man had incurred, his substitution for the actual offence, his complete satisfaction to the Divine justice, his life, his death, for such an end as this, showing the turpitude of sin in the very act of expiating it, and the utterness and hopelessness of our ruin in the very act of retrieving it; oh! if this is not goodness, where shall it be found? or how shall we conceive of it? If this is not transcendent, perfect, heavenly, godlike goodness, let the word be hushed up, and the thought forgotten. Look, though it be but for a moment, at the cross, and him who hangs upon it, and while in breathless silence you count the drops of more than human or angelic blood that fall upon the parched earth, cursed for man's transgression, but now panting for deliverance; by the light that streams from that disfigured brow, read the old lesson written in new characters, "Behold the goodness and severity of God!"

No wonder that the angels bend with an inquiring gaze over this display of the goodness and severity of God! We, too, may well regard it with adoring wonder. But let us not lose sight of the great objects here presented. Let us not forget, in this new exhibition of the divine goodness, that it also involves a grand display of his severity. We are liable here to the same mistake as in a former case. Because God was so good to man at first, we feel surprised that he should be severe when man had fallen. And then, because of that most just severity, the exercise of mercy seems impossible. And now that mercy has been exercised, free favour to the utterly unworthy and the ill-deserving, we are apt to feel as if all danger were escaped forever—as if ruin and damnation were utterly impossible.

This seems to be the effect of the preaching of salvation upon many minds. The very grace of God incites them to go on in sin. Since he has exercised such boundless grace as to sacrifice his own Son for the life of a lost world, they think it utterly incredible that any should be lost; or, if any, that themselves should be among the number. Their whole life is a perpetual practical abuse of the great gospel doctrine—"He that spared not his own Son," &c. The language of their lives, if not that of their lips, is that such transcendent goodness shuts out all severity, as inconsistent and its opposite. Mercy has triumphed over God's inexorable justice, and disarmed, if not destroyed it; so that henceforth it is only in recollection of the past that we can say, "Behold therefore the goodness and severity of God."

This is one of the great practical delusions of the Christian Church, or rather of the Christian dispensation, which prevails among the hearers of the Gospel, and is often nourished by the very advantages which they enjoy, but which must be corrected, or it will go on slaying its thousands and its tens of thousands—the belief that because God is so merciful, he cannot be severe; that because his promise is so gracious, he will not execute his threatenings; that even the rejection of his offered grace will pass unpunished; and that they who refused to be saved through Christ, will magnify the greatness of the divine mercy by being saved without him. The error is refuted by the very nature of the foundation upon which it rests. That foundation is the proof of God's transcendent goodness in the gift of his Son to be a Saviour. But that gift is the strongest imaginable proof that God will not and cannot pardon sin without atonement. How absurd, then, to regard it as a reason for expecting what it proves to be impossible!

It is also refuted by the analogy of all God's previous dispensations, both towards men and angels. If his goodness to the angels in their first estate only sets forth in a stronger light his terrible severity when they had fallen; if his goodness to man in his original condition is enhanced by contrast with severity, which doomed him and his race to everlasting ruin, how can the goodness which provides a Saviour and salvation even for the race thus ruined, exclude the supposition of proportionate severity towards those who will not thus be saved? It does not; it cannot; even in theory the reasoning is unsound, because opposed to all analogy; and in practice, in experience, those who hold it to the end, will one day be effectually undeceived. Yes, the day is coming when those exhibitions of God's goodness and severity, of which we have been speaking, shall be, as it were, lost sight of and forgotten in the presence of a new, and to many souls, an unexpected demonstration, when they who shall have sinned on to the verge of life, refusing to believe in God's severity as something inconsistent with his goodness, shall be made to see both stare them in the face with terrible distress, his goodness embodied in the Saviour whom they have rejected, and on whose blood they have trampled—his severity in that derided hell which they regarded as a phantom, and from which they would not let him save them. Between these two fires—the fire of divine love, and the fire of divine wrath—the one, through their obstinate impenitence and unbelief, beyond their reach; the other, opening its devouring jaws already to receive them—they may cling convulsively to that which is no longer theirs, even as a temporary resting-place; but, as they are thrust off from it forever, they shall find their own perdition added to the numberless examples of the same great truth, and hear the voice of a great multitude, like the rush of many waters, say, " Behold the goodness and severity of God!" The solemn truth cannot be stated too plainly or too strongly. The gospel is a savour of death unto death in them that perish. To hear it is a blessing only to those who believe and embrace it. To all others it is a fearful aggravation of their guilt and their damnation. Better never to have heard the name of Christ, than to reject him; better never to have tasted of God's goodness, than to experience his severity.

The view which we have taken, of God's goodness and severity, has reference strictly only to his dealings with the race as such, just as Paul in the text refers to the dispensation of God's mercy towards Jews and Gentiles. But the truth involved may also be applied to individuals. The general analogy holds good, though not in all particulars. It is true, my hearer, you were never in a state of personal probation. That was past in Adam, and, as his descendant, you are not in danger of perdition, but are lost already. What you want is not so much a way of escape as a method of recovery. But in another sense, you are in a probationary state. Salvation is offered, and on your acceptance or refusal, hangs your everlasting destiny. This possibility, this opportunity, illustrates gloriously the goodness of God; but the neglect or abuse of it will no less conspicuously show forth his severity. Instead of being mitigated by the goodness which precedes, his ultimate severity will by it be unspeakably augmented in intensity.

And, as this is the clearly-defined course of duty and of safety for the preachers of the Gospel, so it is for those who hear it. Let every person who is still within the reach of mercy, look upon his preservation, even thus far, as a signal proof of the divine goodness, and beware how you abuse it! Every gift, every exemption, every prolongation of the period allowed you for repentance and conversion; every providential warning, every fresh appeal to your understanding and conscience, every moment added to the long, long respite of your fearful sentence, every gleam of hope that you may yet escape its execution, every motion of your limbs, every heaving of your lungs, every pulsation of your heart, unless converted by a true faith into priceless blessings, will infallibly plant daggers of supererogatory torment in your ever-dying soul hereafter. While you thank God, therefore, for the gifts which you enjoy, "be not high-minded but fear "—" behold the goodness and severity of God, on them which fell severity, but toward thee goodness, if thou continue in his goodness; otherwise, thou also shalt be cut off."

I exhort you to depart, then, with a deep conviction that the goodness and severity of God are not at variance, or exclusive of each other; but reciprocally magnify each other; that we need not attempt to make the one of these great attributes conceal the other, but may look at them together;—that we must thus view them if we would do justice to the revelation God has given of himself. The faithful presentation of the truth does not require us to exaggerate God's wrath by the denial of his mercy, or to magnify his goodness by denying his severity, or to confound essential distinctions by asserting the identity of both. We can only declare the whole counsel of God by holding up to view these two great phases of his infinite perfections. The ill effect of gazing too exclusively at one, can only be corrected by exhibiting the other.

XIV.

1 Cor. 15, 33.—Be not deceived!

To be deceived is a misfortune so familiar to the every-day experience of all men, that some effort of reflection and abstraction is required to recognize it as an evil in itself, and irrespectively of its effects. And yet it seems to follow from man's very nature as a rational being, that deception, even in the least degree, is both injurious and disgraceful, inasmuch as it implies some weakness, or inaction, or disorder of that faculty by which we are distinguished from the lower animals—the brutes that perish. As the act of deceiving is a certain indication of moral obliquity, so the very liability to be deceived is symptomatic of some intellectual infirmity or depravation. However insensible the mass of men may be to this important feature of their actual condition, there are not wanting partial and occasional perceptions of it, even among those who are commonly regarded as the least intelligent, or the least accustomed to reflect upon the constitution and the exercises of their own minds. Amidst the vast diversity of men's opinions and associations, as to praise and dispraise, honour and reproach, there is scarcely any thing more uniform or universal than the disposition to resent a wilful fraud or imposition as a humiliation and an insult, without any reference to the injury inflicted, or the importance of the subject-matter, as a measure of the conscious degradation. To have been imposed upon or duped, even in a trivial matter, or in jest, is often felt more keenly as a personal dishonour than the foulest wrong or the severest loss, when otherwise inflicted. There are some men, and perhaps some cases in which all men, if abandoned to the government of natural, unsanctified motives, would prefer the imputation of dishonesty to that of weakness; and our Saviour neither spoke at random nor in reference to a merely Jewish custom, when he singled out "thou fool," as one of the severest and least tolerable insults that a man could offer to his fellow. What is all this but the testimony of mankind, so much the stronger if unconscious and involuntary, to its own intellectual disgrace—the protest of the intellect itself against those daily and hourly humiliations which belong to its actual anomalous condition.

But this condition includes something more and something worse than any depravation or derangement purely intellectual. However humbling this might be to man, considered merely as a rational being, it is awfully aggravated by its complication with a spiritual malady, equally real and far more malignant, involving deadly alienation from the standard of all moral rectitude. However distinguishable and indeed distinct this intellectual and moral depravation may be, and however subtilly philosophers may speculate and reason as to their priority and mutual relations, the most interesting fact to us and to all men, as attested both by revelation and experience, is the fact, that the two evils coexist in one case— that to us, at least, they spring from the same cause, and must be healed, if at all, by the same remedy.

That this is really the case, apart from other most conclusive evidence, is proved by the mysterious obliquities of human intellect, in reference precisely to the most momentous subjects, where its genuine and normal operation seems essential to the welfare and even to the safety of the subject; by the strange but certain fact, not only that the weak in other things are weak in these, though even that might be justly regarded as surprising, but that those who seem strong-minded and sagacious, as to matters of the present life, so as to be beyond the reach of all deception, are, in relation to their highest interests, not only liable, but actually, constantly, ruinously, shamefully deceived.

Nor is this a mere accident of man's condition, which might have been otherwise and yet have left him, with respect to all essentials, as he is. A rational being could not be morally depraved without intellectual debasement, whether this be regarded as the cause, or the effect, or the concomitant of that; or if this abstract proposition be disputed, the fact, in reference to our depravity, is settled by our own experience, confirming the incessant exhibition of our fallen state in scripture, as a state of culpable but pitiable weakness, folly, and irrationality—of constant exposure and subjection to the grossest as well as the most subtle and refined delusions. The mysterious influence of evil spirits on the character and destiny of men, is represented in the scriptures, not as a coercive power, but as a deception, from the time of Eve, who, being deceived, was in the first transgression, to the day when the devil that deceived her, shall be cast into the lake of fire. Through the whole of this long interval, there is no description of the race more true to scripture and experience, and at the same time more completely humbling to the pride of man, than that which represents them as "foolish, ($ἀνόητοι$, irrational,) disobedient, *deceived*, serving divers lusts and pleasures"—or that which describes "evil men and seducers" as "waxing worse and worse, *deceiving and being deceived*." There would be something fearfully bewildering and confounding in the sight, if we could view it in a clear light and without obstruction or optical illusion, of a world of intellect, thus crazed and smitten with judicial blindness, mutually leading one another into error and to ultimate perdition—a spectacle of horror from which no relief can be obtained, except by looking up to Him who equally controls the world of matter and the world of mind, and of whom it may be said, in this as well as in a lower sense, that "with him (alone) is strength and wisdom—*the deceived and the deceiver are his.*"— (Job 12, 16.)

Without pausing to determine or enumerate the various instrumental agencies by which this mighty process of deception is continually carried on, and which may all be resolved into the three great sources of delusion and of consequent corruption, our own hearts, our fellow-men, and evil spirits, or, as the scripture more emphatically phrases it, the world, the flesh, and the devil, let me simply press upon your notice and your memory, the intimate connection which in all such scriptural delineations, is established between human depravity and human folly, so that they interpenetrate and mutually qualify each other, making sin inconceivably irrational, and foolishness unutterably sinful; representing every unrenewed heart as "*deceitful* above all things," to itself as well as others, and, for that very reason, "desperately wicked; as hard, not by accident, or by an arbitrary, inevitable effect *ab extra*, but "hardened through the *deceitfulness* of sin," and connecting the perdition of the lost, on the one hand, indeed, with "the working of Satan," but on the other "with all *deceivableness* of unrighteousness in them that perish, because they received not the love of the truth, that they might be saved; for which cause God shall send them strong delusions, to believe a lie, that all might be damned who believed not the truth, but had pleasure in unrighteousness."—(2 Thess. 2, 9—12.)

Now this is the condition from which Christ redeems us. Of him, as a Saviour, no less than of God, as the sovereign arbiter, it may be said, "the deceived and the deceiver are his." The effect of Christianity, *i. e.* of personal regeneration, is, to put an end to this perpetual deception, active and passive, to the habit of deceiving and to the condition of being deceived. Such is undoubtedly the actual experience of every penitent, believing sinner; but, as conversion, though it breaks the power and destroys the dominion of our natural corruption, does not utterly abolish it, but leaves us to struggle with the remnants of it through the present life, this new and strange condition of the soul displays itself in that specific form, or part of our corruption which we have been now considering, as truly as in every other. The fatal spell of sin is broken, the great governing delusion of the mind and of the life has been dispelled, and can never be renewed in the same form or the same degree. But it would be a great and dangerous mistake to think that all deception is henceforth impossible, even in reference to spiritual interests and objects. The continued danger of delusion, even as to these, is one of the peculiar circumstances of the Christian life on earth, or the condition of the church militant, distinguishing it from that of the church triumphant. The cause or ground of its continuance, though certainly mysterious, is not more so in this case than in any other part of that severe but salutary discipline, by which the faith and love of God's elect are to be purified and strengthened before they enter into glory. Of this discipline, for which multitudes who once groaned under it are now thanking God in heaven, the continued possibility of error and deception is a constituted part, and may therefore be regarded as an indispensable ingredient of that "much tribulation," through which "we must enter the kingdom of God," that "great tribulation," out of which they came, who have already "washed their robes and made them white in the blood of the Lamb," and which, even in the mean time, "worketh patience, and patience experience, and experience hope—a hope that maketh not ashamed, because, even now, the love of God is shed abroad in our hearts by the Holy Ghost which is given unto us."

Of the fact itself, that even true believers are in danger of deception, which, though not allowed to be destroying, may be hurtful and distressing to themselves and others, if proof be needed, it is furnished, besides others which I shall not stop to mention, by the frequent warnings against this very peril, addressed by Christ and his apostles, not to unbelieving and impenitent sinners, but to our Saviour's own disciples, and through them to the churches which they founded and instructed. "Take heed lest any man deceive you," was a solemn form of words, employed by Christ himself upon a solemn occasion; and it finds an echo in that phrase which Paul so frequently reiterates, that it has been called one of his favourite expressions, "Be not deceived," "Be not deceived." Can this incessant warning be a false alarm, or have respect to an imaginary danger? If we think so, we have reason to regard it as especially addressed to us, for to nothing more than to the danger of delusion and deception are those warnings of the same apostle more appropriate—" Be not high-minded, but fear"—and—" Let him that thinketh he standeth take heed lest he fall!"

This general view, however, of the danger to which we are exposed, can be practically and effectually useful, only by prompting the inquiry, when and where, or in relation to what specific evils, are we thus in peril? The attempt to ascertain these by conjecture, or by reasoning from abstract principles, would be not only endless, from the infinite variety of cases which might be supposed, but unsafe, from the doubts which might still be entertained, if not as to the actual existence, yet as to the magnitude and nearness of the dangers which might be described. From both these disadvantages we may escape, and at the same time be provided with a valuable safeguard against certain perils, by confining our attention, for the present, to the special cases which occasioned the original utterance of these solemn warnings not to be deceived, and which are all, without exception, common to the general experience of the church and to the personal experience of its members. By pursuing this course, the same passages of scripture which establish the existence of the danger as a general fact, may be employed as clues to guide us in the application of the salutary knowledge thus imparted to specific cases.

1. When our Saviour said, "Take heed lest any man deceive you," the particular deception which he had in view, was that in reference to his second coming, and the assumption of his name and person by pretenders or impostors. The experience of the church has shown that this was not a temporary, transient danger; for although the appearance of false Christs may not have been a frequent occurrence, this is only the gravest or extreme form of the peril against which our Lord forewarned his followers. The more refined and specious form of the deception, consists, not in the personal assumption of Christ's name, but in the confident assurance of his near approach, and the attempt to determine what he has left

indefinite, not as a matter of mere speculation, but as an engine of fanatical excitement, interrupting all the ordinary duties and relations of society, withdrawing men's attention from the claims of personal religion and from preparation for their own departure out of life, to fix it on a great catastrophe supposed to be at hand, and to be dreaded only as the most impious and impenitent of men might dread a deluge and an earthquake; and driving some, through mere excitement and alarm, to madness or to self-destruction. This, if only known to us historically or by a remote tradition, might be thought incredible; and yet it is one of the most recent and familiar forms of popular delusion, the effects of which are still felt in communities and families around us, while stimulating and productive causes are continually seething and fermenting in the caldron of fanatical religion, fanciful interpretation, false philosophy, and social revolution, which is boiling up and bubbling in the very midst of Christian churches and of learned institutions, ready to boil over, when the necessary point of heat or fermentation has been reached, with a fresh inundation of insane disorder, to be followed by a fresh reaction to the opposite extreme of spiritual sloth and deadness.

Nor is the warning thus afforded, to be limited to this precise kind of delusion, but extended to all other enthusiastic and fanatical excitements, which produce analogous effects by like means, and which educated and enlightened Christians are too commonly contented to despise as mere absurdities, from which no danger can be apprehended. There is no intellectual or moral feature of the age more striking and alarming than the frequency with which men of strong and cultivated minds are carried away by forms of error, which to others of the same class appear simply ridiculous. It is not bad logic or erroneous reasoning that produces these results; it is delusion; it is something that prevents the proper use of reason, and by making revelation a mere nose of wax, enables the subject of deception to pass with equal ease over the smallest and the greatest intervals, to leap from truth not only into error, great or small, but into nonsense, contradiction, and fatuity, the practical negation of his own intelligence, as well as the rejection of all previous knowledge and belief. Among the victims of these strong delusions are some who once securely laughed at their pretensions as absurd, and therefore innocent; as most men do until they are bewitched by them. The growing frequency of such irrational conversions, even in high places, and among what we regard as privileged classes, ought to teach us the necessity of something better than intellectual attainments or advantages, to save us even from what now appears to us the drivel of idiocy or the rage of madness, and give us ears to hear the Master saying, even of these things, and even to ourselves, "Take heed, take heed lest any man deceive you."

2. Twice, in the same epistle, Paul says to the church of the Corinthians, "Be not deceived!" In the first of these cases, (1 Cor. 6, 9,) the admonition may to many, seem as needless and superfluous as that addressed by Christ to his disciples. If none of us require to be warned against false prophets or pretended Christs,

how much less can we need to be admonished that the joys of heaven are not reserved for those who practise the most heinous sins, not only of a spiritual and insidious, but of a corporeal and outward kind. Who is, or ever was, in danger of supposing that idolaters, adulterers, extortioners, revilers, thieves, drunkards, and the perpetrators of enormities still worse, are to inherit the kingdom of God? And yet it is precisely this impossible delusion against which Paul warns his readers, not only here but in Ephesians (5, 6,) where a similar enumeration of the blackest crimes is followed by the solemn admonition, "*Let no man deceive you* with vain words, for because of these things cometh the wrath of God upon the children of disobedience." It was not to uninstructed heathen that this language was addressed; for he says expressly in the verse preceding, (Eph. 5, 5,) *Ye know* that no whoremonger, nor unclean person, nor covetous man, who is an idolater, hath any inheritance in the kingdom of Christ and of God." It was not addressed to uninstructed, impenitent or unconverted hearers of the gospel, for he says in the verse following, (Eph. 5, 7,) "Be not ye therefore partakers with them; for ye were sometime darkness, but now are ye light in the Lord." And as in Ephesus, so in Corinth; after enumerating some of the most revolting forms of human wickedness, he adds, (1 Cor. 6, 11,) " and such were some of you; but ye are washed, but ye are sanctified, but ye are justified in the name of the Lord Jesus, and by the Spirit of our God." It was to justified, regenerated, sanctified believers, that the apostle addressed this apparently gratuitous assurance that those who continued in the practice of gross vices could not be saved.

What was the error against which he meant to warn them? Not the mere theoretical or doctrinal absurdity of believing that men could be saved *from* sin, and yet continue *in* it, for of this paralogism the Corinthian and Ephesian converts were in as little danger as ourselves; but the practical paralogism of thinking themselves Christians when their lives belied it; the self-contradiction of a high profession and a lawless life. Is this inconsistency impossible? Alas! it is among the most familiar features of religious life in every age and every country. Ashamed as all would be to teach it or to hold it as a formal proposition, how many practice it and preach it by example, without a scruple and without a blush! It is in vain to say the combination is absurd, it must be an imaginary one. Precisely the same reasoning might be used to demonstrate that there is no sin at all, for all sin is irrational, and every act of sin admits of a reductio ad absurdum. But in this, as in the other case, it is not a mistake in logic, but in morals. It is not weak reasoning, it is strong delusion of the heart as well as of the head, and one to which the highest are as open as the lowest, the wisest as the weakest and the most besotted, if abandoned to their own resources. Here, again, the instances of this delusion are confined to no church, country, or condition of society. Explain it or deny it as you will, the fact is written in the records of the church, and in the memory of the world, that men of eminent endowments and conspicuous position, whatever may have been their creed or theoretical conviction, have lived precisely as they must have lived, if they had really examined and believed the monstrous blasphemy, against which Paul so earnestly forewarns us, saying, *Be not deceived!*

3. But if this delusion, after all, should seem too monstrous in itself, or too remote from our experience, to be made the subject of a serious admonition to professing Christians, let us look for a moment at another case, in which the same apostle uses the same formula, *Be not deceived!* The readers immediately addressed are the Galatians, who had swerved from the simplicity of gospel doctrine under the influence of Judaizing teachers, and besides the fatal error which they had embraced in theory by falling from grace, *i. e.*, from the doctrine of gratuitous salvation, seem to have been betrayed, as might have been expected, into other false opinions, tending more or less to vitiate their Christian character and course of life. Among these there appears to have been one, growing rather out of the abuse than the rejection of the doctrines of free grace; the notion that, provided men are saved, it matters little how they live, since all are to be saved alike, and the imperfections of believers, nay, their worst neglects of duty, and most heinous violations of the law of God, can have no effect upon their ultimate condition or eternal destiny. In opposition to this error, far more specious and insidious than either of the others, and therefore not unlikely to be harboured where the others never gain access, he teaches that the laws of spiritual life are as determinate and uniform as those of nature, that even true

believers will not be, by miracles, exempted from their operation, and that although saved by sovereign mercy from perdition, and made perfect in holiness, the soul's capacity and actual experience of good hereafter will bear due proportion to its progress here; its growth in grace, sanctification, union with Christ, communion with God, separation from sin, and assimilation to the divine nature.

If the subtle perversion of the Gospel doctrine, here corrected, is a natural and almost certain growth of human weakness and corruption, even under the prevailing influence of saving grace, and therefore not confined to certain periods, or places, or conditions of the church, or of society at large, but liable and likely to spring up as tares among the wheat, wherever men are men, and sin is sin; we should require no special pleading to convince us, or impassioned exhortation to persuade us, that the great apostle "being dead yet speaketh" unto us, as he spoke of old to the Galatians, saying, "*Be not deceived;* God is not mocked; for whatsoever a man soweth, that shall he also reap. For he that soweth to the flesh shall of the flesh reap corruption; but he that soweth to the Spirit, shall of the Spirit reap life everlasting." (Gal. 6, 7. 8.)

4. To some of you, my hearers, I rejoice to believe that even this monition, although recognized as resting on Divine authority and certain truth, may not be specially or personally applicable, on the ground of any present and immediate danger, or of actual subjection to the several delusions which have been described, and with which the apostle has asso-

ciated that remarkable expression, *Be not deceived!* I need scarcely say that this exemption from deception, or the risk of it is, even in the best and most favourable case, restricted and precarious, since every human heart, so long as any residue of its corruption still remains is, in itself, exposed to all the evil which that corruption is capable of producing, when free from the restraints of sovereign grace. But since that grace does operate, and those restraints are really imposed, you may undoubtedly be free at this time from the pressure of these strong delusions, from fanatical incitements and hallucinations, and from every form of Antinomian license. If this be so, you will acknowledge your peculiar obligation, not only to thank God for his delivering mercy and restraining grace, but also to abstain from every thing that would endanger the security and liberty which you enjoy. Among the dangers thus to be avoided, I will name but one, and in the choice of that one I shall still be guided by the apostolic warnings not to be deceived. It is the danger of forgetting that the lowest and most moderate degrees of Christianity, though really distinct and distant, to the eye of God, from the highest attainments of a mere morality, and still more from the forms of hypocritical profession, may resemble both in human estimation, and be brought into juxtaposition with them in the ordinary intercourse of life. How natural and amiable is the wish to make this intercourse as peaceable as may be, and for this end to sacrifice whatever seems to be a needless rigour and austerity, endeavouring to obliterate or cover the invidious line of demarkation which unhappily divides the church and world; going as far as the most yielding conscience will allow, in partaking of those pleasures which a more morose religion would proscribe, as dangerous, if not unlawful, under the specious pretext of avoiding sanctimonious preciseness, and of "winning souls" by wise accommodation and concession to the innocent or even to the doubtful customs of society. If any of you are now pursuing this course—as thousands have pursued it in every age—you may not be prepared for the suggestion, that perhaps you are mistaken after all, and that if the warning voice of "Paul the Aged" could now reach you from his grave in Rome or from his throne in heaven, it might only be to say again to you, as he said to the Corinthians 1800 years ago, "*Be not deceived! evil communications corrupt good manners. Awake to righteousness and sin not; for some have not the knowledge of God. I speak this to your shame.*" (1 Cor. 15, 33. 34.)

XV.

ACTS 28, 28.—Be it known therefore unto you, that the salvation of God is sent unto the Gentiles, and that they will hear it.

FAMILIAR as long practice has now made it, there is still something strange in the facility with which we are accustomed to apply to ourselves and our contemporaries, terms that are strictly appropriate only to a former dispensation. I do not here refer to the prevailing practice of appropriating to the Christian church the promises originally uttered to the house of Israel; for this, I doubt not, is in strict accordance with their true design and import. But I mean the habit of transferring to our own times what was really temporary in design, and has in fact long ceased to be. A striking instance is afforded by the way in which we talk about the "Gentiles," as if we were "Jews," and bore the same relation to the heathen that existed between Jews and Gentiles under the restrictive institutions of the old economy. Such is the force of words, to influence as well as to express thought, that by dint of constant repetition, men may actually come at last to think themselves a chosen and peculiar people, not only in the spiritual Christian sense, but in the national external sense.

The very existence of this disposition to confound things so dissimilar affords a proof that with all their dissimilitude, there must be strong points of resemblance, and it may not be unprofitable, therefore, to consider briefly what these points of resemblance are; in what sense, and to what extent, our tacit assumption of the Jewish character and standing may be justified, and also by what dangers and responsibilities, or what advantages and honours this distinction is attended. In attempting this comparison, it will be found to favour concentration and precision to select some one turning point, some critical juncture, in the history of Israel, at which the Jewish character and spirit were peculiarly developed, and if possible brought into immediate juxtaposition with the corresponding traits of Christianity. Such a conjuncture is the one at which the words of the text were uttered, when the old economy had really been abrogated by the advent of the Saviour, and the Jewish world was rent asunder through its whole extent by the great dividing question "What think ye of Christ?" In consequence of this very agitation, Paul becomes a prisoner and is sent to Rome. But even there he preaches the gospel, in obedience to his Lord's command, "beginning at Jerusalem;" even there, the first call is addressed to "the lost sheep of the house of Israel." He convokes the chief men of the Jews, of which race and religion it would seem, from the contemporary statements of Josephus, there were thousands then in Rome. To this representative assembly of his people, he addressed a vindication of himself and of his master; of himself as guiltless even with respect to Judaism, and though groundlessly accused devoid of malice towards his enemies; of Christ, as the "hope of Israel," for whose sake, said he, "I am bound with this chain," thus connecting, in the clearest and most striking form, his personal captivity with that great cause for which he counted it all joy to suffer.

Being assured by those who heard him, of their willingness to do him justice, and their wish to know more of this sect or heresy which everywhere was spoken against, he drops all personal considerations, and to the many who assembled at his lodgings on a day appointed, he "expounds and testifies the kingdom of God," that is to say, the nature of the new dispensation as distinguished from the old, "persuading them concerning Jesus," *i. e.*, proving him to be the promised Christ, the substance of the ancient shadows, and in this sense, as in others, the "end of the law;" proving all this "out of Moses and the Prophets," "from the morning till the evening." When he found, as he no doubt had foreseen, that they were not agreed among themselves, and that "some did not believe," he parted from them after he had spoken "one word," and a fearful word it was, being nothing less than that appalling premonition of judicial blindness, in the sixth chapter of Isaiah, for which the Prophet was himself prepared by a solemn vision and a symbolical assurance of forgiveness. To this application of an awful threatening he adds, "Be it known unto you therefore," *i. e.*, because you thus reject the hope of Israel, for whose sake the Mosaic economy existed, and at whose approach it was to crumble, "be it known unto you, that the salvation of God is sent unto the Gentiles, and that they will hear it." In like manner, Paul and Barnabas had said, long before, to the unbelieving Jews of Antioch in Pisidia, "it was necessary that the word of God should first have been spoken to you; but seeing ye put it from you, and judge yourselves unworthy of eternal life, lo we turn unto the Gentiles." And again, when those of Corinth contradicted and blasphemed, "Paul shook his raiment, and said unto them, Your blood be upon your own heads, I am clean, from henceforth I will go unto the Gentiles."

The same offer, the same refusal, and the same result, are expressed or implied in the passage now before us. Its particular expressions need but little explanation. The "salvation of God," literally, his saving thing, or that by which he saves, does not here mean the actual experience of salvation, but, as appears from the last clause of the verse, in which it is spoken of as something to be heard, the doctrines, message, offer, or glad tidings of salvation; the same that Paul to the Pisidians calls "the word of this salvation." The phrase " and they will hear it " might perhaps be more exactly rendered, " they too shall hear it." By a simple change of emphasis, however, the expression may be made to convey these two ideas, or modifications of the same idea, that they *shall* and that they *will* hear the message of salvation; that they shall, in the dispensations of God's providence, enjoy the opportunity of hearing; and that through the dispensations of his grace, they will give ear to it. All this may therefore be considered as included in the meaning of the text.

But the main point to which I would invite your attention, is the contrast here exhibited between the Christianity of Paul and the Judaism of his hearers, under circumstances singularly suited to bring out, in bold relief, the characteristic attributes of both, so that if we would compare ourselves with either, we could hardly ask a better opportunity. And as one part of the comparison essentially involves the other, let us inquire in what points, if in any, we may claim affinity with these representatives of Judaism, at the eventful epoch of its dying struggle with the infant church.

1. The first resemblance which I would suggest is, that they, like us, had long been in possession of exclusive privileges, and accustomed to survey without emotion the great mass of mankind deprived of them. This is the grand assimilating fact in their condition and in ours, which has led to the habitual adoption of their language, and appropriation to ourselves of what is really peculiar to their insulated and unique position. The ancient Jews were in exclusive possession of the scriptures, a pure worship, and an authorized ministry. So are Christians now, as compared with millions of heathen, and the Protestant churches, in comparison even with millions of nominal Christians. Hence it seems natural and not unreasonable to regard ourselves as bearing just the same relation to the Gentiles of the present day, as that sustained by Israel to the Gentiles of antiquity. But let us not, in looking at the marked points of resemblance, over-

look the no less marked points of diversity between the cases. The exclusive privileges of the ancient Jews, were theirs by an express divine appointment. The barriers, which divided them from other nations, although temporary in design, were reared by an Almighty hand, and could be demolished by no other. Their adherence to these old restrictions, after the set time for their removal had arrived, was indeed an act of flagrant unbelief and disobedience; but until that time came, they had no choice, they were shut up to the necessity of standing aloof, and living apart, and avoiding all communion with the nations as such. Does our situation correspond with this? Are our exclusive privileges forced upon us, as it were by irresistible authority? If not, our insulation from the world is very different from that of ancient Israel. So far as the enclosures which have shut us in are human structures, reared by selfishness and cemented by apathy, they differ wholly from the walls by which the ancient Zion was encompassed, and her sons withheld from all communion with the Gentiles. They had been taught, and by divine authority, to look upon the nations as excluded, for a time, from the covenant of mercy. We have been taught, and by the same authority, that these in all respects are heirs of the same promise. They, as a nation, were in fact the chosen and peculiar people of Jehovah. We, in this respect, have not, and never had, the shadow of a claim to take precedence of our fellow Gentiles. In a word, considering the divine institutions out of which their prejudices grew, and the want of any corresponding pretext for our own, we may say, without irreverence or perversion, that they were straitened in Moses and the Prophets, but that we, if straitened, must be straitened in ourselves. Let this essential difference be kept in view, while we still distinctly recognize the real similarity between the cases in the long-continued undisturbed enjoyment of exclusive privileges.

2. The other points of resemblance, which I shall advert to, all arise from that just mentioned, as its more remote or proximate effects. And in the next place I may specify the influence of long-continued and exclusive privileges on the opinions, the doctrinal belief, of those enjoying them. It is curious, yet melancholy, to observe with what facility advantages possessed by a few for the good of the many may come to be regarded as prerogatives belonging to the few, to the entire exclusion of the many. Of this fatal tendency to abuse, the rise of all despotic power is an illustration. It was never more remarkably exemplified, however, than in the case before us, that of a particular people, made the sole depository of the truth and of the promises of mercy, for a limited time, with a view to their general diffusion afterwards, and seduced by the very possession of this glorious trust, first into forgetfulness, then into ignorance, and then into denial, of the very end for which it was created. That this perversion was facilitated by the peculiar institutions which were necessary to secure the purpose of the temporary system, cannot be denied. But this effect of the Mosaic institutions must be carefully distinguished from their legitimate design and tendency. With all their restrictions and exclu-

sive regulations, they were not intended to create or foster a contracted nationality and a contempt or hatred of mankind. This might be presumed from the divine authority by which they were established.

It may be more certainly inferred from many intimations in the law itself, and still more clearly read in the discourses of the Prophets, its inspired expounders. One grand design of the prophetic office was, to guard the institutions of the law against abuse, and to recall the people from the gross corruptions which its outward forms were apt to generate to more enlarged and spiritual views. A single instance of this general fact, is the prophetic exposition of the sacrificial system, equally distant from fanatical rejection of appointed rites and from superstitious worship of the rites themselves. The very terms of these inspired interpretations seem to show, not only that they were required, but that, with respect to many, and perhaps to most, they were without effect except to blind and harden. The great mass of the people, far from prizing their peculiar and distinguishing advantages, as present or prospective means of general good, valued them only for their own sake, and by so doing showed that they mistook their very nature, and instead of deriving from them an exclusive benefit, were utterly incapable of deriving any benefit at all.

This cardinal error, as to the very purpose of the system under which they lived, could not fail to produce a general distortion in the doctrinal views of those who held it. They who did not know, or could not be persuaded, that " the law must *go forth* from Zion, and the word of the Lord from Jerusalem," could never be expected to appreciate the truth, that the law of the Lord is perfect, converting the soul, and his testimony sure, making wise the simple. They who believed that the truth or mercy of Jehovah existed for themselves alone, could surely never have obtained a glimpse of what his truth and mercy are. Such was the doctrinal effect produced upon the ancient Jews by their long-continued and exclusive privileges.

Now its tendency to this result, was not peculiar to the ancient world or to the house of Israel. It may exist and operate in us, and with a fearful force, proportioned to the magnitude of our advantages. If they, with an unfinished revelation and a heavy ceremonial yoke upon their necks, could dream of an exclusive right to God's compassions, what may not we, without preventing grace, infer from our unclouded light and our unshackled freedom? And if this grand error had a tendency to vitiate their whole view of divine truth, what security have we that an analogous effect may not be realized in our experience? Here, then, to say the least, there is a possible, if not an actual resemblance between us and them. Because they were favoured, for a time, with an exclusive revelation, they forgot the very end for which they had received it, and forgetting this, were naturally led to take distorted views of that religion which they thus regarded as exclusively their own forever. So may *we*, perhaps I ought to say, so *have* we reaped precisely the same fruit from precisely the same seed so far as we have sown it.

3. This view of the matter may be rendered clearer

by selecting from the whole mass of opinions thus injuriously affected by the culpable abuse of long-continued and exclusive privileges, one or two peculiarly important and peculiarly conspicuous in the case before us. Take for example the great doctrine which divided the Apostle of the Gentiles from his Jewish hearers, at the interesting juncture when they went their way after Paul had spoken to them " one word." What was the relative position of the parties? Common to both was a professed belief in Moses and the Prophets, and in the promises of Messiah as the Saviour of his people. But they fatally diverge at an essential point. Paul believes that the Messiah has already come, and that Jesus of Nazareth is he, and as a necessary consequence, that the restrictions of the old economy are at an end, and the diffusion of the true religion through the world the first great duty of God's people. They, on the contrary, regard the advent of Messiah as still future, and the barrier between Jews and Gentiles as still standing. The connexion of these doctrines in their several creeds is not fortuitous. It was *because* Paul believed in the Messiahship of Christ that he believed in the necessity and present duty of extending the blessings of the true religion to the Gentiles no less than the Jews. Believing, as his countrymen at Rome did, that Messiah had not come, they were consistent in believing also that the old restrictive system was still valid and still binding. I say they were consistent, not that they were right, or even excusable, in so believing. Their consistency was nothing but consistency in error, error sinful in its origin and fatal in its issue.

Their mistake was not merely one of chronology. It was not that they put the date of the Messiah's advent too low down. Their rejection of Christ shows that they erred not only as to the fulfilment of the promise, but as to the meaning of the promise itself. Their expectation was not realized because it was a false one. They had corrupted the very doctrine of salvation, upon which all depends. They looked for a Saviour who had never been promised, and could never come. Instead of one who should destroy all national restrictions, they expected a national deliverer, conqueror, and king. This dream of national advancement could be verified only at the cost of other nations. Their mistake as to the Messiah, therefore, tended directly to cherish a spirit of national exclusiveness, and to suppress all rising of a catholic charity. And thus appears the truth of the position, that the doctrinal error of the unbelieving Jews, with respect to the Messiah, and their practical error with respect to the Gentiles, were as really and closely connected as Paul's doctrine with respect to the Messiahship of Christ, and his practice with respect to the conversion of the world.

And the same connexion still exists and will betray itself between a Jewish doctrine and a Jewish practice. For, although it is impossible that any Christian, even one by mere intellectual conviction, should embrace the very error of the old Jews as to the Messiah's kingdom; it is altogether possible and easy to embrace one of a similar description, by unworthy and inadequate conceptions of the Christian system, as designed and suited for a universal faith, as well with respect to its doctrines as its institutions. There is no danger of our thinking that Christ came to be a worldly conqueror and not a Saviour, but there is great danger of our thinking, or at least of our acting, as if we thought that he came to save *us*, and to secure us in the undisturbed enjoyment of our temporal and spiritual comforts, and that the rest of the world must be consigned to his uncovenanted mercy. There is great danger of our looking through the wrong end of the telescope, and seeing that diminished which we ought to have seen magnified, the world reduced to a nut-shell, and our own house or village swelled into a world. There is great danger of our being taught and teaching others this great doctrine as some children learn geography, beginning at the spot on which they stand, and by degrees enlarging their horizon till they take in a whole country, state, or hemisphere, and at the last the world itself. This lesson in geography the church has long been learning, but has stuck fast in the elements. In order to describe the larger circle, we must learn to reverse the process, and begin as the apostles did with the idea of a world to be converted, and from this descend to the particulars included. There are great advantages, no doubt, in rising from particulars to generals, and in making home the starting point of distant operations.

But however necessary this may be in practice, it is well in theory at least to take the other course, and to begin at the beginning, *i. e.* where the apostolic preachers set the ball in motion, who, although they obeyed their Lord's commandment by beginning at

Jerusalem, were careful not to end there, like the
charity of those who in their zeal for the maxim, that
charity begins at home, not unfrequently forget to
let their own begin at all. This preposterous inver-
sion of the grand design of Christianity, by putting
first what ought to be put next, is a doctrinal mistake
to which the church is not a stranger, and which certainly bears some resemblance; although far from
coinciding wholly, or at all, in its external form, with
that of the old Jews in relation to the kingdom of
Messiah. And with this resemblance in the causes,
we need scarcely be surprised at the analogy of their
effects, or wonder that a Jewish spirit should produce
a Jewish practice. If the unbelieving Jews of old
were led by false ideas of the Messiah and his kingdom, to a spurious morality, an outside holiness, a
voluntary humility, and will worship, a deification of
the outward and material, and a laborious groping
in the darkness and the dust of mere observance, to
the neglect of the rain and sunshine and refreshing
airs of genuine religion, why should it be thought incredible that kindred errors among us may lead to
the exchange of spiritual life for dead formality, fac-
titious morals, and a senseless trifle-worship? Would
it in fact be extravagant to state it as a lesson of our
own experience, that a similar contraction of the
views and feelings has been actually found to produce
a similar deterioration; that the truth has not been
kept most pure by those who kept it to themselves;
that the habit of leaving out of view the expansive
nature and design of Christianity has sometimes been
coincident with that of putting mere conventional

arrangements in the place of vital principles and everlasting truths?

But it is not on this general deterioration of the religious life, however real and deplorable, that we are led to dwell at present, as the most important practical effect of long-continued and exclusive privileges, and of the errors which they tend to generate; for in addition to all this, or in the midst of it, there rises up, like a colossus, one practical abuse which may, at least for this time, be allowed to overshadow all the rest. Besides the influence exerted by this error of the Jews, upon themselves, whether doctrinal, moral, spiritual, or ecclesiastical, it led, as we have seen, at the beginning of the Christian dispensation, to a practical denial of the very end for which the old theocracy existed, and a consequent refusal to extend the true religion to the Gentiles, thus converting their own boasted and adored distinctions into a mere historical enigma, to perplex the generations that should follow, by exhibiting the strange sight of a people created to save the world, and yet fondly dreaming to be saved alone! How far it is possible for us to occupy the same position before men and angels, must depend upon the sameness of our opportunities and consequent responsibilities, when tried by the avowed rule of the divine administration, that of those who have much, much will be required, and the cardinal principle of Christian charity, freely ye have received, freely give!

That a marked diversity exists between the situation of the Jews and ours, we have seen already. But let it be remembered, that all the difference is in our favour. If the Jews, even while they were secluded from the Gentiles by divine authority, were bound to keep their eye upon the great ulterior end of that seclusion, and to cherish feelings in accordance with it, how much more does this same obligation rest on us, who have no external disadvantages to hinder its discharge. The Christian world, or, if you please, the reformed part of Christendom, are not intrusted with the oracles of God as an exclusive deposit, *even for a time.* We have them that we may diffuse them. There are no walls built by a divine hand around us, for whose fall we must wait before we go unto the Gentiles. The very dust and rubbish of those old barriers have long since disappeared. A great and effectual door into the heathen world is opened, and the voice of God is calling us to enter it. We have no doubts to solve, and no disputes to settle —as to the fact of the Messiah's advent—as to the question whether Jesus Christ is he. We have no associations with the old economy, or habits acquired under it, to restrain our feelings or impede our movements, even after the judgment and the conscience are convinced. Every thing, both at home and abroad —in the teachings of God's word, and in the leadings of his providence—in the condition of the heathen and our own—makes us as free to think and act for their conversion, as the old Jews were paralyzed and crippled with respect to it. And yet, with all this difference in our favour, may we not be still too Jewish in our spirit and our conduct, with respect to those less favoured than ourselves? The gospel has indeed abolished national distinctions, but have we consented to their abolition? The old middle walls of partition have fallen at the blast of the trumpet, but may we not rear up others in their stead? and, if so, we may imprecate a curse upon ourselves, like that pronounced upon him who should rebuild the walls of Jericho.

This leads me, in the last place, to consider the resemblance which may possibly exist between the cases, with respect to providential retributions. We have seen the effects produced by these errors on the doctrinal views, the affections, and the lives of the anti-christian Jews, and, through their neglect, on the condition of the world. These results they may have partially foreseen, and deliberately ventured on. But there were others which they dreamt not of, and which were, nevertheless, fixed in the divine determination. What means that solemn and repeated declaration of the great apostle, that he turns away from the Jews to the Gentiles? Does it mean merely that his personal ministry should now take that direction? There is evidently more, far more, implied. Does it mean that the Gentiles should, in spite of Jewish prejudice and bigotry, become partakers of their once exclusive privileges, or rather, of others far superior? Even this is not enough. There is an evident allusion, not only to a change, but to an interchange of character and state—not only to the grafting in of foreign branches, but to the excision of the native boughs—not only to the culture of the desert, but to the desolation of the vineyard. "Is it not yet a very little while," said Isaiah, in prophetic anticipation of this very change, "is it not yet a very little while, and Lebanon shall be turned into a fruitful field, and the fruitful field shall be reckoned as a forest?" Had this change literally taken place, it could not have been more complete or striking, than that which has been wrought in the relative condition of the Jews and Gentiles. Left to his cherished notions of hereditary sanctity and safety, and his dreams of a Messiah yet to come, Israel has vanished from his place among the living, to haunt the nations as the restless ghost of a departed people, or to glide about the graveyard where his hopes lie buried, while the dry bones of many nations, who appeared to slumber without hope, have been raised again and clothed with flesh, and new life breathed into their resurrection-bodies. They that dwelt in the dust awake, and the dew of God is as the dew of herbs, and the earth casts forth her dead!

But where are they who once monopolized the promises, and held fast, with a niggard grasp, the keys of heaven? Were it not for prophecies still awaiting their fulfilment, we might well say, in the words of the same prophet, "they are dead, they shall not live —they are deceased, they shall not arise—thou hast visited and destroyed them, and made all their memory to perish. Behold the goodness and severity of God! Behold the vision of the Prophet verified! Lebanon has long since become a fruitful field, and the fruitful field for ages reckoned as a forest!

But how shall I venture to present the other side of this same picture, or to bring ourselves into comparison with Israel as I have just described him? Without pretending to decide what weight is due to such analogies, we can scarcely shut our eyes to the analogy itself, or fail to see that the comparison already pushed so far, admits, at least, of an ideal consummation. We are all disposed, as individuals and nations, to exempt ourselves from the operation of the rules which we apply to others. We can look at the vicissitudes of other times, or of other subjects in our own, without imagining that we or ours may be subjected to the same great providential law. What the heathen called the wheel of fortune, we may call the wheel of providence. However imperceptible it may be on a small scale or within a narrow compass, it is impossible to take large views of human history, without perceiving that its processes are extensively, not to say uniformly, marked by alternation. We may leave altogether out of view the application of this statement to the case of individuals and families. We may pass lightly over those vicissitudes of nations which have ever been the trite theme of declamatory moralizers; by far the most remarkable of which is that presented by the contrast of what Greece and Egypt were to the ancient world, with what they are to us.

Let us dwell, for an instant, on the map of Christendom, as it is and as it was—as it was at the death of the last apostle, or even 1400 years ago—looking particularly at the western coast of Asia Minor and the northern coast of Asia—comparing their innumerable churches and multitudinous councils, not only with their present desolation, but with the actual state of Christianity in Britain and in Scandinavia; and even in these nameless climes of which a Plato may have dreamed, and which Phenicians may have visited, but which have neither name nor place upon the chart of ancient knowledge, is it certain that this process of rotation has been finally arrested? or that its future evolutions will be left to the control of what we call fortuitous or accidental causes, which can neither be computed nor accounted for? Is it not possible, to say the least, that the vicissitudes yet future may sustain the same relation to extraordinary privilege and culpable abuse of it, as those which are already past, and some of which we have been tracing? In a word, is it too much to suppose that the prophetic vision may again be realized—another Lebanon become a fruitful field, and fields now fruitful be transformed into a silent and forsaken forest? What a view does this imagination, if it be no more, open far and wide before us! What a change of absolute condition and of mutual relations! What a levelling of hills and filling up of valleys! What fantastic confusion in the use of names, and in the associations coupled with them! How strange may it yet seem, to remember that Britain once ruled India—that America once talked or dreamed of civilizing Africa—that Australia and the isles of the Pacific once invited missionary labour from the northern continents, instead of lavishing it on them. Should this ever become more than an ideal picture, he who surveys it, may retrace the course of time, as we have done, and, as he speculates on causes and effects, and takes his stand beside the turning point, the critical conjuncture, where the tide of our prosperity began to ebb—he may imagine that he sees Paul standing, as he stood in his own hired house at Rome, and stretching out his arms towards the perishing nations, and saying to the Christian Jews of this day, as he said to the Israelites of that, "Be it known unto you, therefore, that the salvation of God is sent unto the Gentiles, and that they will hear it."

I am far from venturing or wishing to put such anticipations in the place of higher motives, and especially of love to God and love to man, as stimulants to Christian effort. But if the bare imagination of such changes rouses us, and tends, in any measure, to enlarge and elevate our views beyond the dull routine of ordinary duties and of selfish interests, it cannot hurt us, and may do us good. I see not, therefore, why we should refuse to apply the last words of the text to ourselves, in the way of warning. There is no room here for invidious distinctions. None can censure others upon this point without censuring themselves. If we are conscious of inadequate exertions and of cold affections in this great cause, let us think of Israel according to the flesh, and of what he was and what he is—remember that such revolutions are still possible—that if we do not value Christianity enough to share it with the heathen, they may yet become possessed of it at our expense—nay, that while the glorious gospel is so commonly neglected and despised among ourselves, the word of this salvation is already sent unto the Gentiles, and that they will hear it—are hearing it.

But it is not only in the way of warning, that the words may be applied. They are also full of consolation and encouragement—of consolation for the eyes that weep and the hearts that bleed over our own spiritual desolations. Such, with all their zeal for God, are prone to walk by sight and not by faith, and to let their hopes and fears be too much governed by appearances. They are sometimes tempted by a spiritual pride, only more dangerous because insidious and unsuspected, to say, with the desponding prophet of old, "I have been very jealous for the Lord God of Hosts, for the children of Israel have forsaken thy covenant, and I, even I alone, am left." For such grief, and the unbelieving fears that breed it, an appropriate remedy is furnished by the doctrine "that God has visited the Gentiles, to take out of them a people for his name;" and that, although every ear and heart in Christendom should be henceforth and forever stopped against the word of life, "the salvation of God is sent unto the Gentiles, and they will hear it."

But the highest, best, and most important application of the words is yet to come. It is neither right nor salutary to dismiss this subject, with the tones of warning, and reproof, or even consolation, ringing in our ears. We sometimes lose as much by excessive or unreasonable lamentation over our defects and failures as by sheer neglect and apathy. The world is not to be converted, nor our quota of the work contributed, by passionate regrets that it is not yet done. The only profitable sorrow in such cases is that which, like the sorrow of repentance, ends in joy, or leads to it, by prompting to exertion. Our grief, too, must be mixed with gratitude, or it is selfish. Our paramount duty, in contemplation of the future and the past, is neither to presume nor to despair, but to thank God and take courage. To a soul thus humbled and yet excited, the tone of this scripture is encouraging, and I may even say exhilarating. For the truths of which it testifies are these—that this work is the work of God—that the salvation which we preach is his—that he has sent it, yes, and sent it to the Gentiles—and that they will hear it. And though among them, as among ourselves, many be called and few chosen, still this gospel of the kingdom must be preached in all the world, as a witness to all nations, before the end come. As Christ died, not for a nation but a world, so all kindreds, tongues, and peoples, must be represented in that great assembly, to be gathered on Mount Zion, when the kingdoms of the world shall have become the kingdoms of our Lord and of his Christ. As a necessary means to this appointed end, and as a pledge of its accomplishment, in spite of evil omens and discouraging appearances, be it known unto you, you who long for it and hasten towards it, that "the word of this salvation," "the salvation of God," is sent unto the Gentiles, and that they will hear it.

XVI.

1 PETER 1, 5.—Kept by the power of God through faith unto salvation.

THIS is only a fragment of a sentence, occurring in the midst of one of the most pregnant passages in the New Testament—one of the richest and most copious descriptions of the fruits of saving grace, and its effects upon its subjects. But, however undesirable it may be in general to insulate the doctrines of the Bible, and detach them from the context, upon which their just interpretation must depend, there is less objection here, because the clause selected, though really one link in a long chain, is like a literal link, complete in itself, as propounding a great doctrine of the Christian system, which admits of being separately looked at, and, indeed, must be so viewed, if we would see it distinctly, as the field of vision opened in the context is too vast to be embraced at one view, without painful effort and injurious confusion. Withdrawing our eyes, then, from the splendid but confounding spectacle presented in this passage, as a whole, of the divine love to believers, and its influence upon them, let us fix our attention, for a short time, on the apostolical description of them, as a class, "kept by the power of God through faith unto salvation."

The odium theologicum is now a proverb. The admiring cry of the old heathen—"See how these Christians love another," is supplanted by the sneer of the modern infidel—"See how these theologians hate one another." As usual, in the judgments of the world upon the Church, there is here a basis or substratum of truth, with a lofty superstructure of injustice and exaggeration. That earnest contention for the truth, once delivered to the saints, should be mixed with angry passions, is undoubtedly a fruit of human error and corruption. But that men should be most ardent and exacting, in relation to religious doctrines, and especially the doctrines of salvation, is both natural and rational. To expect men to be zealous and enthusiastic, as to minor matters, as to questions connected with their worldly business, their political interests, or even their most frivolous amusements, but entirely calm and self-possessed, dispassionate and even callous, when the points at issue have respect to moral duty and to spiritual truth, to God's glory and to man's salvation, is indirectly to deny the value and importance of religion, as compared with the affairs of this life, or at least to question the sincerity of those who give the former the precedence. If such sincerity exists, it must display itself precisely in the way objected to, by zeal and ardor in defending what is held to be the truth, proportioned to its absolute and relative importance. That is to say, what men value most highly, they not only may, but must defend most earnestly. And where this conviction and its natural effect exist, the purest zeal is too apt to be mixed with passionate excitement, and contaminated by some form of selfishness.

This is not suggested as an apology for such unhallowed mixtures, but simply as an explanation of the fact, that they occur in the defence of great religious truths, which has been often made the ground of an invidious charge against religion itself, as the direct and necessary source of such impure excitements, whereas it is only the occasion of their rising, when they do exist at all, to greater heights of violence, because the subjects which produce them are confessedly the most important that can possibly be made the subject of discussion or dispute. It does not follow, because angry brawls, in private life, are sinful, and should therefore be avoided, that a man is particularly blameable for being angry in defence of those who are nearest and dearest to him; or that his passionate excitability in their behalf is justly chargeable on his affection for them; or that in standing up for them he ought to be more cool and dispassionate, than when contending for a stranger, or for some trivial and indifferent matter. For the same reason, it is not so unreasonable, as some have represented, that when Christians lose their temper, or become too ardent in contending for their own views, these weaknesses should show themselves especially in vindicating what they prize most highly of religious truth, against weak misapprehension, artful misrepresentation, or malevolent aspersion.

Another fact often misrepresented in the same

way, is the fact that theological disputes are often sharpest, and apparently most angry, between those who, as to all important points, except the one directly in debate, are nearest to each other, and most perfectly agreed. This circumstance, though sometimes used to aggravate the alleged tendency of Christianity itself to stir up angry passions, is as easily accounted for as that already mentioned. It is natural, and not at all irrational, to feel especially astonished and displeased at the errors or the faults of those who are in other respects most exempt from both, because this very exemption implies a degree of elevation and intelligence with which it is difficult to reconcile particular obliquities of faith or practice. There may also be included, as contributing to this effect, the same cause, whatever it may be, that makes, and always has made, quarrels between near relations and familiar friends, proverbially violent, if not irreconcilable. Whether this be an effect of the same cause already mentioned—an instinctive application of the principle that from him who hath much, much will be required, and that near approximation to the truth, instead of extenuating, aggravates the guilt of any error still remaining, or the product of something in the state of the affections, or their very nature, which we cannot reach by our analysis or scrutiny, the fact itself is no more strange in one case than another, and can no more be alleged as a peculiar vice of theological dispute, than of private and domestic alienations. If the heat and asperity of family disputes ought to throw no discredit on the family relation, as intrinsically tending to foment such passions, with as little justice can the warmth and even rancour of religious controversy, even and especially between parties otherwise agreed, be justly charged on Christianity itself, or any specific forms of Christian doctrine, as possessing in themselves, or imparting to their votaries, the virus of malignant animosity; but as the intensity of feeling in the one case may be traced to the very nearness of their parties, and that intimate relation, which appears to make it most deplorable, so in the other case, religion and theology, and even the polemic form of Christianity, however vitiated by the presence of this sinful element, is certainly entitled to the benefit of just such explanations as we all admit to be allowable, if not unavoidable, in matters where religious truth is not concerned at all. What we ask for ourselves and our religion is not favour at the hands of men, but "even-handed justice."

But while all this may justly be alleged, if not in vindication, yet at least in explanation, of the violence commonly ascribed to doctrinal disputes between the great divisions of the Christian world, it still remains a lamentable fact that such alienations should exist, not only between those who are in most essential points agreed, but in reference to what they respectively regard as the most precious parts of Christian doctrine, the very parts which they consider as most intimately interwoven with their own experience, and with that of all believers. That alienations, both of judgment and of feeling, should exist just here, however it may be explained, is still to be deplored as an anomaly, to say the least of it, so painful and mysterious, that all affected by it ought to rejoice even in the possibility that it arises from misapprehension, and in all attempts, however feeble, to detect it in specific cases.

A striking illustrative example of these general considerations is afforded by that feature of the Calvinistic system, which is commonly known as the doctrine of final perseverance, as opposed to that of possible defection and perdition on the part of true believers and regenerated sinners. While the former of these doctrines has been cherished, in all ages, by a great body of professed believers, as among the clearest and most precious truths of their religion, it has been rejected by another, not simply as untrue, but as subversive of the Gospel, and as fraught with the most dangerous tendencies, in reference to personal holiness and ultimate salvation. The sincerity of many, upon both sides of this question, both in general as Christians, and in particular as champions of the doctrines thus contrasted, cannot be denied without denouncing all belief in testimony, and indeed in evidence on moral subjects; but this only makes it more desirable, if possible, to reduce the opposition to a mutual misunderstanding.

Without attempting any new or philosphical solution of this ancient problem, upon which so many mighty minds and pious hearts have spent their strength for ages, let us look once more to the objections to this doctrine, as they seem to weigh upon the minds, not of speculative theologians, but of practical experimental Christians, whose belief is in purpose and profession, founded on the word of God, and the experience of his people. How are such, in many cases, affected by the doctrine now in question?

The objections urged to it assume a twofold form, or may at least be readily reduced to two. The first is, that the doctrine is unscriptural; the second, that it is of evil tendency. On close inspection, these two objections will be found to be further reducible to one, or one of them at least so dependent on the other, that they cannot be regarded as entirely distinct. That is to say, the objection to the doctrine as unscriptural, has no substantive existence or foundation, apart from its imputed or alleged pernicious tendencies in practice. It is not denied, or cannot be denied, with any show of probability, that there are expressions in the word of God, which do at first sight, and according to their obvious and superficial import, strongly favor the obnoxious doctrine. It is also certain that the strong presumption thus created, is not shaken, or at least not nullified by any explicit allegation of the contrary, or by the clear and unequivocal assertion of things plainly incompatible and inconsistent with the odious dogma of a final perseverance. That neither of these possible cases is a real one—that is to say, that there is no categorical denial of this doctrine, or any statement absolutely inconsistent with it, is abundantly clear from the existence of so large and so intelligent a class, both of interpreters and ordinary readers, who are thoroughly persuaded that the doctrine, far from being contradicted, is expressly and dogmatically taught in Scripture. They may be mistaken in so thinking; but the error would be inconceivable if there were no ground or even colour for maintaining it, much more if it were formally or certainly condemned. The true cause, therefore, of the confidence with which it is rejected as unscriptural, must be its real or imaginary tendency to practical experimental evil; or, in other words, it is believed to be unscriptural because it is believed to be pernicious. What appears to be said in its favour, is explained away, and what is adverse to it is exaggerated, under the impression of the foregone conclusion, that the doctrine is of evil tendency.

Since, then, the scriptural objection really depends upon the practical or moral one, the question now arises, what the latter is, and wherein it consists? What is the evil tendency imputed to this feared and hated doctrine, not by its spiteful and deliberate calumniators, but by its sincere and honest adversaries —those who really believe that an opinion so pernicious in its influence on character and conduct, cannot be a doctrine of the Bible? When attentively considered, the objectionable features of the doctrine as sincerely viewed by this class, may be said to be these two : That it assumes the final perseverance of the saints, to be secured by a power inherent in themselves, or by something in the very nature of a saving change, precluding all defection as a sheer impossibility, entirely irrespective of the subject's own religious state and dispositions, or of any influence exterior to him, over and above the impulse given at conversion, or the *vis inertiæ* of his new-born nature— a belief which may be justly charged with tending to indulge a proud reliance upon self, and an habitual security, alike dishonouring to God and dangerous to man.

The other feature of this doctrine, as held by its

opponents, is, that the only proof which it requires of the saving change, from which it draws its proud security and absolute immunity from danger, is the consciousness or memory of inward exercises, not susceptible of formal proof, and wholly independent of the actual condition of the subject at the time when he asserts his claim to this prerogative or privilege of absolute exemption from the risk or possibility of a fall from grace. Whatever may be the specific form in which the honest opposition to this doctrine clothes itself, and which may be indefinitely varied by fortuitous or incidental causes, it will always prove, upon a close analysis, or even an accurate inspection, to involve, as the essential grounds of condemnation and rejection, the two assumptions which have just been stated, as to an inherent independent power of self-preservation, and the sufficiency of mere subjective states and exercises, to demonstrate the possession of that power, as belonging to the doctrine of a final perseverance.

Such being, then, the very grounds of the objection to this doctrine as unscriptural, the reasons for believing that it cannot be propounded in the word of God, whatever tends to show that it involves no such assumptions as are thus imputed to it, and then made the proofs of its pernicious tendency, must go so far to clear it from the charge of such a tendency, as necessarily belonging to it, or proceeding from it, and entitle its defenders to insist upon the plain sense, now no longer admissible, at least in this direction, of the places where it seems to be expressly taught. To prove this negative, although the burden of the proof might well be left to rest on those who make the affirmation, is still not difficult, and may indeed be satisfactorily done by an appeal to any of the numerous expressions which are reckoned by the champions of the doctrine as decisive in its favour. Such a proof may be deduced, for example, from the words of the Apostle Peter, in the text, which has always been classed among the clearest recognitions, if not among the most direct and formal affirmations, of the truth in question.

So far, then, is this scripture, as expounded in our system, from referring the continued safety of believers to a power inherent in themselves, or necessarily evolved in the process of regeneration, viewed as a subjective change, that, while it clearly and emphatically represents them as securely kept, garrisoned, or guarded, as the military term in the original denotes, suggesting the idea of complete and perpetual protection from the paramount dominion of their spiritual enemies, this preservation is explicitly described as the effect of a power exterior and superior to themselves; nay, still more unequivocally and expressly, as affected by a sovereign, a divine, an almighty agency, "kept by the *power of God* unto salvation"—not merely capable of being so kept, but in fact, and actually so kept; not as a peculiar favour in the case of some, but as a constant and a necessary incident to the condition of all true believers; not as a mere contingency dependent on the unrevealed design and will of God, but as an ascertained and verified reality, attested by experience at present, and secured for the future by the promised covenant and oath of One who cannot lie.

Of such a doctrine, where is the pernicious tendency? If all depends upon the action of Omnipotence; if perseverance is as much beyond our own control as that original mutation of our spiritual state in which we are said to persevere; if we can no more, in and of ourselves, secure our own continuance in this state, than we could create it, or create ourselves, or than we could create a world;—if this is our position, as defined by the very texts from which we prove the doctrine to be true, "where is boasting then? It is excluded!"

It may be said, however, that although the power which secures our perseverance is entirely exterior and superior to ourselves, and is, in fact, no other than the sovereign and almighty power of God, yet if we look upon its exercise as absolutely and irrevocably pledged for our protection, the tendency of this belief to generate security and license, is as evident and strong as if the power were inherent in ourselves; nay, more so, since the power, instead of being finite, is now infinite; instead of being human, is divine; instead of being ours, is God's; and yet completely under our control. This specious representation quietly assumes that we ascribe the perseverance of believers to an absolute immediate act of power, without the use of means or the prescription of conditions; that God has irrevocably pledged the exercise of his omnipotence to save from the very possibility of falling, every sinner who has once believed and been converted, be his subsequent experience and his actual condition what it may; and, as a necessary consequence, that he who once had satisfying evidence of having undergone a saving change, may now and forever claim the covenanted exercise of God's omnipotence to save him even from the just and natural effects of his own evident apostasy and lapse into a state of impenitence and unbelief; in short, that he who once believed, or rather once believed that he believed, will certainly be "kept by the power of God unto salvation," whether now, or at any future time, or through eternity, be he a believer or an unbeliever. Of such, if any such there be, as live and die in this faith, we may well say, in the words of an apostle, "their damnation slumbereth not."

But see again, how this aspersion on the doctrine in dispute, whether cast in malice or in ignorance, is wiped off, and its foul stain utterly effaced forever, by the simple but authoritative language of the text, which, so far from representing this conservative agency of God's grace and omnipotence, as acting independently of faith in the preserved and persevering subject, holds up faith itself as in a certain sense the means by which the perseverance is secured, by which the preservation is effected, "KEPT BY THE POWER OF GOD THROUGH FAITH UNTO SALVATION."

Now, Faith, as both the parties to this controversy are agreed, is not a thing to be assumed at pleasure or at random, but to be established by conclusive evidence; not that of consciousness or memory or fancy, but of actual experience and practice. "Faith without works is dead." The only true faith is the faith that "works by love," and "overcomes the world," and "purifies the heart," and brings forth "all the fruits of the Spirit," which are also the "fruits meet for repentance." "By their fruits ye shall know them." Where these fruits are not, there is no evidence of faith. Where faith is not, there is no pledge of God's omnipotence to save from falling. It is only those who have this faith and bear this fruit, that have a right to claim a place among the happy souls who are "kept by the power of God through faith unto salvation." If this doctrine, as propounded in this one text, and harmoniously exhibited in many others, and frequently implied or presupposed where it is not expressed, pervading the whole tissue of the system of salvation, like a golden thread, not always visible, but always there; if this doctrine is pernicious in its tendency, then so is truth, and holiness itself. If this view of God's sovereignty and man's dependence, in the matter of salvation and of final perseverance; if this view of the absolute necessity of faith, of vital, operative, fruitful faith, as the only condition on which, the only means by which, the omnipotence of God will act to save us from apostasy; if this doctrine tends of itself to Antinomian license and security, then out of the same fountain may flow salt water and fresh—then men may expect to gather grapes of thorns, and figs of thistles, and may be excused for calling evil good and good evil, putting light for darkness and darkness for light, putting bitter for sweet and sweet for bitter!

But, although the doctrine in itself has no such tendency, its perversion and abuse has. It becomes us, therefore, to consider in conclusion its liability to such abuse. That such a liability exists, is clear from the fact which gave occasion to this whole discussion —the fact that multitudes of seemingly devout and humble Christians have learned to regard it with a holy horror. Erroneous as their judgment may and must be, it is far less likely to have been derived from the weakness of the proofs by which the doctrine is supported, than from the lives in which it is exemplified. There is also something in the very nature of the doctrine which exposes it to misapprehension, not only on the part of its opponents, but of those who plead for it and undertake to act upon it. It presents, as it were, so many points of aberration, where the mind is exposed to a centrifugal impetus towards error. There is so much danger of mistake, and so much actual mistake, with respect to the very nature of salvation, as deliverance from punishment and not from sin, and with respect to perseverance, in the very points which we have been considering, so much danger of mistake as to the power by which it is secured, and which is nothing more nor less than the power of God himself, as to the means by which that power operates, and which is nothing more nor less than faith—a state of saving faith produced and perpetuated by divine grace; and finally, as to the evidence that such a state exists, which is nothing more nor less than holy living or good works, in the highest and most scriptural sense of the expression, there is so much danger of departure from the truth, at all these points, that we who hold the doctrine as a precious part of our religious faith, and as one of the clearest and most unambiguous teachings of the Bible, are under a peculiar obligation to preserve it from abuse, not only by its enemies, but by its friends; not only by others, but by ourselves; not only in our theory, but in our practice; not only in the statement and defence of our belief, but in the commentary on it which is furnished by our lives. To this circumspection we are called by a regard to our own safety, which is jeoparded by nothing more than by the culpable perversion of the most important and most precious doctrines. In this sense, none are more exposed to danger than those who have within their reach the most effective means of safety. Especially let us who preach the gospel, or expect to preach it, see to it that our example and experience afford no confirmation of the old and profound saying: "Nearest the Church furthest from God." We should also be induced to use this caution by a jealous sensibility in reference to the honour of our God and Saviour, lest through our perversion or abuse of this great doctrine, he should seem to be capable of winking at iniquity, or even be a minister of sin.

And, lastly, we should be induced to use a wise precaution, for the sake of those who hate the doctrine which we love, as soul-destroying error, lest their misapprehensions should, through our unfaithfulness and indiscretion, be hopelessly confirmed, and their antipathy to what they reckon false, embittered into hatred of persons who, to say the least, are quite as likely as themselves to be "kept by the power of God through faith unto salvation!"

XVII.

TITUS 2, 11-15.—For the grace of God that bringeth salvation hath appeared to all men, teaching us that, denying ungodliness and worldly lusts, we should live soberly, righteously, and godly, in this present world; looking for that blessed hope, and the glorious appearing of the great God and our Saviour Jesus Christ; who gave himself for us, that he might redeem us from all iniquity, and purify unto himself a peculiar people, zealous of good works. These things speak, and exhort, and rebuke with all authority. Let no man despise thee.

THE being of a God, with all that enters into that conception, being once established or assumed as true, the grand problem of humanity is to determine our relation to him; not as creatures merely, for that is settled by the very conditions of our being, but as sinners. Sin has disturbed and revolutionized the mutual relation between God and man, and as the one is entirely dependent on the other for his being and wellbeing, the inquiry into this effect of sin becomes something more than a curious speculation—it becomes a practical question of the highest import, one of life and death. All other questions, whether speculative or practical, are as nothing until this is solved. Not what is God, but what is God to us? in what aspect are we to behold him? as an absolute sovereign, an inexorable judge, an irresistible avenger, or as a Saviour, a deliverer, or friend? What have we to expect from him, wrath or favour?

If man had never fallen, the answer to this question might have been readily deduced from the essential attributes of the Divine nature, but the intervention of sin seems to bring these into conflict, so that what would otherwise be prompted by God's goodness is forbidden by his justice. The confusion thus introduced into the subject gives it, when seriously considered, an aspect of awful complication and uncertainty, which may be likened to the struggle between light and darkness, clouds and sunshine, on a doubtful day. That the sun is there, no one can doubt, nor that his rays are bright and genial, but between them and the eye of the spectator there is something interposed, and how long this obstruction is to last he knows not. Upon such a sky, the whole race may be said to have been gazing, with more or less attention and solicitude for ages after the fall, as if they expected every moment to see the divine countenance revealed, but knew not whether its expression would be one of unappeased displeasure, or of grace and favour.

The great event in the history of fallen man is, that it was the grace of God that appeared, not merely as benignity in general, but as favour to the lost, the ruined, the condemned; not as an inert though friendly disposition, but as active favour, saving grace, the grace that brings salvation or deliverance from loss, from danger, from actual ruin, and from the wrath to come. Such is the grace of God which has appeared or been revealed, and the epiphany of which is here alleged by the apostle to have been vouchsafed to all men without national or other accidental distinctions; not to the Jews or any other nation, not to the rich or any other class exclusively, but to men in general, to mankind at large.

That this is the true sense of "all men" in the text is clear from the connection. In the foregoing verses, he had urged upon servants their peculiar duties, and assigned as a motive to fidelity, the honour which it would put upon the true religion as revealed and taught by God our Saviour. To some in their exclusive pride, both Jews and Gentiles, this might seem ridiculous; as if the honour of religion could depend upon the conduct of a slave, and therefore the apostle takes occasion to remind such, that the motives by which Christianity operates on character and conduct, are confined to no one class, but are common to the human race, because Christianity itself as a remedial system, as a vehicle by which the saving grace of God is brought to us, has no respect of persons in the sense assumed, but has appeared to all men; or, as the sentence may be construed, is saving to all men; that is, adapted and designed to save them without regard to difference of rank or nation. But as this "grace of God" is not inert but active, so its effect upon its objects is an active one, not only efficacious in itself, but such as to produce activity, to make *them* act, not blindly or at random, but in obedience to an active principle, and in due subjection to a moral discipline. The "saving grace of God which has appeared to all men," is described by the apostle as "teaching us," or rather educating, training us in such a way as to secure the precious fruits that follow. The meaning is not, as it might seem to a superficial reader, that the gospel simply teaches us that we ought to deny ungodliness and so on; *i. e.* makes us understand our obligations so to do; this is indeed included, but far more; the full sense of the language is, that Christianity subjects those who embrace it to a discipline, a systematic training, a moral and spiritual education, so that, as a natural result, nay a necessary consequence, they do in point of fact deny ungodliness and worldly lusts. To "teach" men that they "should" do this is something, it is much, but it is far from being all that Christianity accomplishes. It is a characteristic and essential feature of the gospel that it does men good by putting them to school, by making them disciples, not simply for the purpose of communicating knowledge, but for that of forming and maturing character; for *education* in the highest, largest, and most emphatic sense.

This pedagogical design and character of true religion is stamped upon all its institutions, and legible even in its phraseology. It is not by an unmeaning figure of speech, nor with any attenuation of the primary sense of the expression, that Christians are continually called disciples, *i. e.* learners, pupils, and that the ministers of Christ are spoken of as teachers. Equally false, though false in opposite extremes, is the opinion that knowledge, and consequently teaching, are of no avail in spiritual matters, and the opinion that perfect knowledge is a previous condition of admission to the kingdom of heaven. Some knowledge is indeed an indispensable pre-requisite, but woe to him who imagines that these elements of wisdom are enough, and that he needs no further or more complete indoctrination. Is the child sent to school because it knows so much already, or because it knows so little, and in order that it may know more? Well in this sense too, it may be said to all who seek admission to the body of believers, and a share in the communion of saints, "Except ye be converted, and become as little children, ye shall not enter into the kingdom of heaven." The church is Christ's school; he who enters it must enter as a learner, a disciple, with as real and sincere a deference to his great teacher as the little child feels, when it trembles for the first time in the presence of a master.

Such submission is the more imperative in this case, because more truly than in any other case the process of instruction is moral as well as intellectual; it is not mere teaching, it is training, education; not the mere acquisition of knowledge, although that does lie at the foundation, but the cultivation of the powers and affections, as a preparation for the joys and services of heaven, as well as for the duties and the trials of this present state. The "grace of God" which has appeared as the only means and source of salvation to all men, does not save them by a charm or by a demonstration, but by making them disciples in the school of Christ, by teaching them and training them for earth and heaven, developing their faculties, moulding their affections, forming their characters, determining their lives. The design and the legitimate effect of this disciplinary process are distinctly stated in the text, with reference both to the present and the future; both in a negative and positive form.

The negative design of all this training is that we deny, repudiate, or abjure allegiance, to the sinful dispositions and affections which are paramount in fallen nature, but the objects of which perish in the using, being limited to this world, so that they may be described as "worldly lusts" or desires, and may be said, so far as they predominate, to put man on a level with the brutes, whose highest good is present enjoyment of the lowest kind. By all who would be saved, these worldly, temporal, and short-lived lusts must be denied, renounced; and this is never done without a simultaneous or previous denial of ungodliness, of all indifference and enmity to God, which is indeed the source of the other, for when human hearts are right towards God, the paramount control of worldly lusts becomes impossible. It is because men do not love God that they love the world unduly; it is therefore that the friendship of the world and that of God are represented by another apostle as wholly incompatible. To this denial of the world as our home, and of its lusts as our principles of action, Christianity trains us; not merely informing us of what is wrong, but educating us to hate and shun it.

This however is only the negative part of the effect produced by the spiritual discipline to which we are subjected in the school of Christ. It has a positive side also. It teaches us how we are to live. It does not lose sight of the present state either in profound abstractions, or in fond anticipations of the future. It adapts and purifies the heathen maxim, dum vivimus vivamus, while we live let us live to some good purpose. The positive effect of Christianity as a system of discipline or training, is to rectify the life in all its most momentous aspects and relations in reference to ourselves, our neighbours, and our God. In reference to himself, the true disciple in this school is educated to be sober or sound-minded; the original expression denotes sanity as opposed to madness, not in its extreme forms merely, but in all its more familiar and less violent gradations; all those numberless and nameless aberrations of the judgment which give character to human conduct, even in the absence of gross crime or absolute insanity. From these irrational vagaries, true religion, as a system of discipline and education, tends to free us, and so far as we are really set free, it is by this means and by this alone. The errors thus insensibly corrected are too many to be numbered and too various to be classified.

Among the most important are those visionary estimates of self and of the world by which the mass of men are led astray; those "strong delusions," with respect to good and evil, right and wrong, true and false, happiness and misery, which, both by their absurdity, and by their ruinous effects fully justify that terrible description, "Madness is in their hearts while they live, and after that they go to the dead." In opposition to this "madness," the saving grace of God trains its subjects to be rational or sober, and thus in the highest sense and measure to be faithful to themselves. But at the same time it trains them to be faithful to others, to be just, in the wide sense of the term; one of constant occurrence in the Scriptures, and especially in the Old Testament; including all that one can owe another; including therefore charity and mercy, no less than honesty and rigorous exactness in the discharge of legal obligations. Justice or rectitude, in this enlarged and noble sense, as opposed to every form of selfishness, is no less really a dictate and a consequence of spiritual training, than sanity or soundness of mind, as opposed to the chimeras and hallucinations of our state by nature. But "soberness" and "justice," in the wide sense which has just been put upon the terms have never yet been found divorced from "godliness." As we have seen already, in considering the negative effects of training by divine grace, it is man's relations to his God, that must adjust and determine his relations to his fellow-creatures. The symmetrical position of the points in the circumference arises from their common relation to a common centre. Set a man right with God, and he will certainly be set right with his neighbours. The remaining exceptions as to this point only show the imperfection of his piety, but do not disprove its existence. In spite of all such exceptions, it is still true that the man who loves God loves his neighbour and himself, not with a frenzied, but a rational attachment, and that he who enters as a pupil in the school of Christ must lay his account, not merely in the way of negative abstinence, to deny ungodliness and worldly lusts, but in the way of positive performance to "live soberly, righteously, and godly in this present world."

Such are the objects and effects of Christian training, that is of the method by which Christ trains his disciples, with respect to the present state or stage of man's existence, as distinguished from those future states or stages to which he cannot but look forward. For although the sobriety of mind produced by the discipline of God's grace, causes men of a morbid, penurious disposition to lose sight of present duties and enjoyments in a vague anticipation of the future, it is so far from excluding expectation altogether, that our very salvation is prospective. "We are saved in hope," and that hope is a blessed one; a hope of blessedness to be revealed and realized hereafter; a hope, *i. e.* an object of hope, not yet fully enjoyed, but only "looked for," and to look for which is one of the effects and marks of thorough training in the school of Christ. A religion without hope must have been learned elsewhere. The saving grace of God instructs us, while we "live soberly, righteously, and godly" in this present world, to look for the fulfilment of that blessed hope, in reference to which we are said, by an anticipation of our own experience, to be saved already.

This hope is neither selfish nor indefinite. It does not terminate upon ourselves, our own deliverance from suffering, and our own reception into heaven; nor does it lose itself in vague anticipations of a nameless good to be experienced hereafter. The Christian's hope is in the highest degree generous and well-defined. It is generous, because it rises beyond personal interests, even the highest, even personal salvation, to the glory of the Saviour as the ultimate end to be desired and accomplished. It is well-

defined, because, instead of looking at this glory in
the abstract, it gives it a concrete and personal embodiment;
it is glory, not in the sense of the metaphysician
or of the poet, but in that of the prophets,
saints, and angels; it is manifested and apparent
excellence, a glorious epiphany, analogous to that
which marked Jehovah's presence in the Holy of
Holies, but unspeakably transcending it in permanence
and brightness; the glorious appearance, not of
any mere creature, even the most noble, but of God
himself, and yet not of God in his essence, which is
inaccessible to sense, nor even in some special and
distinct manifestation of the Father, or the Godhead,
under an assumed or borrowed form of which the
senses may take cognizance, but in the well-known
person of his Son, who is the brightness of his glory,
and the express image of his person, in whom dwelleth
all the fulness of the Godhead bodily; and therefore
it is not the untempered brightness of the divine
majesty, and holiness, and justice which to us is, and
must be a consuming fire; and yet it is the manifested
glory of God, of the great God; great in all conceivable
perfections, but as the object of this hope, emphatically
great in mercy, great in the power not to
punish and destroy, but to forgive and save, to save
the sinner, to save us; the glorious appearing of our
great God and Saviour Jesus Christ. This hope is
definite and vast enough to fill the mind and satisfy
the heart, however vague may be its views and apprehensions
with respect to the precise time, and
place, and form, and other circumstances of the epiphany
expected. It is enough to know that it is Christ

our Head who shall appear; and thanks be to God, that when he does appear we shall be like him for we shall see him as he is. These two considerations—the personal identity of that which is to be revealed in glory, and the prospect of personal assimilation to this glorious object—are enough to make us willing to be ignorant of all that concerns merely the chronology, or geography, or poetry of that blessed hope and glorious appearing of our great God and Saviour Jesus Christ, which the word of God not only suffers, but requires us to look for, as a sure sign, because an unavoidable effect, of genuine, thorough, successful training in the school of Christ, and under the educating guidance of that "saving grace," which, for this very purpose, has "appeared," or been revealed "to all men."

Let it not be overlooked, however, that the gospel, while it sets Christ before us as an object of believing expectation, sets him also before us an object of believing recollection, and thus brings into a delightful harmony the hope of favours yet to be experienced with gratitude for those experienced already. It is not simply as a glorious person, human or divine, that we look for his appearing; it is not simply as a Saviour or Deliverer from evil in the general; it is not simply as a potential Saviour or Deliverer, one who can save us if he will, and will if we should need it at some future time; not merely a Saviour whose ability and willingness to save are yet to be displayed and proved, but as an actual deliverer, as one who has already done his saving work, by giving himself for us, the highest gift, it may in a certain sense be said, of which even he was capable, for us, his creatures, his rebellious subjects, his despisers, and his enemies! Had he given infinitely less for us, it might have been too much for justice, too much for mercy, for any mercy but for that of God; but he gave all that he could give, for he gave himself to assume our nature, to be degraded, to be mocked at, to be put to death. He did not merely give his name, his friendship, or his royal favour, but he gave himself! In the highest, strongest, most exhaustive meaning that the words will bear, he "gave *himself*" and "gave himself *for us*." This he *has done*, and he has done it for a purpose, and by every law of gratitude, as well as interest, we are bound, so far as that purpose concerns us, to do what we can for its accomplishment.

What then was his object? To *redeem* us, to buy us back from bondage, to save us by the payment of a ransom-price, not only from the punishment of sin, but from its power, from its love, from its pollution, from its foul and hideous embrace, no less than from its sword and from its chains. It was to set us free from sin itself that Christ redeemed us; not from some sin, but from all sin; not that we should still remain, or afterwards fall back under the dominion of the very tyrant from whose power he redeemed us; not that we should merely exchange one hard master for another, or for many; no, he "gave himself for us," he laid down his life for us, he died upon the cross for us, "that he might redeem us from *all iniquity*."

Nor was this deliverance from sin as well as punishment intended merely for our advantage but for His. He had an end to accomplish for himself. He died to purify us, not merely that we might be pure and therefore happy, but also to purify a people for himself; a peculium, a possession of his own, a church, a body of which he should be the head, a kingdom of which he should be the sovereign. Over none but a purified and holy kingdom could he condescend to reign. Of none but a purified and holy body could he be the Head. Justification would have done but half the work for which Christ died; his end would not have been accomplished if he had not redeemed us from iniquity as well as condemnation, if he had not purified a people for himself, for his own use and his own honour; a people in their measure like himself, his own exclusively, his own forever, his inalienable right, his indefeasible possession, his "peculiar people."

How monstrous then the supposition or pretence that the design of Christ's death is reconcileable with Antinomian license on the part of those for whom he died; that because he died to make men holy, therefore they need not be holy; that because he gave himself for us, to purify a people for himself, therefore we may be his people, and yet not be pure; that because his "good works" have been set to our account, we need do no "good works" for him. The very contrary commends itself as evidently true to gratitude, to conscience, nay to common sense. The body, the church, the kingdom, the peculiar people of Christ, without good works, without fruits meet for repentance, without experimental evidence of union to him by faith, is an absurdity, an odious contradiction, a blasphemous aspersion; as if God could deny himself; as if the Son of God could be the "minister of sin." So far from dispensing with "good works" on our part, he is not even satisfied with good works practised or performed from stress of conscience, or from habit, or from fear, or as a sheer formality. To such works indeed he denies the attribute of goodness, for they lack the very quality by which alone they could be rendered good, at least in His sight. It is not the moral or the physical effect on others, nor the outward conformity to rule, nor the solemnity with which the action is performed, that constitutes it good. It must be wrought in faith and love; not only love to man, but love to God, and love to Christ, or it is worthless. Nay, he asks still more to make good works acceptable. He asks that they be wrought with *strong* affection, with intensity of spirit, with a burning zeal; a zeal of God, according to knowledge. The people whom he died to purify for himself, must be not only pure and diligent, but zealous; not merely passive and submissive, but spontaneous, eager, emulous, to please him, "his peculiar people zealous of good works."

All the doctrines here presented are, or ought to be, familiar to our minds as household words, and elementary ideas. The mode, in which I have endeavoured to exhibit them, is not, as I am well aware, the most agreeable to that taste which prefers points to lines, and lines to surfaces, and surfaces to depth and substance. It is well, however, at least sometimes, to contemplate the familiar truths of Christianity, not merely as they may be picked out, and adjusted in an artificial system, but as they lie upon the face of Scripture, and as they were associated in the minds of the inspired writers, and the primitive disciples. The more attentively we read the word of God, the more highly shall we be disposed to value these original associations, the affinities as well as the intrinsic qualities of saving truth, not merely the more recondite affinities disclosed by philosophical analysis, but those more obvious ones suggested by juxtaposition in the letter of the Scriptures. In this, as in so many other cases, we may learn from experience that "the foolishness of God is wiser than men."

But whatever we may think, as to the form of presentation, let us guard against a mistake as to the truths themselves. They are here exhibited, not only as objects of belief, but as subjects of instruction. The writing which contains them, is a pastoral epistle; filled with the advice and apostolical injunctions of "Paul the aged," to a spiritual child and an official representative, and through him to the ministry of that age, and of this, and every other. In reference to all the foregoing precepts, but especially to those immediately preceding, which have been the subject of discourse this morning, he says to Titus: "These things speak," talk of them, both in public, and in private, make them the theme of conversation, as well as of formal preaching. Do not be content with thinking of them, understanding and believing them, but *speak them*, utter them, impart them to your hearers, to your friends and neighbours, to your pupils and parishioners, your brethren in the ministry, your equals and inferiors in office, to all with whom you come in contact, or to whom you have access, "these things speak."

But how? As curious and interesting matters of opinion, or the dictates of a mere theoretical wisdom? Not at all, but as matters to be acted *on* and acted *out*, as involving not merely truths to be believed, but duties to be done, and to the doing of which, men must be aroused and prompted. "These things speak *and exhort;*" on the basis of sound doctrine rear the superstructure of sound practice, in your own case and in that of others. To yourself, to all who hear you, to all who need the admonition "these things *speak and exhort!*"

But what, if men resist these humbling truths, and angrily reject them? No matter, only add *reproof* to exhortation—not arbitrary and passionate reproof, but, as the word here used denotes, reproof produced by and founded on conviction. Convince them of the truth, and convict them of their guilt, and then reprove them. Appeal not only to their reason, but their conscience, "these things speak, and exhort, and rebuke," not in your own name, nor in mine, but in His name, whose you are, and whom you serve; as asserting his rights, and as holding his commission, be not afraid or ashamed to speak the truth, but whenever the occasion is afforded, "these things speak and exhort, and rebuke with all authority!"

But what if men treat you and your message with levity. "Let no man despise thee." This suggests two ideas, both of which are useful and appropriate to us. Let no man despising thee, prevent the full discharge of certain duty. "He that despiseth you, despiseth me, and he that despiseth me, despiseth him that sent me." If men will despise God and Christ, the human messenger may well consent to be despised along with them. Let them despise thee, but let not the effect be caused by cowardly supression, or disingenuous corruption of the truth on your part. As a faithful messenger of God and an ambassador of Christ, let men despise you, if they will or if they must, let them despise you at their peril. But as a traitor to the truth and to its author, let no man despise thee. "For this is thankworthy, if a man for conscience toward God endure grief, suffering wrongfully. For what glory is it, if when ye be buffeted for your faults, ye shall take it patiently; but if, when ye do well, and suffer for it, ye take it patiently, this is acceptable with God. For even hereunto were ye called, because Christ also suffered for us, leaving us an example that ye should follow his steps." . . . . . "Who is he that will harm you, if ye be followers of that which is good? But and if ye suffer for righteousness' sake, happy are ye." . . . . . "For it is better, if the will of God be so, that ye suffer for well-doing than for evil-doing.". . . . . "If ye be reproached for the name of Christ, happy are ye, for the spirit of glory and of God resteth upon you; on their part he is evil-spoken of, but on your part, he is glorified." . . . . . "If any man suffer as a Christian, let him not be ashamed, but let him glorify God on this behalf." These consolatory warnings drawn from the experience of another great apostle, and one who well knew what it was to suffer both for his own faults, and the name of Christ, may serve to illustrate and to qualify Paul's pointed charge. "Let no man despise thee." To us, my brethren, who preach the gospel or expect to

preach it, and especially to those of you who are
soon to enter on that difficult but necessary, dangerous
but blessed work, the words of the apostle have
peculiar interest; for in reference to these simple but
essential truths, which we have been considering, and
to the risk of error or unfaithfulness in teaching them,
"he being dead yet speaketh," saying, not only to
the church at large, but more directly to each one of
us, "These things speak, and exhort, and rebuke with
all authority. Let no man despise thee!"

XVIII.

Luke 22, 32.—When thou art converted, strengthen thy brethren.

There is nothing in which self-ignorance displays itself more frequently than in men's estimation of their own strength and weakness. It is enough that they consider themselves strong when they are weak. They go still further, and consider themselves strongest at the very points where they are weakest. Hence the easy conquest of the tempter by assailing men at those points which require protection most, but which enjoy it least. Nothing is more familiar as a trait of human character, than the disposition to be vain or proud of foibles and weaknesses. A striking historical example of this error and its fruits is afforded by the character of Peter. His intrepidity and self-reliance might have seemed to constitute his strength, and yet we find them lying at the root of his defections. This was the case even in those minor aberrations which incurred our Lord's rebuke from time to time.

But it is still more clear, in reference to his great fall, the denial of his master. To himself this seemed incredible, even when predicted, as it is in the passage whence the text is taken. But along with his fall our Lord predicts his restoration or conversion.

"When thou art converted." This might seem to imply that Peter was before an unconverted man, or that his fall was an entire fall from grace. Both these conclusions are forbidden by the promise which immediately precedes the exhortation of the text. "Simon, Simon, Satan hath desired to have you that he may sift you as wheat; but I have prayed for thee that thy faith fail not." These last words prove (1) that he had faith, and (2) that his faith was not entirely to fail. Nor will the context bear any other explanation of the word "faith" but as meaning that which constitutes a true believer. The conversion, therefore, here immediately referred to, is not the primary original conversion of a sinner from his natural condition to the love of God, but a reconversion of one who had been before converted.

This reconversion is connected in the text with a peculiar influence to be exerted on his brethren, *i. e.*, those in the same situation, exposed to the same temptations, in danger of a like fall. "Strengthen thy brethren," *i. e.*, confirm their faith, preserve them from the same disgrace which has befallen thee. This strengthening effect was not to be wrought by any natural power of Peter, nor by any official authority conferred upon him. It was only to be the product of a moral influence created by the very circumstances of the case, *i. e.*, by the very fact of his conversion. And as this conversion may exist in other cases, too, it will, perhaps, afford a profitable theme for meditation to inquire what it is and how it operates. The only division of the subject needed, is the one presented by the text itself—(1) When thou art converted, (2) strengthen thy brethren. (1) Conversion: (2) Strengthening the brethren.

In speaking briefly of the first, I shall begin with conversion in general, and afterwards advert to reconversion in particular. The term conversion is so familiar in its spiritual sense and application, that we seldom think of it as metaphorical. But the original terms corresponding both to this word and its cognate forms convért and cónvert, are applied even in the New Testament to physical as well as moral changes. To this primary usage of the words it may be useful to revert, not only for the purpose of determining their essential import, but to mark certain gradations in their meaning as applied both to natural and spiritual objects. The essential primary idea is that of a corporeal turning round, without any thing to limit it. The act described may be that of turning round and round indefinitely, still coming back to the original position, and then leaving it again, in a perpetual succession of rotations. But to this original notion which is inseparable from the word, usage in many cases adds certain accessory notions. One of these is the idea of turning in a definite direction, *i. e.*, towards a certain object. The difference is that between a wheel's turning on its axis and a flower turning towards the sun. But in some connections there is a still further accession to the primary idea; so that the words necessarily suggest not the mere act of turning, nor the act of turning in a definite direction, but the act of turning from one object to another, which are then, of course, presented in direct antithesis to one another.

VOL. I.—15

Thus the magnetic needle, if mechanically pointed towards the south, is no sooner set at liberty than it will turn from that point to the north. In this case, however, there is still another accessory motion added to the simple one of turning, namely, that of turning back to a point from which it had before been turned away. And this idea of return or retroversion may of course be repeated without limit, and without any further variation of the meaning of the term used, which is still the same, whether the turning back be for the first or second, tenth or hundredth time. All these distinctions or gradations may be traced also in the spiritual uses of the term. As thus applied, conversion is a change of character, *i. e.*, of principles and affections, with a corresponding change of outward life.

Now, such a change may be conceived of, as a vague, unsettled, frequently repeated revolution of the views and feelings, without any determinate character or end. But the conversion spoken of in Scripture is relieved from this indefiniteness by a constant reference to one specific object to which the convert turns. It is to God, that all conversion is described as taking place. But how, in what sense, does man turn to God? The least and lowest that can be supposed to enter into this conception, is a turning to God, as an object of attention or consideration, turning, as it were, for the first time, to look at him, just as we might turn towards any object of sense which had before escaped attention or been out of sight. This is, in fact, a necessary part of the experimental process of conversion.

To the mind in its natural condition, God is absent or unseen as an object of attentive contemplation. When a change is effected, one of the first symptoms is a turning of the soul to look at him, to gaze upon him, often with wonder at the blindness or stupidity which kept him so long out of view. This change of feeling can by no corporeal movement be so well represented as by that of turning round to look at something which before was out of sight. But the same influence which brings about this simple contemplation of God as an object before unknown or disregarded, gives it a higher character by fixing the attention on the attributes of the object, so that what might have been a gaze of curiosity, is deepened into one of admiration; and, as the absolute perfection of the excellence admired becomes apparent, into one of adoration; and as the personal affections become more and more enlisted, into one of love and confidence and self-devotion. Thus the turning which the word of God describes as necessary to salvation, is a turning to God as an object of admiring and adoring, loving and confiding contemplation. This may be so presented to the mind as to exclude or swallow up all accessory notions, by concentrating the thoughts upon Him to whom the sinner turns. But sometimes, perhaps commonly, the Scriptures so speak of conversion as to suggest distinctly the idea of that from which, as well as of that to which, we turn. We do not turn to God from nothing or neutrality. We turn from his opposites, his enemies, his rivals. God is never the first object of supreme affection to his fallen creatures. The change is not from loving nothing, but from loving self, from loving sin. When we turn, we turn from darkness to light, from death to life, from hell to heaven, from the power of Satan unto God.

The state from which we turn determines the method of conversion, or defines what acts and exercises are included in it. If our natural condition were only one of ignorance or innocent infirmity, conversion would involve nothing more than intellectual illumination and increase of strength, both which it really includes. But if our native state be one of guilt and condemnation, and of utter impotence to all good, then conversion necessarily implies deliverance from guilt by a power independent of our own; and this presupposes faith in that gratuitous deliverance, while the very act of turning from a state of sin implies a change of mind, *i. e.*, of judgment and of feeling with respect to it. Conversion, therefore, as exhibited in Scripture, is inseparable from repentance toward God and faith toward our Lord Jesus Christ; because, from the nature of the case, without these it is utterly impossible, in any truly scriptural sense, to turn from sin and Satan unto God.

Sometimes, again, the idea is suggested that we not only turn to God, but turn back to him. This may at first sight appear inconsistent with the fact just stated, that our first affections are invariably given to the world and to ourselves. But even those who are converted, for the first time, from a state of total alienation, may be said to turn back to God, in reference to the great original apostasy in which we are all implicated. As individuals, we never know God till we are converted. As a race, we have all departed from Him, and conversion is but *turning back* to him. But this expression is still more appropriate, even in its strict sense, to the case of those who have already been converted, and are only reclaimed from a partial and temporary alienation, from relapsing into sin, or what is called, in religious phraseology, declension, and, in the word of God itself, backsliding. That the term conversion may be properly applied to such a secondary restoration, is apparent from the language of the text, where it is used by Christ himself, of one who is expressly said to have had faith, and faith which did not absolutely fail. This usage agrees fully with the nature of conversion as described in Scripture, and with the primary import of the figurative term itself. Suppose a person to have turned completely round from one object toward another, from the west, for instance, to the rising sun, and to be so attracted and absorbed by this grand sight, that he cannot wholly turn away from it, we may still conceive of him as turning partially away, and even trying to embrace both objects in his field of vision. This is no bad illustration of the case in question. The perseverance of the saints is not secured by any thing inherent in themselves, nor even by the nature of the change wrought in conversion, but by an almighty intervention, rendered certain by a special promise. They are "kept by the power of God through faith unto salvation." Upon this same power, and this same promise, they would be dependent even if transferred at once to heaven; how much more when left to struggle with temptation and the remains of their original corruption. They who have once truly turned to God, can never wholly turn away from him, so as to lose sight of him forever. But they may turn partly round, they may turn half round, they may try to look both ways at once, as all do who endeavor to serve God and mammon, or who, like heathen settlers in Samaria, fear the Lord and serve their own god. They may turn more than half round, so as scarcely to see any thing of that towards which they lately looked with such delight, and so as to be reckoned by the world with those who have their eyes and hearts fixed upon *it*.

There is something fearful in the length to which this retroversion may be carried, in the gradual approximation of the convert to his old position, and the little that seems wanting sometimes to complete the counter-revolution when he is arrested and turned back again. When thus recovered, he must pass through much of the same process as at first. His second turning no less necessarily involves repentance and belief. The object of his faith is still the same. The pangs of godly sorrow, far from being soothed, are exasperated by the recollection of a previous repentance and a subsequent relapse. It *is* a new conversion, then, in all respects but one—the point at which the convert sets out, and the distance over which he passes. The neglect or rejection of this doctrine has a pernicious practical effect. The idea that conversion can in no sense be repeated, and that erring Christians must return to duty in a way generically different from that by which they came to God at first, has a necessary tendency to foster spiritual pride. by making all defection seem impossible; and then, when pride has had its fall, to breed despondency by leaving no means of recovery.

The truths opposed to these pernicious errors are, that even true believers may depart from God, and though, through Christ's intercession, their faith cannot wholly fail, they must experience a new conversion—must repent, believe, submit, as really as if they had been always in the gall of bitterness and the bond of iniquity. Often, when men are using palliative remedies or resting wholly on remote experience, what they really need is to be converted, to repent and do their first works. Peter had faith, and it was not to fail, even in that fiery trial, because Christ prayed that it might not fail; but it was to be severely tried, and he was to experience a fearful, ignominious fall, from which he could only be recovered by a new conversion, by a new repentance, and new acts of faith. "I have prayed for thee, that thy faith fail not; and when thou art converted, strengthen thy brethren."

This brings us again to the second point suggested by the text, to wit, that conversion, whether primary or secondary, total or partial, tends to the strengthening of others, *i. e.*, to their preservation or recovery from the evils which the convert has himself escaped. In answer to the question, how does conversion tend to this result? the general fact may be thus resolved into three distinct particulars: 1. It enables men to strengthen others. 2. It obliges men to strengthen others. 3. It disposes men to strengthen others. The convert is enabled to confirm or rescue others by his knowledge of their character and state. He knows,

not only what he sees in them, but what he feels or
has felt in himself. Take, for instance, the new convert from a state of total unbelief and impenitence.
He knows the misery of that state, as it cannot possibly be known by those who still continue in it.
They know what he knew once, but he knows in addition, what he never knew at all until awakened and
enlightened by the grace of God. Their view of it
tends only to despair or false security. His, rouses to
exertion. He looks at the reality as well from their
point of observation as his own, and the very insensibility which he perceives in them, excites him to
new efforts for their rescue, for he knows that he was
once as stupid and as much in danger. He knows,
too, the inefficacy of the means which they employ to
strengthen or to save themselves. For he remembers
his own struggles in the slough, and the momentum
with which every effort sunk him deeper and deeper.
This remembrance helps him to discern what is truly
needed in the case of others, and prevents his relying,
as he once did in his own case, upon any thing except
the true foundation.

On the other hand, he knows the sovereign virtue
of the means which God provides—the truth, the
blood of Christ, the influences of the Spirit. He ap-
preciates the freeness with which these are offered,
and the simplicity of God's way of salvation, which,
without experience, men are always sure to under-
rate or misconceive. He knows too, by experience,
how their hearts are most accessible, what are their
difficulties, doubts, and scruples, what are the vulnerable points at which they may be best assailed, as

well for evil as for good, as well by Satan as by God. From this experimental knowledge of the evil, the remedy, and the application, even the new convert is peculiarly able to do good to others. It is accordingly a lesson of experience that men are or may be more particularly useful in this way to those who are most like their former selves.

The same thing is true of the secondary, subsequent conversion from a state of declension or backsliding, to which the text more immediately refers. The person thus reclaimed knows better than his brethren who have not yet fallen, the peculiar dangers which environ them, the weakness of their faith, the strength of their temptations, the illusions of the adversary. He knows the hideous shame of the relapse, and the remorseful anguish of the first convulsive movements towards repentance. He knows the difficulties of the restoration—how much harder it is now to excite hope or confirm faith, how much less effective, either warning, or encouragement, or argument is now than it once was—how precarious even the most specious reformation and repentance must be after such deflections. All that tends to make him watchful in his own case, and to arm him against those insidious foes by whom he was betrayed or vanquished, at the same time enables him to strengthen others. This advantage of experimental knowledge is accompanied, moreover, by a corresponding liveliness of feeling, a more energetic impulse, such as always springs from recent restorations or escapes. It is a matter of proverbial notoriety, that young converts, as a class, have more intensity of zeal and more promptness to engage in active effort. This zeal is often indiscreet, but when sufficiently informed and guided, it secures to those who have it an immense advantage over those whose hearts have been becoming cold, in due proportion to the increase of their knowledge and the ripeness of their judgment. It is this elastic spring of the affections, this spontaneous movement of the active powers to exertion, which, united with the experimental knowledge before mentioned, enables the new convert or reclaimed backslider, above all other men, to "strengthen his brethren."

Out of this increased ability arises, by a logical and moral necessity, a special obligation. This is only a specific application of a principle which all acknowledge, and which the word of God explicitly propounds, "To him that knoweth to do good and doeth it not, to him it is sin." It needs not so much to be explained or established, as to be exemplified from real life. The recognition of the principle is there unhesitating and unanimous. He who has been recovered from the power of a desperate disease by a new or unknown remedy, is under a peculiar obligation to apply it, or at least to make it known, to all affected in like manner. Hence the unsparing, universal condemnation of the man who, from mercenary motives, holds in his possession secrets of importance to the health or happiness of others. The man who has just escaped, as if by miracle, from the devouring flames, often feels that, if he can, he is particularly bound to save those who are still unconscious of the danger or unable to escape it. He who is mercifully saved from shipwreck, often feels especially incumbent on himself the rescue of his fellows. He must do what he can, even though he be exhausted; how much more if he is strengthened. For there is a circumstance which makes the obligation of the spiritual convert to confirm or rescue others, greater, even in proportion, than that of the escaped from fire or shipwreck. These are often, if not always, more or less disabled by the very circumstances of their own deliverance from helping others. The one, though saved as by fire, may be scorched and bruised, the other stiffened and benumbed—both stupified—so that long before they have recovered their capacity to act, the opportunity of saving others is gone by forever. But conversion is attended by no such contusions, swoons, or burnings. On the contrary, it always strengthens and prepares for spiritual action, so that they who do not act for the deliverance of others, are without excuse.

It seems to me that these considerations are sufficient to establish the existence of the obligation, if indeed there can be any disposition to dispute it. But in this, as in other cases, the bare conviction or oppressive sense of duty is not always followed by an inclination to perform it. And without this inclination, no effects of a salutary kind can be expected. It is not the naked knowledge or belief of what is right, that prompts to virtuous obedience. Such knowledge and belief may coexist with hatred of the thing required, and with a fixed determination not to do it. This state of mind is probably included in the torments of the damned. The heart must beat in concord with the reason and the conscience. And it does so in the case of the true convert, both in general and in reference to this specific duty. For conversion moves him to discharge it, first of all, by a general softening of the heart and the excitement of benevolent affections. But this, though indispensable, is not enough. There must be higher motives even, to secure good will and charitable acts to men. There must be love to God and zeal for Christ, as the grand motives even to benevolent exertion, or the fruit will fail.

But we may go still further, and assign a more specific principle of action prompting to the same result. This is gratitude for what the convert has himself experienced. You may possibly remember that, when one of the great vessels which long maintained a constant intercourse between the old world and the new, had weathered what was looked upon as an extraordinary storm, the passengers resolved to testify their gratitude to God by establishing a fund for the relief of shipwrecked seamen and their families. The principle involved in this proceeding was a sound one, and the feeling altogether natural. True thankfulness invariably creates the desire of requital; and, as God cannot be its object, it is natural to spend it upon others, with a view, however, to glorify, please, and honor him. There is reason to believe that a large proportion of the purest charities of life are directly prompted by the gratitude of those who practise them. The mere conviction of right and sense of obligation would do nothing; mere benevolence to others would do little; and even a general desire to perform the will of God and glorify his name would do less than it does, without the operation of that special motive recognized in Christ's argumentative command: " Freely ye have received, freely give."

From all this it sufficiently appears that true conversion, whether primary or secondary, tends to the strengthening of others, by enabling, by obliging, by disposing the convert to seek the rescue of the lost, and the deliverance of those in danger. This view of the subject sets before us an important test of character and an invaluable means of usefulness. If it be true that conversion always more or less disposes to the strengthening of others, it would seem to follow, that wherever there is no sense of the obligation, much less any strong desire to discharge it, there is reason to suspect that we have never been converted, or at least that we need to be converted again. If, on the other hand, so large a part of the efficient charities of life depends upon the influence excited by conversion on the convert himself, we may infer that the spiritual labours of the unconverted are of little worth. This is a general proposition, but admits of a specific application to the labours of the ministry. Without this, genius, learning, eloquence, may please, they may improve, they may even in a higher sense do good, but how can we expect them to be savingly effectual, to strengthen those who are ready to perish, to confirm in good, and to deliver or protect from evil? Perhaps much of the unfruitfulness which we lament, proceeds directly from this very cause. How shall we strengthen our brethren, unless we are converted? This applies even to declension and backsliding—how much more to sheer impenitence and unbelief. The consciousness, or even the well-grounded apprehension of this grand defect *must* paralyze exertion. Self-deception no less certainly must make it ineffectual. Nay, the very recollection of conversion as a past event, perhaps a distant one, although correct, may have the same result by hindering the soul from turning back to God, however gross and long-continued its declensions. Instead of seeking re-conversion by renewed acts of repentance, faith, and love, we linger on in a condition half dependant, half presumptuous, in expectation of some special and extraordinary grace adapted to the case of " Christians," as distinguished from those whom we are wont to call " impenitent sinners." We forget that every interruption of repentance makes ourselves impenitent; that every lapse of faith converts us so far into unbelievers; and that from this new state of impenitence and unbelief, the way of restoration and recovery is the same as from the old.

It is easy to imagine the effect of this mistake, whenever it exists, in rendering abortive the most zealous efforts even of men really converted, but estranged from their first love and their first works through the deceitfulness of sin. Through the Saviour's intercession, their faith does not fail; but they must be converted before they can confirm their brethren. Here, then, is the test, and here the means before referred to. Would you prove yourself converted? Strengthen the brethren. Would you strengthen the brethren? Be converted. This last is indeed the best and safest course in any case. We may err in our attempts to strengthen the brethren, but we cannot err in aiming at our own conversion.

Let us secure this, and the rest will follow. We have every inducement, personal and public, to seek reconversion. There are always some conversions going on among us and around us. The wicked are becoming worse. The Christian, if not growing, is declining. In the world one form of sin is constantly exchanging for another. There are many conversions from ambition to avarice, and from pleasure to ambition. And even in countries professedly religious, there is scarcely any interruption of the same mysterious process.

The best preventive of these retrograde conversions, is conversion in the right direction, turning continually back to him from whom we have revolted. Let not this be hindered by the evidence of former conversion. As long as there is sin, there will be something to turn *from*. And, thanks be to God, there is always something to turn *to*. While *we* change, He remains the same. Amidst all our fluctuations, the capricious ebb and flow of our affections, there is no change or motion in the everlasting rock against which they are beating. Through all our vicissitudes of light and darkness, night and morning, noon and twilight, lightning and eclipse, *he* still remains the Father of Lights, with whom is no variableness, neither shadow of turning. Even when we wander furthest, if we look back, we still see him where he was. It is this sublime immutability and constancy that furnishes a basis for our hopes. If at every fresh return to God, we found some change in the attributes of his nature, or in the offers of his gospel; if we had to make acquaintance with another

Saviour, and to seek the aid of an unknown Spirit, we might well despair. But, thanks be to God, there is always something, and always the same thing, to turn to, and the same altar, the same laver, the same mercy-seat, the same Sovereign, the same Saviour, the same Comforter—in one word, the same Father, Son, and Spirit, God over all blessed forever. There is always something to turn *to ;* and lastly, there is always something to turn *for*. For the honour of Christ— he may be glorified in our growth rather than in our decay, in our salvation rather than our ruin. For ourselves—that we may redeem lost time, and wipe off the reproach which we have justly incurred upon the cause. For our brethren—that they may be strengthened; if impenitent, converted; if backsliding, reclaimed; if assailed, confirmed.

Let us give ear, then, to the two great lessons which the text affords. The one is, Be converted, for the first time, or afresh. And oh! when thus converted, Remember those whom you have left behind. You who are raised up by the great Physician from the bed of spiritual languishment, do not forget the sufferers still lying there, fevered, or palsied, or convulsed with pain. You who are plucked as brands from the burning, oh remember the poor victims who are still asleep beneath the curtain of that stifling smoke, and with that horrid glare upon their eyelids, or perhaps just aroused to a benumbing sense of their condition. You who have reached the shore of mercy from that scene of spiritual shipwreck, oh, look back upon those still unconscious victims, lying just as you lay but a little while ago, or on those pallid faces, mutely pleading for deliverance, or those hands lifted up above the surface of the bubbling waves, before they sink forever. When you go hence, you will go to witness just such scenes as this, to stand upon the wreck-strewed shore, and there see thousands perish, while perhaps you may be able to save one! But how precious even that one in the sight of God and holy angels. How well worthy of your best exertions and most fervent prayers. But forget not, in addition to the training through which you are passing, and which claims your most assiduous attention; oh, forget not that without which, this must be forever unavailing; forget not to prepare your hearts, yourselves, for future toil and future usefulness, by giving present, constant heed to the first great commandment of the Saviour—" Be converted;" and to the second, which is like unto it—" When thou art converted, strengthen thy brethren."

XIX.

Luke 9, 60.—Let the dead bury their dead; but go thou and preach the kingdom of God.

The gospel history is distinguished from all others by the intrinsic dignity of its subject—the sayings and doings of our Lord and Saviour. In such a record, if inspired, there can be nothing small or unimportant. The slightest hint or trace of the Redeemer's words and deeds is precious to his people in all ages. And yet there is a secret disposition to regard these books as only fit for children, and to slight the gems of godlike wisdom which are scattered through them—always invaluable, although sometimes, as, for instance, in the text which I have read, they may be strange and enigmatical. These remarkable words are recorded by two of the evangelists—*i. e.*, the words of the first clause—and in precisely the same form, which shows how carefully the apostolical tradition has preserved our Saviour's very words there, while in the other clause the two accounts agree only in substance. According to both accounts, our Lord said, "Let the dead bury their dead;" but according to Matthew, he began by saying, "Follow me;" according to Luke, he ended by saying, "Go thou and preach the kingdom of God." Both these versions may be literally accurate, though each has been preserved by only one historian. Or both may be paraphrases, giving the spirit, not the letter, of our Lord's reply. Or one may be such a paraphrase, and the other a statement of the words actually uttered. Upon any of these suppositions, all of which are natural and easy, and according to analogy and usage, the consistency of the accounts may be completely vindicated. At the same time, this diversity, however it may be explained, renders still more striking the exact agreement of the gospels in the other words. Whatever else our Saviour may have said besides, he certainly said, "Let the dead bury their (own) dead."

There is also a remarkable agreement and diversity in the accompanying circumstances, as related by the two evangelists. Both connect this little dialogue, in which the text occurs, with another of the same kind, and both put this other first. But Luke adds a third of the very same description, which Matthew does not give at all. They also agree in representing these brief conversations as taking place upon the road, or as our Lord was setting out upon a journey. Luke merely says, as they went in the way, or were proceeding on their journey, without specifying time or place. In the absence of all other information, it would be most natural to understand him as referring to the immediately preceding context, which is generally supposed to record the commencement of our Lord's last journey to Jerusalem. But observe, the writer does not say so; it is a mere inference, and more than half, perhaps nine-tenths, of the alleged variations in the gospels, have arisen from confounding mere sequence or juxtaposition in the record, with exact or immediate chronological succession. All that Luke says is, that they were journeying, or on their way.

If this were all we knew about it, we might well infer that it was on the journey previously mentioned. But that inference is gone when Matthew tells us that this very conversation happened at an earlier period of Christ's ministry, when he was just embarking on that voyage across the sea of Galilee, which furnished the occasion of a miracle, evincing, for the first time, his dominion over nature and the elements, as well as over demons and diseases. It was just before the stilling of the storm that Matthew places this occurrence; and as Luke's expressions are entirely indefinite, those of Matthew must of course determine the chronology, not in opposition to Luke's statement, or even in correction of it, but in addition to it, as a supplement or specification.

This view of the matter involves no invidious distinction between Luke and Matthew, as more or less exact or complete in their statements, because Luke, in other cases, supplies facts and incidents omitted by Matthew, and in this very case, it is only by a reference to Mark—who does not give the dialogues at all, but does give what precedes and follows—it is only by a reference to this third witness, that we learn with certainty that all this happened on the very day when Christ uttered that remarkable series of parables beginning with the sower, or at least a part of them. Matthew prefaces the dialogue from which the text is taken, by saying that "when Jesus saw great multitudes about him, he gave commandment to depart unto the other side." This, taken by itself, might seem to mean that what follows in the narrative, held the same position in the order of events. But he does not say so, and he may mean that it happened on a different occasion, when he saw a multitude around him. This possibility becomes a certainty when Mark informs us that this passage of the lake took place "on the same day, in the evening." This is perfectly definite as to the time, as well as the events. It cannot possibly be referred to any other day or hour, without impugning Mark's authority. There may have been a thousand days on which our Lord found himself surrounded by a crowd, and escaped them by embarking on the lake; and this is all that Matthew says. We are, therefore, at liberty, nay, bound to fix the date of this vague statement, in accordance with the light obtained from other sources. Such a source is Mark, and such a light is his explicit statement (4, 35), that the voyage across Genessaret, in which our Saviour stilled the storm, occurred in the evening of the same day—what day? why of course the day of which he had just been speaking.

Now the immediately preceding context in Mark's narrative contains a series of parables, beginning with that of the sower, and ending with that of the mustard seed—the same series that occurs, with some additions, in the 13th of Matthew, long after he has recorded the dialogue from which the text is taken, but which Mark, without giving it all, assigns to its exact place in the order of events, by telling us what happened just before and after. Luke merely says that they were on the way; Matthew, more distinctly, on their way to cross the lake; and Mark, still more explicitly, that they did cross it, and that Christ did still the storm, upon the evening of the same day when those parables were uttered.

This is only one out of a multitude of instances in which one of the gospels gives the actual order of events, while another gives them in another order suited to his own immediate purpose. This deviation from the order of actual occurrence is practised by the historians of every age, and can only be condemned as unhistorical by those who do not know the difference between history and chronology, or rather between dates and the events to which they owe their value. This practice is peculiar to no one of the evangelists, but common to them all, the attempt to make one of them the standard in chronology, to which the others are to be conformed, having proved as impracticable in execution, as it is arbitrary and gratuitous in theory. As Mark here furnishes a date which neither Luke nor Matthew gives us, so in other cases he receives from them the same additional specification. The *reason* for departing from the rigid chronological arrangement is not always the same, nor always apparent; but the one most generally applicable is, that the historian means to put together facts resembling one another, although not immediately successive in the order of occurrence.

Thus Matthew, in recording several parables that Mark gives, omits one and adds another, as more suited to his purpose, and inserts the whole series at a different point in the narrative from that to which it properly or rather chronologically belongs. Thus, too, Luke, in giving the two dialogues between our Lord and two new followers, which Matthew had recorded, not only adds a third, which may have happened at a different time, but places the whole series in a different connection, yet without the slightest intimation as to time, beyond the mere juxtaposition, and therefore without the slightest contradiction to the more specific statements of the other gospels.

A biographer of Washington, who wished to give that great man's views on some important subject—say the subject of religion—not only might, but must, in order to attain his end, collect the expression of those views from different periods of his history, and give them seriatim, without any risk of being charged, as the evangelists are charged by shallow and dishonest infidels, with contradicting those biographers who give the very same facts or words, not together—having no such purpose to answer as the one first mentioned—but in connection with the times and places at which they happened or were uttered.

In the case supposed, too, no one dreams of charging the respective writers with mutual contradiction, simply because, in illustration of the point which they are proving, they may differ in the choice or the arrangement of their proofs, because one passes over what another has recorded, or repeats a certain part of it without the rest. When will the same principles and modes of judgment which experience and common sense are constantly applying on the bench and in the jury-box, and even in the ordinary intercourse of life, be fairly extended to the real or alleged variations in the gospel history or life of Christ?

These considerations are abundantly sufficient for my purpose in proposing them, viz., that of showing that the question as of time and order, in the case before us, though admitting of an easy and satisfactory solution, is of little moment as an element of sound interpretation. Whether these three replies of Christ were uttered on the same or on different occasions, whether earlier or later in his public ministry, are questions which can have no effect, either upon their intrinsic value, or upon their mutual connection, which arises from their common bearing on a single subject of great practical importance.

It is also a subject of peculiar interest to such an audience as this—composed almost entirely of persons looking forward to the ministry, or actually in it—being nothing more nor less than the spirit which should actuate those seeking this high office, and the principle on which it should be chosen as the business of a lifetime, and on which its claims should be adjusted, when apparently or really in conflict with attractions or demands from any other quarter. This is a subject which can never be wholly inappropriate to us, and on which it may sometimes be expedient to let Jesus Christ speak in his own way, however paradoxical or strange it may appear when compared with the maxims of worldly wisdom, or even with those of casuistical theology.

Let this be my apology for asking your attention to this text and context, just as it lies upon the face of

Scripture, or with only such departures from the form, as may render its consideration more convenient and more practically useful. In order to secure all the light which the connection can afford to the obscure words of the text, I shall include in my proposed examination all the similar or homogeneous cases here referred to, whether by one of the evangelists or both. At the very threshold we are met, however, by a striking instance of the way in which the gospels mutually specify and supplement each other.

The first case mentioned, both by Luke and Matthew, is that of one who volunteered to follow Christ wherever he should go. Besides the unimportant variation in the title, by which this man addressed him, and which Matthew gives as Master or Teacher, Luke, as Sir or Lord, there is another more material and interesting difference, though not the slightest discrepance or contradiction, the difference being only in the degree of definiteness and precision. Luke's account, by itself, might suggest the idea, that this volunteer disciple was an ordinary man, of little knowledge or intelligence, and his proposal a vague offer of discipleship in general, without reference to any special or official service. Both these impressions, although perfectly legitimate and natural, if we had only Luke's description, are removed by Matthew's statement, that this "certain man," of whom Luke speaks, was a scribe, or literally, "one scribe,"—an unusual expression, which may either mean a certain individual of that class, or more definitely, one of the scribes, known to have been present then and there. Remembering, as we should do, whenever scribes are mentioned, that they were not clerks or secretaries, nor simple copyists of the law, but its official conservators and professional expounders—the successors of Ezra, without his inspiration, but aspiring to the same high trust of guarding the Old Testament canon, which he closed, from mutilation and corruption, and unauthorized addition; yes, and recognized by Christ himself as the legitimate interpreters of Moses, although grossly inconsistent in their lives, and forming a part, either collectively or representatively, of the Sanhedrim, the great national presbytery or senate—you will see, at once, that this was no fortuitous or vague proposal, from an unknown or unimportant person, to enrol himself as one of our Lord's followers—as multitudes were, no doubt, doing every day—but an extraordinary overture, of which there seems to have been few examples, from an educated student and interpreter of Scripture, to assume the same position in the new religion that he held already in the old; in other words, it was an offer to become what Christ himself is elsewhere said to have described as "a scribe instructed, or discipled, into and unto, *i. e.*, into the fellowship, and for the service of, the new dispensation or kingdom of heaven," Matthew 13, 52; and that not merely upon certain terms, or in a certain place, to be selected by the offerer, but wherever he, whom by this act he owns as the Messiah, should be pleased to lead the way. Upon every principle of worldly wisdom, or of selfish policy, or even of what some regard as Christian prudence, how would this offer have been received and answered? as a flattering compliment? a condescension? a remarkable example of distinguished gifts and lofty station laid upon the altar of religion, and entitled therefore to a high place in the synagogue or church, and to a grateful recognition, even at the hands, and from the lips, of Christ himself?

With such prepossessions and anticipations of our Lord's reply to this attractive offer, how should we, and how may some of his attendants upon that day, have been shocked and startled, by its seeming harshness and irrelevance? Instead of thanks, instead of praise, instead of courtly acquiescence, and a graceful welcome, the poor scribe gets nothing in return for his proposal, but that wild and melancholy sentence, which has ever since been ringing in the ears of all who read or hear the gospel, like the burden of some funeral song, a snatch of some unearthly chant by "airy tongues, that syllable men's names on sands, and shores, and desert wildernesses"—" Foxes have holes, and birds of the air have nests; but the Son of man hath not where to lay his head."

Sublimely touching as the weakest intellect and meanest taste must feel these words to be, considered in themselves, how strange do they appear to most, considered as an answer. How evasive, incoherent, and unmeaning have they been declared to be by many a pedantic critic! Yet the world has never heard, and the records of the world do not contain a more direct, conclusive, and exhaustive answer—not to the scribe's words; there is the error that gives birth to all these false and foolish judgments, of which every one of us has had his share—not to his words, but to his thoughts, his wishes; those desires and purposes which lay so closely coiled about his very heart that he may have had no clear view of them himself. Not to his lips, or to his eye, or to his ear, but to his inmost soul, and to the hidden core of his corrupt affections, to his proud conceit and secular ambition, to his love of ease, and fame, and power, to his sordid, carnal, and concealed hope of distinction and enjoyment in the kingdom of this untaught teacher, this unbribed benefactor, this amazing, wonderworking Son of Man; to these, to all these, as seen by an omniscient eye to constitute the man, did that unsparing, unexpected answer speak in articulate annihilating thunder.

But even in attempting to do feeble justice to our Master's greatness upon this occasion, let us not be led astray by any false interpretation of his language, however natural, however common. Let us not impair its simple grandeur by forcing quaint conceits upon it, by supposing an allusion, in the foxes and the birds, which he seems almost to envy, to the cunning or the other evil attributes of those who hated him, but give the expressions their most obvious import, as descriptive of familiar living things, perhaps presented at the moment to the eyes of those who heard him, or at least to their memory and imagination. Nor let us rush into the opposite extreme of giving to the words that follow too obvious and easy an interpretation, as expressive of extreme want and privation, not only of the luxuries and comforts, but of the necessary means of life. Such a description would have been at variance with the known facts of our Saviour's history, the apparent circumstances of his nearest relatives and friends, including some at least of his apostles, and still more of his disciples in the wider sense, the various comfortable homes in which we find him a most welcome guest, and the extreme devotion of a few choice spirits, whose substance and whose lives existed only for his service, and among whom, while none were poor, one was connected with the royal household. The glory of the Saviour stands in no need of romantic or poetical embellishment. Starvation, penury, formed no part of his sufferings, though often gloried in as chief points of resemblance by ascetic bearers of his cross. His food and raiment seem to have been those of the society in which he lived, and he expressly describes himself as " eating and drinking " with his neighbours, in contrast with the austere life of his forerunner, who came " neither eating nor drinking," and was therefore thought to have a devil.

The idea of extreme want and a state of beggary, is not suggested by his words on the occasion now before us. To the scribe's ambitious expectations of a long triumphant reign of the Messiah upon earth, and of distinction and enjoyment in his service, he opposes that of a mere transient visit and unsettled life; the absence, not of ordinary food and shelter, but of a permanent and settled home, much more of a luxurious court and palace, using the very figure long before employed by Tiberius Gracchus, when complaining that the champions of Italian freedom were compelled to lead a homeless life, and flit from place to place, while the very beasts that ravaged Italy had lairs and pasture-grounds. The spirit of our Lord's reply to this deceived or hypocritical pretender is: "You know not what you ask or what you offer; you are utterly mistaken in relation to my presence upon earth and its design. Instead of being here, as you imagine, for the purpose of establishing a temporal and worldly kingdom, I am only here to die and rise again. I am here, not as a conqueror or a sovereign, but as a servant and a stranger, less at home than even the inferior animals; "the foxes have holes, and the birds of the air have nests," &c.

The next place, both in Luke and Matthew, is assigned to the discourse from which the text is taken; but it may be more convenient to reserve this till we have considered the additional case found in Luke, and closing his account of the whole matter. From this we learn that, on the same occasion, or one like it, another person offered to follow him, but asked permission first to bid farewell to those at home. This request was so much like that of Elisha to Elijah, when he called him from the plough to the prophetic office, that our Lord, with a beautiful accommodation in the form of his reply to this designed or undesigned allusion, speaks of his own service under the figure of husbandry or plowing, recommended also by the agricultural employments of the multitude before whom he was speaking, and perhaps suggested, as so many of his parables are thought to have been, by the sight of some one actually so employed. That sight, or even recollection, was sufficient to suggest the necessity of close attention, undivided thoughts, and undiverted eyes, in order to accomplish a straight furrow. The man, who with his hand upon the plough for such a purpose, could look idly back, in sport or in stupidity, would be pronounced by every ploughman present, utterly unfit for that humble but important duty. Here too, as in the first case, the reply is to the thoughts, or to the state of mind; the character or disposition, rather than the language. And to those the answer is adjusted; having reference, in this case, not to proud ambitious hopes, but to distracted views, and a divided heart-wish, and purpose to serve Christ, combined with a presumptuous desire to continue the enjoyment of what ought to have been sacrificed or left behind by one who sought his service. To this very different, but perhaps more common class of false professors and unfaithful servants, our Lord spoke once for all and forever, when he said in answer to that new proposal, "No man, having put his hand to the plough, and looking back, is fit for the kingdom of God."

There is, however, still another question raised and answered in these few words; that of the comparative or relative demands of natural affection, duty and regard to relatives and friends, when brought into real or apparent conflict with the service of our Lord, or with his positive commands. But this is a subject still more clearly and impressively presented in the third reply from which the text is taken. The person speaking and addressed in this case is by Luke simply called "another," but by Matthew, "another of his disciples;" in the wide sense of one who was already a believer in our Lord's Messiahship, and a receiver of his doctrine, but desired to sustain a more intimate relation to him, as an attendant on his person, and a messenger to carry his commands to others. Although mere sequence or juxtaposition, as we have already seen, is no sure sign of chronological succession, it is not perhaps unmeaning or fortuitous, that this whole narrative in Luke immediately precedes the mission of the seventy disciples, nor entirely improbable that these offers of service had respect to that important mission. If so, this renders it still more certain that the propositions and replies in all the cases, referred, as they unquestionably did in one, not merely to discipleship in general, but to preaching in particular. If any thing were needed, this would seem to be sufficient, to awaken our attention to a passage, so directly bearing, not on Christian character only, but on the very office which we seek or hold already.

In one point, Luke is here more definite than Matthew, taking up the conversation at an earlier stage, and showing that the words which Matthew puts into the mouth of this disciple were occasioned by an express command from Christ to follow him, *i. e.* to attend upon his person, with a view to being sent out by him. The same command may be implied, though not expressed, in one or both the other cases. Unless it be, we must regard the one before us as a more direct evasion of acknowledged duty than the others, where the proposition seems to be a voluntary one, and not in answer to a special call. Be this as it may, the proposition itself is not unconditional, as in the first case, nor on the condition of a simple opportunity of bidding farewell to friends at home, as in the second, but turns upon a still more solemn and affecting duty, that of burying a father; not of waiting upon him till he died, as some interpreters have understood it, for such a proposition would have been absurd, asking to wait until his father's death before he followed Christ on this occasion. Nor is it the natural meaning of the words, Let me *first* go away and bury my father; referring just as plainly to a momentary and immediate interruption as the following request to bid farewell to those at home. Even this has sometimes been explained as meaning to adjust or wind up one's affairs, or dispose of one's possessions; but the only natural hypothesis, in either case, is that which concentrates the attention on a single act, and one connected with the tenderest domestic ties and personal affections; in the one case, that of parting from the nearest living friends, and in the other, that of burying the body of a father.

Here, again, a different answer might have been expected, not by policy or selfishness alone, but by the kindliest sentiments of human nature; and our Lord's reply may therefore seem abrupt and harsh to a much larger and more elevated class than those who are offended by his former answer. The difficulty here felt has betrayed itself in exegetical expedients to impose some other meaning on the words than that which can be gained by any natural interpretation. As a single but extreme specimen of such expedients, I may name the monstrous supposition that the dead first mentioned are those charged with the burial of the dead, so that our Lord's words are only a consolatory or encouraging assurance that this sacred duty would not be neglected, even if the son should instantly obey his call.

To the same class may be referred the supposition that his words have reference to ceremonial defilement, and that his refusal is no more severe than that which would have been received from any priest, whether Jew or Gentile. The total silence of the narrative on this point, and the inconsistency of such a meaning with the whole spirit of our Lord's instructions, may serve as a sufficient refutation of this notion, and of every other which supposes the permission to have been withheld on any other ground than that suggested in the accompanying words, viz., the paramount necessity of following Christ and preaching or proclaiming the kingdom of God.

Of the enigmatical words "Let the dead bury their dead," there are only two interpretations which appear in any age to have commanded the assent of sober and judicious minds; and of these two, one has always had so great a majority of suffrages that it may be regarded as established by the voice of the church and exegetical tradition. This is the old interpretation which assumes two entirely different senses of the word *dead*, in the two parts of the sentence; the first figurative or spiritual, the second literal or natural. "Let those dead in sin bury the bodies of the naturally dead." There are enough of worldly, unconverted men or of men not called into my immediate service, to render these last offices to lifeless bodies, but do thou go and preach the kingdom of God.

To this it has been objected, not without some

force, that the very assumption of a double sense within so short a compass is not to be assumed without necessity, and also that the sense obtained is not entirely satisfactory, since it is not consistent with the letter or spirit of Christianity, to devolve such duties on the unconverted, to the exclusion of "devout men," such as carried the first martyr to his burial. Without pausing now to show how these objections may be answered, I may simply state that they have led some eminent, though few interpreters, to give the same sense to the word *dead* in both clauses, and to understand the whole as meaning, "leave the dead to bury one another." This, it is objected, is impossible; but that impossibility is looked upon, by those who take this view as constituting the whole force and point of the expression, like the camel passing through the eye of a needle. It is then equivalent to saying, and saying in the boldest and the strongest form, "If necessary, leave the dead unburied, but at all events, obey my call to go and proclaim the kingdom of God."

According to this last view of the passage, it belongs to what have sometimes been, perhaps improperly, described as the *paradoxes* of our Lord's instructions; those unexpected and surprising forms of speech, by which he first awakens the attention of his hearers, and then states a principle or rule of action, not in its abstract form, nor yet in application to an ordinary case, but to an *extreme* case, so that every other may be readily disposed of. Thus instead of laying down in general terms, the rule of charity or Christian love, he commanded the young ruler, whom he saw to be enamoured of his wealth, to sell all that he had and come and follow him; thus showing him at once, by an extreme test, where his weakness lay, which might have been untouched by requisitions of another kind or of inferior degree. So too, instead of giving rules for the mortification of sin in ordinary cases, he at once supposes the extreme case of a choice between wilful indulgence and the loss of a limb, and teaches, not that such a case is likely to be expected to occur, much less that we may lawfully produce it, but that if it did occur, we ought to be prepared to sacrifice the body to the soul. Instead of dealing out empirical prescriptions for the regulation of our duties and regards to God and man respectively, he assumes abruptly the extreme case of our love to God excluding or forbidding that to any relative, however near or dear, and then requires his followers, *in that case*, not only to prefer God, but to HATE even father or mother. Not that the case itself is one to be expected, but because the principle of paramount affection to the Saviour reaches even such a case, however rare and unexampled, and must therefore of course cover every other, just as every Christian at the present day is bound to suffer martyrdom rather than deny Christ, although actual martyrdom has been unknown, in most parts of the earth, for ages.

This seems to me to be the true key to the enigmas of our Saviour's Sermon on the Mount, and to the fallacies by which so many Christian men have been seduced into the effort to convert the extreme cases thus employed into formal rules of ordinary conduct.

In the case before us, the same principle would lead to the conclusion that the Christian should be willing and prepared to leave his dearest dead unburied, or to slight any other tender natural affection, the indulgence of which would be in conflict with a plain command or call of God, but not that such a conflict commonly exists, or may be brought about at pleasure, which so far from being pleasing in the sight of God, is really the sin committed by the hypocrites who said, "Corban," when they ought to have supplied the wants of their dependent parents. These are the grounds on which the literal interpretation of the words has been defended and explained, but as I said before, almost the whole weight of authority and long prescription is in favour of the other explanation, which requires the follower, and especially the minister of Christ to leave all natural attentions, even the most tender duties of affection, to the men of this world, when they would conflict with his obedience to the call of God.

As topics of reflection on this interesting passage, I suggest

1. That there is still a special call of Christ to individuals, not only to believe in him, but to preach his kingdom. Without attempting to define this call at present, I may observe, that it is neither miraculous on one hand, nor a matter of business calculation on the other, but a complete judgment or conclusion to which various elements contribute, such as intellectual and physical capacity, without which a call is inconceivable; providential facilities and opportunities, opening the way to this employment

more than to all others; the judgment and desire of others, and especially of those best qualified, by character and situation, to sit in judgment on the case. I might add a desire for the work, which, in a certain sense is certainly included in a call, but which is apt to be confounded with a mere liking for the outward part of the profession, for example with that mania for preaching which is sometimes found in grossly wicked men, and has been known to follow them, not only to their haunts of vice, but to the prison and the madhouse. There is also a desire which results from early habit and association, the known wish of parents, pastors, and other friends, or the fixed inveterate habit of regarding this as a man's chosen calling, even when every evidence of piety is wanting. The desire which can be referred to any of these causes is entirely distinct from that which God produces in the heart of his true servants, as a part of their vocation to the ministry.

2. This vocation, where it really exists, is paramount to every personal and selfish plan, to every natural affection, even the most tender, which conflicts with it.

3. This conflict is not usually unavoidable, though often so regarded by fanatics. The first duty of the Christian is not to desire or create, but to avoid it; but if unavoidable, his next is to obey God rather than man.

4. Our Saviour did not deal indiscriminately with all cases of desire to enter his immediate service. The remark is at least as old as Calvin, that in this case he repelled the man who wanted to go with him

everywhere, and urged the man to follow him at once, who wanted to go home for what appeared to be most necessary purposes. So far as his example is a guide to us in these things, we are bound not only to persuade, but to discourage as the case may be.

5. There is no more danger of excluding those whom God has called by faithful presentation of the whole truth, than there is of preventing the conversion of his chosen ones, by showing them the true tests of faith and repentance. The man who can be finally driven back in this way ought to be so driven. He whom God has called will only be confirmed in his desire and resolution by such warnings against self-deception, though he may pass through the discipline of painful doubt and hesitation for a season. To you, my young brethren, whose presence here to-day is a profession that you believe yourselves called of God to this high office, my desire and prayer is, that the Lord would speak directly as he sees your case to need; that if any of you are anticipating only ease, and honour, and enjoyment of a selfish nature in his service; though you honestly believe yourselves prepared to follow him wherever he may lead you, he may say to you this morning, as he said to that deluded scribe of old, "the foxes have holes, and birds of the air have nests; but the Son of man hath not where to lay his head;" that if any of you, although willing and desirous to engage in this service, have your hearts divided between it and that which you have left, the business or the pleasures of the world, or its mere natural attachments and enjoyments, you may this day hear him say, and say with a medicinal

effect, "No man having put his hand, to the plow, and looking back, is fit for the kingdom of God." And lastly, that if even one among you is distracted and distressed by imaginary obligations to your nearest friends, at variance with your duty to your Lord and Master, he may nerve your courage and dispel your doubts, by saying as he said to him whose father lay unburied, "Let the dead bury their dead, but go thou and preach the kingdom of God."

XX.

MARK 13, 37.—What I say unto you, I say unto all: Watch!

THE personal ministry of Christ was limited to one small country. On two occasions only do we read of his having crossed the frontiers of Palestine. The first was in his infancy, when he was carried into Egypt, to escape the sanguinary spite of Herod. The second was in later life, when he visited the coasts of Tyre and Sidon in Phenicia, and there wrought a miracle of healing on the daughter of a Syrophenician woman, and in compliance with her urgent prayer, as if to show, by one signal action of his public life, that he came to be the Saviour of the Gentiles as well as of the Jews. With these exceptions, his whole life was passed in the land of Israel; its earlier years chiefly in the northern part called Galilee; its later years partly in that region, partly in Judea, partly beyond Jordan.

We read repeatedly in Scripture, that his fame was spread, not only through these provinces, but over the surrounding countries, and that wherever he went, he was accompanied or followed by vast multitudes. These multitudes were no doubt always changing, as he passed from one part of the country to another. There is reason to believe, however, that a large number followed him from place to place, forming a permanent body of attendants. These were influenced no doubt by various motives; some by vague curiosity, and a desire to see new and wonderful performances; some by a desire to be healed, or to obtain healing for their friends; some by gratitude for such gifts experienced already; some by a wish to be instructed; some by a conviction of sin and a desire of salvation. Those who were governed by the higher class of motives, the desire of instruction and salvation, may be comprehended under the general description of "disciples," *i. e.* such as acknowledged Christ's authority and received his doctrines.

Out of this undefined and shifting body of disciples he selected twelve, that they might constantly attend him or be sent out by him. These were called apostles. But even among these we read of three who were admitted to more intimate and confidential intercourse, as appears from the frequency and prominence with which their names are mentioned in the gospel history, and from the fact that they accompanied their Master upon some occasions when the rest were left behind. The three thus specially distinguished were Simon Peter and the two sons of Zebedee, James and John. In this point of view our Lord appears surrounded by a succession of concentric circles; first, the narrow circle of his confidential followers, then the wider circle of his twelve apostles, then the still wider circle of disciples, beyond which spreads the less defined and constant circle of his hearers and spectators, like a circle on the surface of the water spreading till it merges in the smooth face of the lake or stream.

Corresponding to these various sets of hearers is the various design of the discourses which our Lord addressed to them. Some were intended for the ear of the few nearest to him, some for the whole body of apostles, some for his disciples generally, some for the vast mixed multitude who happened to be present. In some cases, what was said had reference to the wants of his contemporaries generally, not of those merely whom he immediately addressed. Sometimes his instructions had a universal application to all countries and all ages. Sometimes, though immediately adapted to one purpose, they admitted of a wider or a more specific application. Thus the text has reference directly to the downfall of the Jewish nation, and to the dangers in which Christ's disciples were to be involved. It was against these dangers that he meant to warn them. But the warning was applicable to the case of all then living, as he intimates himself, by adding, what I say unto you I say unto all.

On the same principle, we may make a still further application of the precept to ourselves and to our spiritual dangers. For if such a warning was appropriate in reference to temporal calamities however fearful, it can be no perversion to extend it to perils no less real, and as much more tremendous as the soul is more important than the body, and eternity than time. We need not therefore hesitate to look upon ourselves as comprehended in the wide scope of our Saviour's exhortation, though addressed to his immediate hearers, " What I say unto you, I say unto all, Watch! "

Let us consider then the duty and necessity of watchfulness in reference to spiritual dangers. The exhortation to watch may be resolved into two others; be awake, and be upon your guard. The last necessarily implies the first. No one can be upon his guard unless he is awake: but the converse is not true. A man may be awake, and yet not on his guard. Let us therefore consider them successively.

And first, what is meant by spiritual watchfulness? This again may be resolved into several particulars. In the first place, the mind must be awake, the understanding, the rational powers. And in order to this, it is essential that the powers should be exercised; in other words, that the man should think. There is, indeed, a sense in which the mind must always think. Thought is inseparable from its very being. In another sense, which although less philosophical is equally intelligible, mind may be said not to think. Hence the familiar terms, unthinking, thoughtless, and the like. The thing required is not the mere possession of rational faculties, but their use. The man must think in earnest, think with vigour, think coherently. Some thinking is not so much active as passive, not so much an exertion as an indulgence. This dreamy, indolent condition of the soul is the lowest stage of intellectual life, and that state of opinion must be morbid and corrupt which represents it as the highest mode of thought, and even as a kind of inspiration. To be mentally awake, there must be life, spontaneous action and coherence in the thoughts.

But this is not enough. The mind may be awake in this sense, and yet dreaming in another. It may act, and yet the world in which it acts may be not the present but another. Some minds operate too fast, and some too slow. Some men's thoughts are forever in advance of that which claims their present attention. This is the case with those who habitually dwell upon the circumstances of our future being, and attempt to discover that which has not been revealed, and therefore has no bearing on our present duties or interests. The same is true of some who do not look so far off, who confine themselves to this life, but who constantly anticipate a state of things still future, and do now what they ought to do hereafter. On the other hand, some are either constitutionally or habitually slow; they are constantly behindhand; they think, but think too late, when the necessity for thinking has gone by. Both these mental states and habits have analogy to sleep; the first to the condition of the fitful, feverish, visionary dreamer, the last to that of the more drowsy slumberer.

Both however are asleep. The mind, to be awake, must not only think, and think with vigour and coherence, but think seasonably also. Even this is not enough. This may be done, and yet the mind remain absorbed in spiritual slumber. For what can vigour, coherence, or promptness avail, if the thoughts are exercised on trifling or unimportant objects. However thoroughly the mind is roused, however actively it may exert itself, however ready it be to act precisely at the juncture when its action is required, if it does not act upon the proper objects, it might just as well not act at all, it may still be figuratively represented as asleep. This is the spiritual state of many. Their powers appear to be in active exercise, but they are spent on trifles. Even when they think of serious things in general, it is not of the great doctrines of religion—the substantial truth of God, but of enigmas, difficulties, puzzles in theology, about which men may speculate for ages, without reaching any satisfactory result, or doing any good to themselves or others. Such minds may seem wide awake, but they are walking and talking in their sleep; just as in real life we meet with cases where the person performs certain acts with vigour and precision, but not such as belong to his present situation: he is asleep. The mind which is asleep in this sense, never proves itself awake, until it turns away from its beloved theme of speculation to the matters which deserve and claim its attention.

But even when it does this, it may still come short of the desired and necessary end, by thinking to no practical purpose. We may think, think in earnest, think with vigour, think coherently, think seasonably, think of the right things, yet think of them merely as themes of speculation, without any reference to our own duty, or practical concern in them. This is the case of those who hear the gospel, and read the Scriptures, and think much of religion, but still keep it at arm's length, or still further off from any personal contact with themselves, or with any thing beyond their understandings or their speculative faculties.

This leads me in the next place to observe, that the conscience as well as the intellect must be awake —the moral as well as the purely intellectual faculties. There must be perception, not only of what is true, but of what is right. A power of distinguishing not only between true and false, but also between right and wrong; and that, not only in the abstract, but in reference to ourselves, our own duty, and our own transgressions. If the conscience is asleep, no liveliness of intellect can make up the deficiency. We are but talking in our sleep. We are not spiritually awake. And lastly, in addition to all this, the heart must be awake. There must be liveliness of affection no less than of intellect. We must not only feel bound, but feel disposed to do the will of God. We must see the coincidence of what is right with what is good and pleasant. When all these conditions are complied with—when the mind, the conscience, and the heart, all act, and act in harmony— when the man thinks in earnest, and coherently, and seasonably of right objects and to practical purpose— when he feels his obligations, and his failures to discharge them—when he earnestly desires, and sincerely loves what he admits to be true and binding —then indeed he may be said, in the highest spiritual sense, to be awake. And being thus awake, he is a proper subject of the second precept comprehended in the text—Be on your guard!

The figure is a military one. So much may depend upon the vigilance even of a single soldier—so many lives—so many personal and public interests— so many subsequent and seemingly remote events—

that there is scarcely any situation in real life more responsible. Hence the severity with which a breach of trust or even an involuntary lapse of attention has been punished in all ages. To sleep upon one's post might seem, at first sight, to be rather a pitiable weakness than a crime—at least a crime deserving the extreme penalty of death, which has so often been inflicted. But when the remote as well as the immediate consequences of neglect in such a station are considered, the venial offence swells into a crime of awful magnitude, and worthy of the highest penalty.

But what is there analogous to this in the spiritual warfare? At whose door are we stationed as sentinels to watch, upon pain of death? If I should answer, at the door of every neighbour, friend, or fellow-christian, some might be disposed to ask as Cain did—Am I my brother's keeper? For this cause, although there is a real and important sense in which we may be, figuratively, represented as sentinels over one another, I shall confine myself to that watch which every man is bound to keep over the citadel of his own heart. The order given by the captain of our salvation, is, "keep thy heart with all diligence, for out of it are the issues of life." If a dereliction of this duty were not liable to be punished by virtue of a positive decree, it would still be punished by the loss incurred, the total loss of that which can never be supplied; for what is a man profited if he gain the whole world and lose his own soul, or what shall a man give in exchange for his soul?

With these views of the importance of the charge,

let me again remind you that, although it is essential, it is not enough to be awake. This admits of illustration from the case of literal, external watching. See that sentry at the gate of an encampment or a fortress—mark his measured tread, his martial port, his anxious though determined countenance—his quiet and searching glance, as he repeats his constant walk—that soldier is awake, but he is more—he is upon his guard—his mind is full of his important trust—he feels the weight of his responsibility. But see—his frame becomes relaxed, his form grows less erect, his movements lose their regular mechanical succession—his look is vacant or abstracted, he no longer looks afar off and at hand in search of approaching danger, he has either forgotten it, or ceased to reckon it so imminent. And yet the man is wide awake; not only are his eyes still open, but they see surrounding objects; all his senses are still active and his mind, though distracted from his present duty, is as much at work as ever; for no sooner does the slightest sound arouse him, than, as if by magic, he recovers his position, and the tension of his muscles, he resumes his measured walk, his mingled air of circumspection and defiance, and his look of bold but anxious scrutiny. Even before, he was awake; but now he is awake, and at the same time on his guard.

Precisely the same difference exists between a simple wakefulness in spiritual matters—a wakefulness of understanding, conscience, and affection—and the active exercise of spiritual vigilance; this is impossible without the other, but the other does not necessarily involve this. In both cases, *i. e.*, in the literal and spiritual case supposed, there is a sensible gradation of remissness or the opposite. We have seen the sentry wholly losing, for a moment, the recollection of his solemn trust; but this is not the only way in which he may unconsciously betray it. Look at him again. Every look, every motion, now betokens concentration of his thoughts and feelings on the danger which impends, and against which he is set to watch. Perhaps he is now motionless, but it is only that his eye may be more steadfastly fixed upon the point from which the enemy's approach is apprehended. In that point his whole being seems to be absorbed. And you can see at a glance that he is ready, even for the first and faintest intimation of a moving object on that dim horizon. But while he stands like a statue, with his face turned towards that dreaded point, look beyond him and behind him, at those forms which are becoming every moment more and more defined against the opposite quarter of the heavens. He hears them not, because their step is noiseless; he sees them not, because his eye and all his faculties are employed in an opposite direction. While he strains every sense to catch the first intimations of approaching danger, it is creeping stealthily behind him, and when at last his ear distinguishes the tramp of armed men, it is too late, for a hostile hand is already on his shoulder, and if his life is spared, it is only to be overpowered and disarmed, without resistance. And yet that soldier was not only awake but on his guard—his whole being was absorbed in contemplation of the danger which impended; but alas, he viewed it as impending only from one quarter, and lost sight of it as really approaching from another. We may even suppose that he was right in looking where he did, and only wrong in looking there exclusively. There was an enemy to be expected from that quarter, and if this had been the only one, the sentry's duty would have been successfully performed; but he was not aware, or had forgotten that the danger was a complex one—that while the enemy delayed his coming, another might be just at hand, and thus the very concentration of his watchfulness on one point, defeated its own purpose, by withdrawing his attention from all others.

By a slight shifting in the scene, I might present to you the same man or another, gazing, not at one point only, but at all, sweeping the whole visible horizon with his eye as he maintains his martial vigil. See with what restless activity his looks pass from one distant point to another, as if resolved that nothing shall escape him, that no imaginable source of danger shall remain unwatched. That man might seem to be in every sense awake and on his guard—surprise might seem to be impossible—but hark! what sound is that which suddenly disturbs him in his solitary vigils? he looks hastily around him but sees nothing, yet the sound is growing every moment louder and more distinct—" a voice of noise from the city"—"the voice of them that shout for mastery"—" the voice of them that cry for being overcome!" Doubt is no longer possible—it is—it is behind him—yes, the enemy for whom he looked so vigilantly, is within the walls, and the banner which he thought to have seen waving at a distance, is floating in triumph just above his head.

The cases which I have supposed, are not mere appeals to your imagination. They are full of instruction as to practical realities. They vividly present to us, in figurative forms, the actual condition of the soul in reference to spiritual dangers. It is just as true of us, as of the soldier in the case supposed, that we may fail of our duty and expose ourselves to ruin, not only by actually falling asleep, but by want of proper caution when awake—by forgetting the danger or by underrating it—by admitting its reality and magnitude, but losing sight of its proximity and imminence—by looking for it from a quarter whence it is not likely to proceed, while we turn our backs on that from which it ought to be expected—by looking for it with good reason from one quarter, but forgetting that it may proceed from others also—by looking for one enemy instead of many—and above all, by looking at a distance when the danger is at hand—by exercising vigilance without, when the danger is within—and vainly hoping to anticipate its first approaches, when the fight is finished and the battle lost.

If it be asked, Who is the enemy against which spiritual vigilance is called for, I reply, his name is Legion. There is no end to the forms under which he can disguise himself, nor to the arts which he can practise—" We are not (wholly) ignorant of his devices." But our spiritual dangers, although endlessly diversified in their specific characters, may all be resolved into one, and that is sin. Indeed, all danger, whether physical or moral, may be traced back to this source, for it is wholly incredible that suffering could ever have existed without sin. But in reference to spiritual dangers, it is still more emphatically true that they are all reducible by ultimate analysis to this same form. There is nothing to be spiritually dreaded except sin and its effects. Whatever therefore tends to sin, not merely to the overt act, nor even to specific acts of will, but to the love, the practice, the dominion of iniquity, in any form or measure whatsoever, is a danger to be dreaded and assiduously watched against. And this extends not only to the actual commission or indulgence, but to all exciting and facilitating causes, such as are usually comprehended in the name temptation. However little you may be aware of it, I tell you that temptation is your danger, and the tempter your enemy. This danger, this enemy, as I have said, appears in various disguises, and assails us from a thousand different quarters. Our vigilance must, therefore, be a constant and a universal vigilance, or we can have no confidence of safety.

To concentrate and define our vague conceptions of a multiform peril, we may group the innumerable dangers which surround us, under several descriptive heads; and these, in accordance with the figure hitherto adopted, and as I think implicitly suggested by the text, may be enumerated as so many distinct quarters from which danger threatens us, and towards which our vigilance must therefore be directed.

The first that I shall mention is the devil, both as an individual spirit and as representing the collective hosts of hell, the aggregate of the powers of darkness. This, of all spiritual dangers, is the one which most men look upon as most remote and least substantial. However readily they may assent to what is theoretically taught upon the subject, they are practically less afraid of this than of any other adverse power. Nay, some professed believers in the Bible are by no means loth to join in the derisive language of the irreligious as to this mysterious subject. Be it so. Let those who can, derive amusement from the doctrine of a fallen spirit, far superior to ourselves in original intelligence, and now possessed of faculties strengthened and sharpened by the malignant activity of ages, allowed access to the minds of men, and suffered to exert a moral influence upon them, though deprived of all coercive power. But let such, even while they laugh, remember that the time may not be far off when they shall perceive their situation to be that of the soldier or the general who denies and even laughs at the existence of a certain enemy, until he is suddenly convinced, by being crushed beneath the very force which he derided as imaginary. If the sentinel be justly doomed to death who jeopards his own life and that of others by neglect, or even by too narrow an attention to his trust, what shall be said of him who does the same by making light of the existence of the danger. With this premonition of the change which may take place hereafter in your views upon this subject, I am not ashamed to say to the most incredulous among you, in the words of the apostle Peter, "be sober, be vigilant, because your adversary, the devil, like a roaring lion, goeth about, seeking whom he may devour."

Another quarter from which danger is always to be apprehended, is the World, a term by which the Scriptures designate the complex influence exerted by mankind upon each other, not as individuals merely, but as elements of human society, whether this influence be brought to bear upon the opinions, the passions, or the appetites; whether the bait presented be that of sensual enjoyment, social popularity, official rank, civil power or military glory, intellectual fame, or mere inglorious ease and exemption from annoyance. The reality of this danger, few will dare to question. Some may be ready to exclaim, we know what this is, we believe in its existence, we have felt its power. Whether there be an infernal devil or not, we know that there are devilish powers at work in human society. The young and inexperienced, who have not been sucked into this fearful whirlpool, may swim carelessly around it, but you whose hearts have been already blighted, and your consciences seared perhaps as with a hot iron; you know, although you may not choose to tell, what depths of meaning are contained in that one syllable—the world, the world. You know too, that it is not, as the young sometimes imagine, the enmity, the scorn, the hatred, the oppressions, wrongs, or persecutions, of the wicked world, that constitute the danger, but its smiles, its blandishments, its friendship; "know ye not," says the apostle James, "that the friendship of the world is enmity with God; whosoever therefore will be a friend of the world is the enemy of God."

But neither world nor devil would be objects of alarm and apprehension, if they always remained without us and external to us; what makes them dangerous is that they get within us, they obtain a lodgment in our hearts, they are leagued with our own corruptions; hence the third and most alarming source of spiritual danger is ourselves, the last to be suspected and the hardest to be watched, and yet the most in need of our suspicion and our vigilance, because one enemy within the camp or fortress is worse than many foes without; because one traitor is more to be dreaded than a host of open enemies. Yet such is our condition, exposed all at once to these three dangers, any one of which would seem sufficient to destroy us; the World, the Flesh, and the Devil; seduced to evil by human example, urged to it by demoniacal suggestion, and inclined to it already by the very dispositions of our fallen nature; assailed without by the united hosts of earth and hell, betrayed within by our own corruptions, bound hand and foot, and left to float upon the rapid current which every hour brings us nearer to the judgment seat of Christ.

While such is our condition, how can we look forward with joy to his appearing? This is a painful thought, but one which cannot be avoided, that to these three dangers which have been already mentioned, we must add as a fourth the coming of our Lord. Is he then our enemy, from whose approach we ought to shrink back in terror? It may be so. Let us see to it that it is not so; let us so resist our spiritual foes, and watch against them, as to meet him when he comes with joy and not with grief. Let us so live as to show that we are not of those who shall hereafter call upon the rocks and mountains to conceal us from his view, but of those who sincerely love his appearing. We have surely no need of additional inducements to obey the exhortation of the text.

The only question that remains is, how shall we obey it? We have seen the necessity and duty of spiritual watchfulness and wherein it essentially consists, but we are like the sick man who is told of his disease and of the remedy, but still looks round for some one to apply it. It is natural to ask: is there not some safeguard, some appointed tried means of spiritual safety, something that will at once secure our vigilance and make it efficacious? Yes, there is such a talisman, and its name is prayer; not the mere act of supplication or devotion, whether audible or mental, but that prayerful attitude or frame of mind, which is ever ready to commune with God, and of which Paul could say, without extravagance, and meaning to the letter what he did say: "Pray without ceasing;" that settled bent of the affections which makes actual devotion not a rare experience, but the normal condition of the soul, to which it naturally flies back whenever it escapes from any temporary pressure. This prayerful habit is repeatedly connected in the word of God with watch; "Watch and pray lest ye enter into temptation." "Continue in prayer, and watch in the same with thanksgiving." And Paul in that sublime description of the panoply of God (Eph. 6,) seems to add this as essential to the efficacy of the rest, for after urging them to take the girdle of truth, the breastplate of righteousness, the shield of faith, the helmet of salvation, and the sword of the Spirit which is the word of God, he crowns all with this closing exhortation, "praying always with all prayer and supplication in the Spirit, and watching thereunto with all perseverance." Thus it seems we must watch that we may pray, and pray that we may watch. The influence which prayer exerts is easily explained. It operates by keeping the mind ever awake and in a state of healthful activity, by keeping it in contact with the best and highest objects, and bringing the affections and the powers to bear primarily upon them.

If then we would watch to any good effect against our spiritual dangers, let us pray without ceasing, let us breathe the atmosphere of genuine devotion. And in this way we shall do far more than escape injury. The benefit of prayerful vigilance is not merely negative but positive, a blessing is suspended on it. In the present state; the best of us are like men that wait for their lord, that when he cometh and knocketh we may open unto him. Already the flashing of his torches is beginning to illuminate the darkness, already the voice of his forerunners comes through the silent night saying, Be ye also ready; and amidst these cries, his own voice may be heard still afar off, saying, "What I say unto you, I say unto all, Watch." "Watch and pray that ye enter not into temptation." "Blessed are those servants whom the Lord, when he cometh, shall find watching; whether he come in the second watch, or come in the third watch, and find them so, blessed are those servants."

XXI.

MATTHEW 24, 6.—The end is not yet.

THE prophetical discourse, of which thsi sentence forms a part, has been the subject of conflicting explanation, ever since it was originally uttered. The grand difficulty lies in the appropriateness of its terms to two distinct and distant events, the end of the world and the destruction of Jerusalem.

But whether we assume, with some interpreters, that the one catastrophe was meant to typify the other; or with another class, that the discourse may be mechanically divided, by assuming a transition at a certain point from one of these great subjects to the other; or with a third, that it describes a sequence of events to be repeated more than once, a prediction to be verified, not once for all, nor yet by a continuous progressive series of events, but in stages and at intervals, like repeated flashes of lightning, or the periodical germination of the fig-tree, or the re-assembling of the birds of prey, whenever and wherever a new carcass tempts them; upon any of these various suppositions, it is still true that the primary fulfilment of the prophecy was in the downfall of the Jewish state, with the previous or accompanying change of dispensations; and yet that it was so framed, as to leave it doubtful, until the event, whether a still more terrible catastrophe was not intended. However clear the contrary may now seem to us, there was nothing absurd in the opinion which so many entertained that the end of the world and of the old economy might be coincident. This ambiguity is not accidental but designed, as in many other prophecies of Scripture.

Another striking feature in the form of this discourse, is the precision with which several stages or degrees of the fulfilment are distinguished from each other, each affording the occasion and the premonition of the next until the close of the whole series. Of these successive periods or scenes of the great drama, each might, considered in itself, have seemed to be the last. And no doubt each as it occurred was so regarded even by some who had been forewarned by Christ himself. To correct this error and prepare the minds of true believers for the whole that was to come upon them, he says, at the close of the first scene, "see that ye be not troubled, for all these things must come to pass, but the end is not yet;" or, as Luke expresses it, "the end is not by and by," *i. e.* immediately. And again at the close of the next stage of this great revolution, "all these are the beginning of sorrows."

The same intimation, although not expressed, may be supplied throughout the prophecy. At every solemn pause, until the last, a kind of echo seems to say again, "the end is not yet." When the prediction was fulfilled, we may easily imagine the impres-

sion which this well-remembered formula would make
upon the minds of the disciples. As each new sign
appeared, they were no doubt ready to exclaim, *the
end cometh*, and as each gave way to another, *the end
is not yet*. And what was thus true of the several
stages of this great catastrophe was also true of the
whole. The impression made on many by the very
structure of the prophecy, that the Jewish state and
the world would come to an end together, was no
sooner rectified by the event, than multitudes who
had been breathlessly awaiting the result, as they
again respired freely, cried out to themselves or
others, *the end is not yet*. The need of this caution
has not ceased. Men have ever since been and are
still too much disposed to precipitate the fulfilment
of God's purposes, and to confound "the beginning
of sorrow" with "the end." They are slow to learn
the lesson that "the believer will not make haste,"
that an important element of faith in the divine en-
gagements is a disposition to leave time and every
other circumstance to God himself, a disposition perfectly consistent with intense desire and urgent im-
portunity. There is something curious in the difference of men's feelings and opinions with respect to
the life of individuals, and to that of the race or the
continued existence of this present world. The great
majority of men live as if they were to live for ever.
The effect of this upon their character and lives affords a constant theme to moralists and preachers of
the gospel. In all this there is only a misapplication
or undue restriction of a principle inherent in our
very constitution. Man *is* immortal, and was made

for immortality. He cannot, if he would, look only at the present and the past. He must feel and act for the future also. And that not only for a definite or proximate futurity, but also for one more remote and undefined, the boundless field of what is yet to be. The practical error lies in confounding endless existence with an endless prolongation of the present life. The negation of all end is confounded with exemption from all change. The more profoundly men reflect, the more they are brought off from this illusion. But so long as they are heedless and controlled by natural feeling, they expect to live forever. No extent of observation, no degree of familiarity with death and its accompanying changes is sufficient to correct this practical error, for of course it can have no theoretical existence.

But the most surprising fact of all is that these views may co-exist with a strong disposition to expect a speedy termination of the whole system under which we live. The certainty of this fact is clear from the effect of those fanatical predictions which at different times have agitated Christendom. In all such cases the panic has had reference to the end of the world. Let this be quelled, and all fear is extinguished. It does not occur to the alarmist that however probable the near approach of the event may be made by calculation or by reasoning, it never can be rendered half so certain as his own death in the course of nature at no distant period. Nay, the probability of this inevitable change occurring even speedily must always transcend that of a speedy occurrence of the final consummation. Yet the oldest and the least prepared to die remain unmoved by this appalling certainty, although they would be terrified by any intimation that the world was to continue but a twelvemonth longer. It matters not that they may die to-morrow or to-day, if they can only be assured that the end of the world is not immediately at hand.

In some cases it is easy to refer these very different effects to one and the same cause. The self-love which forbids some men to look upon themselves as mortal, makes them equally unwilling, when this truth is forced upon them, to allow a longer term to others. If they must die, let humanity die with them. Something of this selfish feeling no doubt enters into the strong disposition of some good men in all ages, to regard their own times as the last, and to fix the winding up of the great drama as near as may be to their own disappearance from the stage. As Herod the Great is said to have ordered a large number of distinguished persons to be massacred as soon as he was dead, in order that his death might not be wholly unaccompanied by mourning, so the class in question seem to look upon the end of the world as a necessary part of their own obsequies. The impression of approaching change and dissolution, which is perfectly appropriate to their own case, is transferred by a natural association to the scene which they are leaving, as if it were out of the question that the world can get along without them.

This pardonable vanity, if such it may be called, seeks, of course, to justify itself by the authority of scripture. Hence the prophecies are tortured into confirmation of the fact assumed, and every art of calculation and construction is employed to bring the end of the world as near as may be into coincidence with that of the interpreter. Nor have these been barren and inoperative speculations. Their effect has been immense and sometimes long continued, both on individuals and whole communities. The most remarkable exemplification of the general statement, is afforded by the memorable panic which diffused itself through Christendom at the approach of the year 1,000. The belief had been gradually gaining ground that the close of this millennium, or first period of a thousand years, was to be the final close of human history. As the fatal term drew near, the superstitious dread associated with it grew continually more intense and powerful in its effects. These, as disclosed by the historical research of modern times, have more the aspect of romance than of true history. They might indeed be thought incredible, but for the like effects of the same causes in our own times, on a smaller scale and in less imposing circumstances. One of the most striking facts recorded, is, that a large portion of those massive, medieval structures which now constitute the monuments of those times, were, at least, projected under the first impulse of recovered hope, occasioned by the transit of the fatal era. They who, a little while before, were throwing away treasures and abandoning estates as henceforth worthless, by a natural reaction, now rushed into the opposite extreme, and began to build as for eternity.

However improbable the actual recurrence of such scenes may now appear, the principle from which they spring has been too often manifested, to be looked upon as temporary or accidental. It continues to exist and to exert its power, not always with the same effect or to the same extent, but so far constantly and uniformly, as to make it an interesting subject of inquiry what we ought to think, and how we ought to feel and act in reference to it, as connected with our own times and circumstances. What I believe to be the true solution of this question may be reduced to these two propositions:

1. So far as we have any means of judging, *the end is not yet.*

2. So far as it remains a matter of doubt, it is better to assume that *the end is not yet*, than to assume the contrary.

1. So far as we have any means of judging, *the end is not yet.* This may be argued negatively and positively. The negative argument is this, that there are no conclusive indications of a speedy end, afforded either by the word of God or the condition of the world. Such indications are indeed alleged, and that with confidence, but they have no conclusive force, because, in the first place, they rest upon gratuitous assumptions. It is assumed, for instance, that a certain form or pitch of moral depravation is incompatible with the continued existence of society. That there is or may be a degree of wickedness irreconcilable with any social organization, is too clear to be disputed. But it does not follow that the present condition of the world is such. Such a conclusion is not warranted by the mere degree of actual corruption, however great, because we do not know how much is necessary to the end in question, and any at-

tempt to determine it must rest on a gratuitous assumption.

The same thing is true as to the real or supposed predictions of the final consummation in the word of God. That these were meant, not merely to assert the general fact, and in some cases to describe the attendant circumstances, but to afford specific indications of the very time of its occurrence, so that it may be distinctly known beforehand; all this is assumed in the usual reasoning on the subject, but assumed without proof. It is not more easy to affirm than to deny it. Whatever plausibility there may be in the sense thus put upon the passage in question, there can be no certainty. It is not necessary to maintain that this *cannot* be the meaning. It is enough to know that it *may* not be. The position taken is not that the proofs alleged are manifestly false, but that they are inconclusive; they prove nothing, because they rest upon gratuitous assumptions. This, by itself, would be enough to justify the negative position, that we have no sufficient reason to believe that the end is at hand.

But the same thing is still clearer from experience. These signs have all been misapplied before. There is perhaps not a single indication now made use of for this purpose, that has not been so employed in former ages. Every striking coincidence, every verbal allusion, has been weighed already in this balance and found wanting. Nay, arithmetic itself, of which it has been said, the figures cannot lie, has here misled its thousands. The most positive numerical specifications may be varied indefinitely by the variation of the term from which they are to be computed. The millennium of the Book of Revelation has by turns been proved to be present, past, and future. All this argues no defect or error in the Scriptures, but only something wrong in the interpretation. When any thing can thus be made to mean any thing, we have reason to believe that it was not intended to reveal so much as we imagine. In other words, the passages of scripture thus appealed to, having been applied before in the same way and with equal plausibility, and the application falsified by the event, we are naturally brought to the conclusion, that they never were intended to disclose so much as some are able to perceive in them.

We may reason in the same way, from experience, with respect to the condition of society and the degree of actual corruption. The extraordinary abounding of iniquity at any one time, in itself considered, might well lead us to believe that such depravation must be preparatory to the final dissolution of society. But when we find analogous appearances insisted on, from age to age, with equal confidence, in proof of the same thing, and the proof as constantly annulled by the event, we may not unreasonably hesitate to rest upon such evidence in this case, and conclude that tests, which have always led to false results before, must be at least defective, and their testimony inconclusive. Whether we look, then, at the word of God or at the world around us, or compare the condition of the one with the predictions of the other, we have no satisfactory or adequate ground for the conclusion that "the end of all things is at hand" in this sense.

Let us now look for a moment at the positive argument in favour of the same position, which may be conveniently reduced to this form, that the fulfilment of the Scriptures is still incomplete, and will require a long time for its completion.

In support of this, we may appeal in general to the grand and comprehensive scale on which the divine purposes are projected in the Scriptures. The natural impression made, perhaps, on all unbiassed readers, is, that in the Bible there are vast beginnings, which require proportionate conclusions even in the present life. There are germs which were never meant to be developed in the stunted shrub, but in the spreading oak. There are springs in tracing which we cannot stop short at the brook or even at the river, but are hurried on, as if against our will, to the lake, the estuary, and the ocean. Every such reader of the Bible feels that it conducts him to the threshold of a mighty pile, and opens many doors, through which he gets a distant glimpse of long-drawn aisles, vast halls, and endless passages; and how can he believe that this glimpse is the last that he shall see, and that the edifice itself is to be razed, before he steps across the threshold.

This impression made by the very structure of the Scriptures is confirmed by their peculiar phraseology, the constant use of language pointing not to sudden instantaneous revolutions, but to long-continued dilatory processes of change, decay, and restoration, dissolution, and relapse, which have as yet but had their beginning, and the full course of which can only be completed in a cycle of ages. And besides these general considerations, founded on the structure of the dialect of Scripture, we can specify particular changes which have scarcely yet become perceptible, but of which the Bible leads us to anticipate the end and the completion before " the end cometh."

One of these is the universal spread of the gospel. Without insisting on particular predictions of this great event, we may appeal to the general impression made upon all readers of the Bible, that it must and will take place before the end of the existing dispensation. Closely allied to this, as one of its conspicuous effects, is the regeneration of the race, the reconstruction of society, the realization of those glowing pictures of the earth and its inhabitants, which can neither be explained as day-dreams of an imaginary golden age, nor as poetical anticipations of the joys of heaven. Nor do the Scriptures lead us to expect a mere restoration, but a continued exhibition of the race, and of society in its normal state, contrasted with its previous corruptions and distortions.

To these and other mighty changes we must look, not only as important means of human elevation, but as necessary to the vindication of the truth of prophecy. The longer its fulfilment is delayed, provided it is clearly verified at last, the stronger is the proof of divine foresight. This is enhanced still further if the fulfilment of the prophecy is gradual, or marked by a series of gradations. The longer the intervals between these the more striking the fulfilment, if the several gradations can be clearly ascertained and their mutual connection rendered palpable. Now there certainly are such predictions even now in the process of fulfilment, and the very fact of their existence is a strong proof that *the end is not yet.*

Before this comes, there is still another object which must be accomplished. This is the vindication of the Scriptures generally from the doubts engendered by apparent inconsistencies not only with itself but with history, with science, with the principles of morals. These clouds are not to rest forever on the word of God, nor are they merely to be scattered by the brightness of the final conflagration or the clear sunlight of eternal day. We have cheering reason to believe that the reconciliations which have been effected in our own day between different forms of truth, are but the foretaste and the pledge of what is to be done hereafter and before the end cometh.

It may indeed be urged in opposition to this argument, that all these changes may be suddenly and speedily effected, so that their necessity proves nothing as to the nearness or remoteness of the final consummation. That such an issue is within the reach of the divine omnipotence, cannot be doubted. But it does not follow that because God can, he will produce a certain effect, or that his power is the measure of his wisdom or his actual purpose. His wisdom, on the contrary, controls the exercise of his power. Such a sudden termination of the system, therefore, although possible, is far from being probable, because some of the proofs, by which the truth of the divine word is to be established, from their very nature seem to require time for their perfect exhibition.

If, for example, it is one of the great purposes disclosed in Scripture to exhibit human society in its normal state, and the effects of holiness compared with those of sin, it is not easy to imagine how this could be brought about by any sudden, partial, transient revolution, which, although it might illustrate the omnipotence of God, could scarcely serve to show the operation of moral causes. And even where a longer period does not seem to be required by the very nature of the proof itself, it may be necessary to its full effect, as in the case of prophecy, which, as we have already seen, becomes impressive and conclusive, as an evidence of prescience, in proportion to the number and remoteness of the points at which its fulfilment may be verified. A prophecy fulfilled the day after its date may leave no doubt as to its origin, but what a cumulative increase in the clearness of the evidence and in the scope of its effect would be produced by successively enlarging the interval between the date and the fulfilment to a week, a month, a year, a generation, a century, a millennium!

Now if some signal prophecies have as yet been but partially fulfilled, and the fulfilment thus far has been marked by numerous gradations and divided by long intervals, there is at least a probability that what remains will exhibit the same aspect, and will therefore require time for its development. The sum of these considerations, negative and positive, appears to be, that there is no conclusive indication of a speedy end; that, on the contrary, there are strong reasons for believing that it is remote; but that even these are insufficient to decide the question absolutely; so that, after all, it is a doubtful point. Regarding it as such, we may naturally hesitate between two courses. Shall we, on the one hand, follow the preponderating evidence in favour of a distant consummation? or shall we, on the other, take what seems to be the safer course of looking for that soon which *may* be still far distant, but which *may* be already at the very door? In other words, considering the case as doubtful, is it better to proceed upon the supposition that the end is near, or upon the supposition that the end is not yet?

This is a question both of principle and practice, and the way in which it is decided may exert, as we shall see, no feeble influence upon the character and life. It is therefore worthy of a brief but serious consideration, the result of which may serve as the practical improvement of a subject that might otherwise seem rather to belong to the class of curious and subtle speculations, than to that of experimental truths or Christian duties. To what quarter shall we look then for an adequate solution of this question?

The first consideration that presents itself is this: that the very doubt in which the Scriptures leave the thing involved, creates a presumption that it was not meant to influence our conduct by the expectation of this great event as just at hand. This, however, is at variance with the general analogy of revelation, in which, though every thing of absolute necessity is clear, yet many things of high practical importance are left to be determined by laborious scrutiny and processes of reasoning. There is nothing therefore in the mere dubiety of this case to forbid the supposition that its practical design was to keep men in a constant attitude of expectation. But the probability of this is greatly lessened by the fact, already shown, that the proofs are not in equilibrio, but preponderate in favour of the negative conclusion, although insufficient to establish it. It can hardly be supposed that in order to maintain a healthful expectation of approaching change, they would be so mentioned as to favour the belief that they are still far distant. Nothing indeed could warrant this assumption but experimental proof that the belief just mentioned has necessarily a bad effect. But so far is this from being certain or admitted, that the contrary admits of a most plausible defence. The expectation of a speedy end seems naturally suited to enervate, nay to paralyze exertion, while the opposite belief invigorates it.

No less dissimilar is the effect of these two causes, in relation to the credit and authority of Scripture. The perpetual failure of the signs, which some see there, of instant dissolution, though it only proves the falsehood of the principle assumed, has a practical tendency to bring the word of God itself into discredit, as if these ever-shifting whims and fancies of professed interpreters were really expedients necessary to disguise or palliate the failure of predictions which events have falsified. The existence of this danger is apparent from the ill-concealed contempt with which the irreligious argue, from the failure of fanatical predictions, to the worthlessness of prophecy in general. But no such inconvenience could result from the other supposition, even if it should be falsified by the speedy occurrence of the thing which it assumes to be remote, because the failure could occur but once, and then in circumstances utterly exclusive of effects like those which have been just described as flowing from the constant repetition of mistake and failure on the part of those who undertake to fix an early day and hour for the end of the world.

The other doctrine would seem therefore to be safer, both as respects the honour of the Scriptures, and the zeal of Christian enterprise. The only practical advantage of the same kind which can well be claimed for the opposite opinion is that it leads men to be always ready, as our Lord requires. This is, in fact, the grand recommendation of the theory, and that to which it owes its currency among some truly devout Christians. Yet it rests upon a fallacy, for it confounds the life of individuals with the existence of the race on earth. The readiness which Christ requires of us is a personal readiness to leave the world and meet our God. This has existed in the case of thousands who had no such expectation as the one in question. The necessity of this individual preparation cannot justify the sacrifice of higher interests, or dispense with the discharge of duties which we owe not only to ourselves but to our successors, to the church, to society, to human kind.

This preparation too for personal departure is not secured by a belief in the approach of the great final catastrophe. No such belief has ever wrought it. Where it really exists, it is preceded by a due sense of the shortness and uncertainty of life, and the importance of the interests suspended on it, without any reference whatever to the subsequent continuation or destruction of the world. The strongest possible persuasion that this world is yet to last for ages, may exist, because it has existed, in connection with the deepest sense of men's mortality and need of constant preparation for the great change which awaits them all without exception. But if the two convictions are thus perfectly compatible, we cannot of course argue from the requisition of the one to the exclusion of the other. The duty of constant preparation for the end of our career, may be truly and successfully performed by those who honestly believe that the existing state of things is to continue perhaps ages after they are themselves forgotten.

It may still be urged, however, that this state of mind exposes those who entertain it to be taken by surprise. What, it is sometimes said, if after all, the great event should be at hand, how fearful the surprise of those who fancy it to be still distant! Here again we may see traces of that same confusion of ideas which has been already mentioned. If men are unprepared to die, they will be just as much surprised by death, as by the coming of the end while they are living. If prepared to die, they are prepared for any thing. However great or sudden the surprise, it cannot be to them a fearful one. And if divested of this attribute, surprise is not an evil. Joy involves surprise as well as horror. Some of the most exquisite sensations of delight which have ever been experienced, have taken those who felt them by surprise. Nay, exclude all thought of danger, doubt, or fear from your conception of surprise, and most men would deliberately choose it, in preference even to the fullest opportunity of calculation, measurement, and deliberate foresight. But whether this be so or not, we know that the catastrophe in question will take most men by surprise at last, and not only the unthinking and the reckless, but the sober, the considerate, the wise.

This seems to be a necessary feature of the providential scheme imperfectly disclosed to us in Scripture; and among the means by which it is secured, may probably be reckoned that very ambiguity of Scripture which has given rise to so much fruitless controversy, and to so many vain attempts to render clear and definite, what God has left obscure and vague until the time for a fuller revelation shall have come. There is no advantage, therefore, upon either side in this respect, and if there were, there would be nothing in the mere risk of surprise, even though it were unavoidable, to make the state of the believer less secure, or that of the unbeliever more so.

If it be true, then, that the supposition of a distant end diverts the thoughts of men from this great change, it is only by transferring them to one still more momentous, because more closely connected with the loss or gain of personal salvation, because perfectly inevitable in reference to every individual of every generation but the last, and because according to the most indulgent computation, "not far from every one of us." Whether we look then at the absence of all certain indications that the end of the world is at hand, or at the existence of some striking proof that it is still far distant, or at the practical effect of both opinions, we may safely rest in the conclusion, that so far as we can judge at all, the end is not yet, and that so far as we are in doubt, it is better for ourselves and others to suppose that the end is not yet than to suppose the contrary.

The practical conclusion to which these theoretical conclusions point is obvious enough. Let us first of all prepare to die, and thus in the most effectual way prepare to live. This preparation is of course not to be made by needlessly anticipating cares which are appropriate only to the time of actual departure, but by the doing of our present duty, in reliance upon that grace which provides for all emergencies, but seldom grants to one the aid appropriate to another. Having made this indispensable provision for the future, let us cease to look upon our own salvation as the final cause of all that God is doing. Let us look away from our minute concerns to that stupendous whole, of which they form an indispensable though humble part. Instead of feeling and acting as if all must die with us, let us continue, until God shall teach us otherwise, to cherish the belief and expectation of a glorious work yet to be accomplished even here, of which the changes which we now behold are not the end but the beginning. Let us not shrink even from the thought that unknown evils are yet to be experienced before the good can be finally triumphant. Through the clouds of such anticipations we may still discern the clear sky of better days to come; nay even in the mean time, we may see the storm and sunshine striving for the mastery, and although we may be forced to say, as one disaster treads upon the heels of its forerunner, "these are but the beginning of sorrows," we may still console ourselves by looking further off to still remoter changes, saying the end is not yet.

Let this not only solace but incite us. At every new stage of our course, when we are tempted to imagine our work done, let this word rouse us, the end is not yet. Let the same conviction follow through life. Whatever you may seem to have already suffered or accomplished, still remember that the end is not yet; and from the midst of your trials, your perplexities, your errors, your temptations, yes, your doubts of God himself, still force yourselves to look even on the beginning of sorrows as prophetic of their end, and to take refuge from the worst that can befall you, or the cause for which you live, for which you die, in the fixed persuasion that with reference both to labour and reward, "the end is not by and by." The time, indeed, is coming when the same thing can no longer be said equally of both. Yes, the time is coming when these present light afflictions shall be past, forgotten, "as a dream when one awaketh," but at no point of your history more truly than at that, will you be justified in saying as you look forward to the glory that awaits you, "these are but the beginnings of an everlasting life,—the end is not yet."

Some Other SGCB Classic Reprints

In addition to *Theology on Fire* which you hold in your hand, we are delighted to list several other titles available from Solid Ground Christian Books, many for the first time in a century or more:

A SHEPHERD'S HEART: *Sermons from the Pastoral Ministry of J.W. Alexander*
THE ASSURANCE OF FAITH *by Louis Berkhof*
OPENING SCRIPTURE: *A Hermeneutical Manual* by Patrick Fairbairn
THE PASTOR IN THE SICK ROOM by John D. Wells
THE NATIONAL PREACHER: *Revival Sermons from the 2nd Great Awakening*
THE POOR MAN'S NT COMMENTARY by Robert Hawker
THE POOR MAN'S OT COMMENTARY by Robert Hawker
THE POOR MAN'S MORNING & EVENING PORTION by Robert Hawker
FIRST THINGS by Gardiner Spring
BIBLICAL & THEOLOGICAL STUDIES by Princeton Professors of 1912
THE POWER OF GOD UNTO SALVATION by B.B. Warfield
THE LORD OF GLORY by B.B. Warfield
CHRIST ON THE CROSS by John Stevenson
SERMONS TO THE NATURAL MAN by W.G.T. Shedd
SERMONS TO THE SPIRITUAL MAN by W.G.T. Shedd
HOMILETICS & PASTORAL THEOLOGY by W.G.T. Shedd
A PASTOR'S SKETCHES 1 & 2 by B.B. Warfield
CHRIST IN SONG: *Hymns of Immanuel from all ages* by Philip Schaff
THE PREACHER & HIS MODELS by James Stalker
IMAGO CHRISTI by James Stalker
LECTURES ON THE HISTORY OF PREACHING by John A. Broadus
A HISTORY OF PREACHING (2 VOLS.) by E.C. Dargan
THE SHORTER CATECHISM ILLUSTRATED by John Whitecross
THE CHURCH MEMBER'S GUIDE by John Angell James
THE SUNDAY SCHOOL TEACHER'S GUIDE by John Angell James
THE DEVOTIONAL LIFE OF THE SS TEACHER by J.R. Miller
And several more....

Call us Toll Free at **1-877-666-9469**
Visit us on the web at **http://solid-ground-books.com**

www.ingramcontent.com/pod-product-compliance
Lightning Source LLC
Chambersburg PA
CBHW021758220426
43662CB00006B/106